77th New York Volunteers

Former Private William A. Baker, 77th New York State Volunteers, Company H, nicknamed "Yankee Bill"

Courtesy of the Author

77th New York Volunteers
"Sojering" in the VI Corps

By
Robert F. Morrow Jr.

Clifton Park - Halfmoon Public Library
47 Clifton Country Road
Clifton Park, New York 12065

WHITE MANE BOOKS
SHIPPENSBURG, PENNSYLVANIA

Copyright © 2004 by Robert F. Morrow Jr.

ALL RIGHTS RESERVED—No part of this book may be reproduced in any form without permission in writing from the publisher, except by a reviewer who wishes to quote brief passages in connection with a review.

This White Mane Books publication
was printed by
Beidel Printing House, Inc.
63 West Burd Street
Shippensburg, PA 17257-0708 USA

The acid-free paper used in this book meets the guidelines for permanence and durability of the Committee on Production Guidelines for Book Longevity of the Council on Library Resources.

For a complete list of available publications
please write
White Mane Books
Division of White Mane Publishing Company, Inc.
P.O. Box 708
Shippensburg, PA 17257-0708 USA

Library of Congress Cataloging-in-Publication Data

Morrow, Robert F., 1949-
  77th New York Volunteers : "sojering" in the VI Corps / by Robert F. Morrow Jr.
    p. cm.
  Includes bibliographical references (p.) and index.
  ISBN 1-57249-352-6 (alk. paper)
    1. United States. Army. New York Infantry Regiment, 77th (1861-1865) 2. New York (State)--History--Civil War, 1861-1865--Regimental histories. 3. United States (State)--History--Civil War, 1861-1865--Regimental histories. 4. United States (State)--History--Civil War, 1861-1865--Campaigns. 5. New York (State)--History--Civil War, 1861-1865--Personal narratives. 6. United States (State)--History--Civil War, 1861-1865--Personal narratives. I. Title: Seventy-seventh New York Volunteers. II. Title.

E523.577th .M67 2004
973.7'447--dc22

2003070505

PRINTED IN THE UNITED STATES OF AMERICA

*To remembering the men and deeds of the
77th New York State Volunteers
and to my wife and best friend, Mary*

—the heroes in my life.

Contents

List of Illustrations ix
Acknowledgments xi
Introduction xiii

1. Formation of the 77th New York Volunteers 1
   The Bemis Heights Regiment (Summer–Fall 1861)

2. Rendezvous at Camp Schuyler 5
   (Fall 1861)

3. Tenting on Abe's Lawn 11
   To Washington & Camp Hill House (Winter 1861–1862)

4. Hello Baldy 21
   Camp Griffin (Winter 1862)

5. Siege Yorktown 26
   Peninsular Campaign (Spring 1862)

6. Advance—Williamsburg & Mechanicsville 36
   Peninsular Campaign (Late Spring 1862)

7. Seven Pines & Retreat—The Seven Days Battles 43
   Peninsular Campaign (Early Summer 1862)

8. The 77th Needs a Few Good Men 52
   Harrison's Landing & Bull Run (Summer 1862)

9. Baldy Ordered Them to Fall Back 59
   Antietam (Fall 1862)

10. Good Generals Are Hard to Find 67
    Fredericksburg & the Mud March (Winter 1862–1863)

11. Legend of the Greek Cross Begins 75
    Marye's Heights to Banks' Ford (Spring 1863)

12. Chasing Bobby Lee 86
    The March to Gettysburg (Summer–Fall 1863)

Contents

13. Besides Sojering 98
    Winter Camp (Winter 1863–1864)
14. Fighting in the Wilderness 106
    Overland Campaign (Spring 1864)
15. Good-bye Uncle John 117
    Overland Campaign, Spotsylvania (Late Spring 1864)
16. Three One-Legged Jims 127
    *Overland Campaign, Cold Harbor & Petersburg
    (Early Summer 1864)*
17. Pursuing Old Jube 135
    Battle at Fort Stevens (Summer 1864)
18. Little Phil Takes Charge 146
    *Shenandoah Campaign, Winchester & Fisher's Hill
    (Early Fall 1864)*
19. Have to Drive Them from the Field 157
    Shenandoah Campaign, Cedar Creek (Late Fall 1864)
20. The 77th New York Battalion 170
    Petersburg to Appomattox (Winter 1864–Spring 1865)
21. The 77th Marched Home 181
22. The Reunion Years from 1873 188
23. The Hard-Fighting Seventy-Seventh 197
Appendix A—77th New York Battle Guide 205
Appendix B—77th New York Officers Chart 209
Appendix C—77th New York Roster 217
Notes 232
Bibliography 259
Index 270

Illustrations

Former Private William A. Baker, 77th New York
    State Volunteers, Company H .... frontispiece
Congressman James B. McKean 4
Lieutenant Colonel Winsor B. French 4
Lieutenant John J. Cameron 10
Private John D. Riley 10
Sketch of Camp Hill House 19
Chaplain David Tully 20
Brigadier General John W. Davidson 25
Sergeant William H. Wright 25
Surgeon George T. Stevens 35
Confederate gunboat CSS *Teaser* 35
Sketch of the 77th's charge at Mechanicsville, Va. 41
Portrait of Colonel James B. McKean 42
Brigadier General William "Baldy" Smith 51
Sketch of the Seven Days Battle, White Oak Swamp ... 51
Captains Luther Wheeler, Orrin Rugg, Martin Lennon,
    and Lieutenant John Belding 57
Lieutenant Joseph H. Loveland 58
Major Nathan S. Babcock 66
Sergeant Henry Allen and daughter 66
Major General John Sedgwick 73
The Stone Wall at Marye's Heights 74
Corporal Altus Jewel and Private William Deyoe 84
Sketch of the 77th's charge of Marye's Heights 85
Lieutenant Sidney Cromack 96
Sketch of the 77th on Powers Hill, Gettysburg 97
Chaplain Norman Fox Jr. 105
Private James Daivenson 105

Illustrations

Brigadier General Daniel Bidwell	116
Assistant Surgeon Justin Thompson	116
Lieutenant Thomas H. Fowler	125
Sketch of the fighting at the Salient	126
Private William A. Baker	134
Union Generals: David A. Russell, Thomas H. Neill, and John H. Martindale	134
Sketch of the battle at Fort Stevens	144
Captain Charles H. Davis	145
Sketch of the battle of Winchester	155
Sketch of Sheridan's army chasing Early up the Shenandoah Valley	156
General George W. Getty	168
Painting of General Philip Sheridan on Renzi	169
Captain David J. Caw	178
Sketch of the Petersburg assault	179
Captain Sumner Oakley	180
The VI Corps' Grand Review in Washington, June 1865	186
The 77th's guidon	187
The 77th's national flag	187
77th Monument dedication in Saratoga Springs, September 2, 1875	194
77th Monument dedication at Gettysburg, October 19, 1889	195
Veterans reunion in Ballston Spa, late 1890s	195
77th Monument in Congress Park, Saratoga Springs	196
77th Survivors	201
Former Lieutenant Cyrille Fountain with grandson	202
Former Sergeant David Wetherwax	203
John Clements, 77th Regimental Band	203
77th New York State Volunteers artifacts inherited by the author	204

Acknowledgments

Thanks to my wife, Mary, whose faith in me exceeds my own. Proofreader, sounding board, English major, muse, cheerleader, and nurse—she has done it all. To my dad and mom, who were always there for me. What my dad and I shared while researching this project has already made it a success. Stan Spencer, who gallantly edited my first manuscript—all 600 plus pages. Family members who helped in various ways include Lee-Ann and Dan Dullea, Tina Charbonneau VanEvera, and Jon, Jan, and Will Charbonneau.

Individuals who went the extra step include James Morrison, Marsha Goss, West Point's Susan Lintelmann, Chris Morley, Lorraine Westcott, Jeannine Woutersz, Daniel Lorello, Tom DuClose, Rachael Clothier, Joseph Covais, Karen Ufford Campola, Doris Lamont, Ed Italo, Dave Handy, and Mike O'Donnel. Institutions that also went the extra step include the Williamstown Public Library, William's College Sawyer Library, Union College's Schaffer Library, the Saratoga Room at the Saratoga Springs Public Library, and Saratoga Springs Historical Society. Descendants of the 77th who helped include Gayland Wojtowicz, Susan Weatherwax Bishop, Dan Cole, Professor Donald Chipman, Louise Barker, Leona Biard, Robert E. Lingow, Richard Geho, and Minnie Clark Bolster. The doctors who kept me moving include George Plotkin, Lewis Sudarsky, Reese Cosgrove, James Corkins, John Penny, and Ellen Doyle.

Special recognition goes to Edward Fuller, Dr. George T. Stevens, Winsor B. French, Martin Lennon, Robert H. Skinner, Cyrille Fountain, T. Scott Fuller, David Wetherwax, William G. Watson, William A. Baker, Nathan S. Babcock,

Acknowledgments

Benjamin Judson, Norman Fox Jr., the *Saratogian*, the *Ballston Journal*, and the others who in one form or another left the pieces of the puzzle that are the basis of this book.

A first-time writer, I appreciate the patience shown by the staff at White Mane.

Introduction

About the most originality that any writer can hope to achieve honestly, is to steal with good judgment.

—Josh Billings, Yankee Humorist

Cyril Clemens, *Josh Billings—Yankee Humorist*

The 77th's chaplain, Norman Fox, stated: "The man who makes the good soldier was not the swaggering swash-buckler, not the street brawler, but the plain respectable man who at home had always done his duty, faithfully, whatever it might be. The man who being set to hoe corn on a hot day would hoe his row without watching, even when the day was hot, was the man who, when assigned a station on the field of battle, would stay there till recalled, even though it was apparent that the recall would be given by the resurrection angel."[1] I would like to assume that my great-great-grandfather William A. Baker was this type of a man.

Inspired by a PBS documentary, I began to research my great-great-grandfather's part in the Civil War. I had always known that he served in the 77th New York, but other than having possession of a few artifacts, that was the extent of my knowledge. Making his mark with an "x" at 36 years of age, he enlisted for three years as a private in Company H. He left his wife, children, and farm to fight in Mr. Lincoln's war. The more information that I collected on the 77th, the more evident it became that the boys from Bemis Heights were arguably one of the better regiments in the Union army, and their stories should be told. In 1995, I was forced to leave my job because of my struggle with Parkinson's disease. During my good times, I began writing about the regiment, the results of which were a couple of magazine articles in *America's Civil War* and this book. Whoop her up, take yourself back to the years of 1861 through 1865. The times when the gallant men of the 77th touched elbows and formed battle lines in over 50 battles when "sojering" was their business.

–1–
Formation of the 77th New York Volunteers
The Bemis Heights Regiment
Summer–Fall 1861

Let us organize a Bemis Heights Battalion, and vie with each other in serving our country.
—James B. McKean, Congressman
Nathaniel B. Sylvester, *History of Saratoga County, New York*

During the spring of 1861, Washington was cut off from the North, and for two weeks Congressman James Bedell McKean put aside his own safety and stood guard outside the White House protecting President Lincoln and his family. When the opening shots of the Civil War were fired at Fort Sumter, there was not a single company of Federal soldiers anywhere near the capital city. Representative for the 15th Congressional District, McKean volunteered as a private in Clay's Battalion.[1] During July he witnessed the Union rout at the first battle of Bull Run. Immediately after the battle, President Lincoln called for 75,000 more volunteers. In response, Congressman McKean returned home to upstate New York to raise a regiment.[2]

James B. McKean was born in 1821 on Bennington Battlefield and raised on Saratoga Battlefield. Elected superintendent of Halfmoon schools at the age of 21, a few years later he was voted in as colonel of the local militia regiment. Next, McKean dedicated himself to the law, and within seven years he was elected county judge. He was elected to Congress in 1858 and 1860.[3]

On August 22, 1861, McKean posted an invitation to his constituents in Essex, Fulton, and Saratoga Counties to form a regiment to defend the constitution and protect the capital. He called all classes to step forward to protect their imperiled liberty. McKean proclaimed: "Let us organize a Bemis Heights Battalion, and vie with each other in serving our country, thus showing we are inspirited by the holy memories of the Revolutionary Battlefields upon and near which we are living."[4]

There was an immediate response, and others took up the torch, setting up recruiting stations in the district's various towns. Throughout the 15th district, the blood-stirring beat of the fife and drum summoned men to arms, and the patriotic men of upstate New York enthusiastically responded. The congressman took to the field in a campaign of war meetings held throughout the district. All of the working classes turned out to listen. Before enlisting, they always asked him if he was going to war with the regiment, and McKean responded: "Yes, I will not ask you to do what I will not do myself."[5] At a recruiting meeting for Ballston Spa's company, Steven Smith Horton stated: "We follow the flag first unfurled on our soil, and for our country we will live, and for our country we will die."[6] Winsor Brown French attended a war meeting at the old school house in Wilton, New York, with no intention of enlisting. But soon after arriving, he found himself caught up in the enthusiasm of John Carr and 12 other men. French and the others all enlisted in the Wilton Company.[7] Later, French posted a recruiting ad that proclaimed, "Young men, come out! If our country is worth living in—it is worth defending Liberty and Union, now and forever, one country inseparable."[8]

Amiable Winsor B. French was born during 1832 in Vermont, and raised on a farm south of Wilton, New York. A skilled violinist, French financed most of his studies by teaching music. He graduated from Tufts College with a bachelor of the arts degree and returned to Saratoga Springs to pursue a legal career. Employed by the law firm of McKean, Pond, and Lester, French was admitted to the bar in May of 1861.[9]

Based on his prior service in the militia, McKean became the regiment's first commanding officer with the rank of colonel. The New York State Adjutant General's Office issued Special Order No. 360 in August to establish a branch location at Saratoga Springs for the companies of the new regiment to rendezvous. Originally assigned as the 44th Regiment, McKean petitioned Governor Edwin D. Morgan to change the regiment's number. He wanted his men to have a sense of tradition that connected with the region's rich historical past. The governor approved the petition and the regiment became the 77th New York State Foot Volunteers, honoring the British surrender to the colonials after the Battle of Saratoga at Bemis Heights in 1777. The 77th was probably the only regiment in the army to be numbered for purely sentimental reasons.[10]

Early in September, Colonel McKean's personal solicitations secured the Saratoga County Agricultural Society's Fairgrounds. The location on Nelson Avenue had level terrain, ample buildings, and was easily accessible. The camp was named Camp Schuyler to honor Revolutionary War hero General Philip Schuyler and was to be a branch of the Albany Depot.[11] By mid-September, McKean's regiment was rapidly coming together, and the conversion of the fairgrounds into Camp Schuyler was almost completed. Floral Hall was nearly filled up with bunks for the soldiers. They erected a hospital on the western side of the grounds, and expanded the dining house to meet the needs of the regiment. Everything was proceeding as planned, with the camp scheduled to open on Tuesday, September 24, 1861.

The Honorable James B. McKean

McKean was the 77th Regiment's first colonel and representative of the 15th Congressional District.

Courtesy of the National Archives

Lieutenant Colonel Winsor B. French, 77th New York State Volunteers

He enlisted as the regiment's first adjutant and was wounded in action at Fort Stevens.

Courtesy of the Roger D. Hunt Collection at the United States Army Military History Institute (USAMHI)

– 2 –
Rendezvous at Camp Schuyler
Fall 1861

The Wilton Boys will stand by that flag to the last man.
—Captain Winsor B. French
"The Bemis Heights Regiment," *Saratogian*

From the start, the public had expectations that this regiment composed of men with character would perform their duty with honor. Ready and eager, these stout and healthy farmers' sons left home by the hundreds to seek glory with the new regiment. On September 24, 1861, the new recruits marched into Camp Schuyler for the rendezvous of the Bemis Heights Regiment. Bursting with confidence and eager to fight, some of the new recruits were troubled by the possibility that they might arrive too late for the battle.

Albert Beach and the Charlton Union Guards were the first to parade into Camp Schuyler, followed by Clement Hill with the Ballston Spa Company. Next came Benjamin Judson and a company from Saratoga Springs. Reed Arnold and the Westport Company made part of their journey from Essex County by boat. Winsor French's Wilton Company and Lewis Wood's Greenfield group also marched into camp on the first day.[1]

Their time was spent drilling and learning the fundamentals of being a soldier, or "sojering" as some would say. One anonymous soldier described army days as starting with morning drill, then drill, followed by drill again, next drill, more drill, and lastly drill. Despite six hours of drill each day, Corporal Robert Skinner wrote to a friend that he enjoyed life in the military and found the quarters and fare to be adequate. New York State allotted 30 cents per day for a subsistence allowance for each recruit.[2] Mr. Richard H. McMichael, one of the Congress Hall proprietors, took over the job of feeding the regiment. The Bemis Heights Boys quickly became accustomed to the routine of tin-plate, pint cup, roll call, reveille, and tattoo.[3] One corporal likened the barracks society to a frog pond, where some croaked, a number of them sang, several swore, a few told yarns, and the rest slept.

The commander of the Albany Depot, Brigadier General John F. Rathbone, sent an aide to Camp Schuyler to give the companies their first inspection. Doctor John L. Perry of Saratoga Springs gave each enlistee a medical examination. A few days later, Colonel Charles T. Peek resigned from the position of commandant and Rathbone assigned Major Joseph C. Henderson to fill the position. Henderson, an Albany hardware merchant, was promoted to lieutenant colonel.[4]

Even within the confines of Camp Schuyler, the reality of death was never very far from the regiment. During daily drill practice, one soldier became ill and died of an apparent heart attack, and in late October the regiment lost its first man to diphtheria. The daily dress parade and ceremonial firing of a cannon at sunset began attracting spectators. After the dress parade on November 3, the regiment was drawn up in formation, awaiting the cannon firing. Private Thomas Joyce from Bleecker, New York, commented to those in the ranks nearby that he would cross the mouth of the cannon without being touched. The short fuse on the cannon had just been lit when Private Joyce deliberately stepped out in front of the barrel. The surprised gunner had no way to stop it. Joyce's boast proved false—he was not faster than a cannon. The ball hit him squarely in the back of the head, and killed him instantly.[5]

By October 1, seven companies composed of over 600 men had marched into Camp Schuyler. Within a few more weeks they numbered 900 and later 1,000. The arriving recruits included Calvin Rice and the Northumberland group; Judson B. Andrews and the Mechanicville Company with their band; John Cameron with the Edinburgh and Providence unit; and Wendell Lansing with the Adirondack Guards from Keeseville, New York. Nathan Babcock and the boys from Gloversville were the last company to march into camp. Smaller groups were consolidated into companies. Each company elected a second lieutenant, and the captains drew lots for their companies' line position.[6]

The communities took great pride in the men who volunteered to serve. Many chose to honor their new officers with the finest swords and pistols available. The proud citizens of Ballston Spa presented a sword and sash to Company B's Captain Hill and Lieutenant Horton. The ladies of Wilton hand made a flag, and Reverend George Bell presented the flag and staff to Captain French. The captain responded that the Wilton Boys will stand by that flag to the last man.[7] Lieutenant Colonel Henderson's friends and neighbors held a ceremony for the colonel in Albany, New York. They outfitted Henderson with a sword, sash, belt, saddle, trunk, and two hundred dollars in gold. Three companies represented the regiment at a rally celebrating the anniversary of the Battle of Bemis Heights. Dressed in full uniform, they entertained the crowd with an excellent display of marching.[8] The people of Greenfield hosted a Soldiers Festival for Captain Wood and Company E. The festival started with speeches, a meal, and concluded with the presentation of a sword and revolver to the captain. On November 27 the regiment marched to Saratoga Springs High School for Boys to witness the presentation of a sword to Second Lieutenant John J. Cameron. Prior to his enlistment, the lieutenant taught at the school. To appease the insistent crowd both Cameron and Lieutenant Horton gave patriotic speeches. In closing, the regiment traded cheers with the audience of students and citizens.

To provide relief from the daily routine, Colonel McKean, the son of a reverend, made provisions for his men to attend religious services. Every Saturday, Corporal Skinner, Sergeant Rugg, and a number of others could be found in attendance at the regiment's weekly Bible class. The soldiers were permitted to attend prayer meetings three times a week, weekly Bible class, and Sunday church services in Saratoga Springs.

McKean needed someone he could trust and depend upon as his adjutant, and the young attorney who worked in his law office was the perfect man for the position. At McKean's request, Winsor French gave up his captaincy in Company D and became the regiment's first adjutant with the rank of first lieutenant. John Carr was promoted to captain.[9]

On November 23, each of the men in the 77th was given a new uniform, consisting of dark blue pants and a dark blue frock coat. Dressed in their new uniforms with caps in hand, the men were mustered into the United States Military Service. The captains of each new company began the swearing-in ceremony: "O honor that this muster-in roll exhibits the true state of Company —— of the Seventy-seventh Regiment, New York Foot Volunteers, for the period herein mentioned: that each man answered to his own proper name, and that the remarks set opposite each officer and soldier's name are accurate and just."[10] Thus, the regiment was formed into the United States service as the 77th New York State (Foot) Volunteer Regiment under James B. McKean, Colonel.[11] Following the ceremony, the boys gave three rousing cheers for the Union.

On Thanksgiving Day, camp was broken and the regiment marched out of Camp Schuyler. On the way to the train station, they halted at the Temple Grove Seminary for Women. The proprietor and principal, Reverend L. F. Beecher, presented them with a United States National Flag handmade by the lady scholars. Made of fine silk, it was handsomely embroidered in gilt "77TH REG'T. N. Y. S. V."[12] Mary Carleton Beecher read her poem to the Bemis Heights Regiment. The flag "wrought by fair hands and true"[13] was entrusted to the regiment in the good faith that it would be defended at any price and never be lost. The boys responded with loud cheers and resumed marching to the Rensselear and Saratoga Railroad Station on Division Street.

Shortly before noon, the 77th boarded the 18 old passenger cars that made up their train. A large crowd had gathered at the train station to see them off, illustrating Saratoga Springs' deep support and interest in the regiment. According to Private Abram Cramer, they left in a lighthearted frame of mind as if they were going on a picnic. The people gathered on the train platform shouted, cheered, and waved their handkerchiefs or hats. The boys of the 77th responded with cheer after cheer. At noon the whistles blew and the train chugged out of the station while the crowd and regiment battled for the loudest cheer. "We left Saratoga, November 28, 1861, with cheerful hearts and young and vigorous bodies."[14] The next town on the train route was Ballston Spa, but much to the disappointment of both the soldiers and well-wishers, the train did not stop. As it passed, the people cheered, a cannon was fired, bells were rung, and whistles tooted.

Exactly 99 days since McKean's posting and 64 days after Camp Schuyler opened, the Bemis Heights regiment left for the battle to save the Union and to become "Saratoga's Favorite Regiment."[15]

Lieutenant John J. Cameron, 77th New York State Volunteers, Company F

Cameron died of disease at Yorktown.

Courtesy of the USAMHI and the New York State Division of Military & Naval Affairs Adjutant General's Office, Albany, N.Y.

Private John D. Riley, 77th New York State Volunteers, Company H

Riley enlisted on September 20, 1861. He was discharged for disability during August of 1862.

Courtesy of Gay Wojtowicz

– 3 –
Tenting on Abe's Lawn
To Washington & Camp Hill House
Winter 1861–1862

The change from a house with good beds to a tent and government blankets will ever be fresh in our memories.
—Adjutant Lieutenant Winsor B. French
"Letters from the Army," *Saratogian*

Three hours after leaving Saratoga Springs, the regiment arrived in Albany, New York. They marched to the steamboat landing and began boarding the *Knickerbocker*, a decrepit old steamer. Several hours were required to stow away the regiment's 960 men, stores, and baggage. There was not enough covered space on the boat to accommodate the entire regiment, and two companies were forced to endure the voyage on the exposed deck. These hardships gave some men an excuse to sip the liquor smuggled aboard in their canteens. While there was no disorderly conduct aboard, there were quite a number of jovial fellows. Throughout the long night, the old boat churned southward down the Hudson River. The night's darkness gave way to a foggy and rainy morning. The steamship docked on November 29, 1861, in New York City at the foot of Fourteenth Street and the regiment disembarked into a pouring rain.[1]

The welcoming committee of the Sons of Saratoga residing in New York and a lively band escorted the 77th to the barracks in the park. After lunch, Captain Benjamin Judson assisted in the distribution of 862 British Enfield .577 caliber rifles. Deadly accurate at 200 to 300 yards, the rifle in the hands of a trained soldier could fire three shots per minute.² Later, in front of a large crowd, the 77th formed up on the steps of New York City Hall. After numerous speeches, the Sons of Saratoga presented one regimental flag and two small national flags to the regiment. McKean did not make any boastful promises. He assured their friends that they would never be ashamed of the Bemis Heights Regiment. The colonel placed the regimental flag in the hands of Sergeant Isaac Bemis, a distant relative of the farmer on whose land the Battle of Bemis Heights was fought.

The handsome flag was made with deep blue silk surrounded by a thick fringe of fine yellow silk cord. The flag had gilt lettering with "Bemis Heights Regt. 77TH N. Y. S. V." across the top, and the state motto "Excelsior" on the bottom. Painted on both sides, the top center area had an eagle with spread wings, perched on a globe. Below the globe was the furled flag of stars and stripes. Beneath this was a large shield, half of which represents the sun rising over a lake; the other half stars and stripes. The right side displayed a Revolutionary War Battle with men in continental uniforms loading a cannon under the colonial flag. The left side depicted British General John Burgoyne surrendering his sword to the American commander with the Stars and Stripes waving overhead. Mounted on the head of the flagstaff was a spontoon captured from the British in 1777.³

The regiment marched to a pier near the battery and boarded a large ferry that transported them across the Hudson River. In New Jersey, they were directed to a number of dirty, dilapidated cattle cars. Caked with filth and reeking disgusting odors, the cars were judged unfit for human occupation. The officers protested unsuccessfully and the regiment spent the night riding in those wretched cars.⁴

The following morning, November 30, the regiment pulled into Philadelphia. To provide for the tired and hungry troops, the people of Philadelphia set up two saloons that accommodated 500 men. At the Cooper Shop Volunteer Refreshment Saloon, or simply the Old Cooper Shop, the men made barrels during the day, and at night the ladies fed the troops. The bill of fare consisted of the best that the market could supply.[5] They marched into the building in perfect order, demonstrating precise military decorum as they dined. The previous regiment had behaved poorly, and the ladies were overheard whispering about how gentlemanly this regiment conducted itself. One of the ladies asked for the name of the regiment. In response, an officer saluted in true military style and bellowed, "The 77th New York, Colonel McKean commanding."[6] When the lunch ended, the colonel called for three cheers for the loyal ladies of the City of Brotherly Love. The men responded loudly with rousing hurrahs and passed quietly out of the building. The kindness shown by the citizens of Philadelphia was never forgotten.[7]

It took the regiment 12 hours to cover the 100 miles from Philadelphia to Baltimore. The reception in Baltimore was not warm and previous regiments had been fired upon. The boys were ordered to fix bayonets, keep their comments to themselves, and to maintain a tight formation while marching to the railroad station.[8]

At 4:00 a.m. Sunday, December 1, the exhausted regiment rolled into the Washington railroad station near the Capitol building. The train ride in unheated freight cars from Baltimore to Washington had taken seven hours to cover 37 miles. Adjutant French and Quartermaster Lucas F. Shurtleff rode out to Meridian Hill to select the best available campsite. The regiment ate a hearty breakfast at the Soldiers Rest, a temporary relief station. Later that afternoon, the 77th arrived at their campsite located by the old Porter mansion, about one mile and a half outside of Washington. The sun set while the regiment prepared supper and pitched tents for their first night under canvas. According to Lieutenant French, the change from good beds and a house to a small tent and government blankets would always be fresh in their memory.[9]

The tents used by the regiment housed four men and measured eight feet by seven feet and seven feet high in the center. Tent floors were covered with straw, cedar boughs, or boards. The typical contents of a tent included a bed, stove, and plank seats.[10] The comforts of each tent varied with the ingenuity of its occupants. Many of the soldiers modified their tents to gain extra headroom. They bought boards about nine inches wide and made a pen for the tent to sit upon, which raised the tent and provided them with more headroom.

The camp, named Camp Hill House, was laid out in 10 long straight rows of 25 tents each. Each row was named for a familiar street back home. Commodore William Porter's mansion was within the boundaries of the 77th's camp. The building was utilized as the regiment's headquarters, hospital, and also for religious services. The various functions like quartermaster, commissary, post office, barber, suttler, headquarters, and the hospital were in operation.

Everywhere in view, which included the dome and the river, were tents and encampments. "The neighborhood looks like a forest of bayonets when they are all on drill."[11] Drill here, as at Camp Schuyler, was the primary duty of the day. Days were spent with officers studying infantry tactics and drill regulations and the men learning the manual of arms, and duties of a soldier. They were taught everything from reveille to tattoo.[12]

Drill and discipline were instilled in the boys. Profanity and drunkenness were forbidden. The common form of punishment was the cordwood drill. The soldier being punished was required to stand guard or march while carrying a heavy four-foot-long section of cordwood. The regiment averaged about one soldier per day on the cordwood drill. When two of the 77th's soldiers were caught sleeping on guard duty, Colonel McKean immediately placed the guilty pair under guard and ordered the whole regiment turned out. The prisoners were escorted to the front by armed guards, and informed that death was the penalty for their crime. McKean told the regiment that he would take responsibility for pardoning them, "but the next man who is convicted of a similar offense, dies."[13] Later in the war the whole brigade would be assembled to witness the punishment for those convicted of cowardice. Private Lewis Burke, sentenced for cowardice in the 77th, served his time at hard labor in the Dry Tortugas. Burke was brought before the regiment, his sentence was read aloud, his buttons and the blue cord on his uniform were cut off, and a sign marked "Coward" was hung on his back. Guards with fixed bayonets marched him off as the band played "The Rogues March."[14] During 1863, their entire division assembled to witness the executions of two deserters from the Vermont Brigade. "The men knelt down on their coffins and the provost guard shot them. One of them did not even groan; the other said 'Oh dear me.' "[15]

At Meridian Hill, the 77th was provisionally brigaded along with the 85th, 87th, and later the 76th Regiments of New York State Volunteers to form the Third Provisional Brigade in Brigadier General Silas Casey's division. Casey frequently reviewed and drilled his brigades. The training was not wasted on the Bemis Heights' regiment; their drill performance rapidly improved.[16] Although they were only under Casey's command for a few weeks, the general quickly earned the respect of both the officers and men of the 77th.[17] He appointed Colonel McKean as the provisional brigade commander. When Congress was in session, the colonel maintained a busy schedule. He slept in camp every night, and each morning he attended to the needs of his regiment and brigade. After the morning drill, McKean mounted his horse and rode to the Capitol. After the day's session in the house, he made his way back to the camp.[18] The colonel established a guard around his brigade. A man from the 87th was shot when he tried to run one of the 77th's guards. An investigation cleared the guard.

Morale was high among the 77th on the day before Christmas. The weather was pleasant, and during the previous two weeks, a steady stream of packages from home had arrived. The people of New York State had certainly not forgotten their boys in blue. Boxes and cash arrived for the regiment from Saratoga Springs, Ballston Spa, Wilton, Essex County, and Fulton County. The Christmas packages contained mittens, socks, pillows, and other items to make a soldier's life in field a bit easier.[19] On Christmas Day 1861, many of the boys were homesick. Corporal Skinner remarked: "Some have the blues and some a lack of patience. In our tent we are beguiling the hours, each in his own way. Fowler smokes his pipe, McNeal likewise, Sid King is singing, Perkins is on guard, and Skinner is trying to write."[20]

Throughout the entire month of December, the days began with misty mornings that cleared off at midday to bright sunshine; the weather seemed more like September than December to the displaced Northerners. On New Year's Eve at midnight, it was warm enough that no fires were needed for warmth, and some of the boys danced in the moonlight to celebrate. Since their formation the previous year, the 77th lost 10 men to disease and 27 deserted. January 1, 1862, was designated as a gala day and no one in the regiment was required to perform any duty. Richard McMichael, of Saratoga Springs, felt the boys in the 77th should celebrate the New Year with a good meal. He arranged for 400 pounds of cooked chicken and turkey to be sent to them, but the eagerly anticipated shipment did not arrive on time. The bountiful gifts arrived the next day, Thursday, January 2. The earth literally shook with spontaneous cheers from the troops as the food was distributed. McMichael was brevetted the regiment's unofficial quartermaster at Saratoga.[21]

Every Sunday the regiment assembled in front of the mansion and from a balcony the chaplain delivered his sermon. The troops sang hymns, listened to the sermon, and sang some more. A choir was even formed to enhance the regiment's services. Colonel McKean established a rule that each and every man of the 77th was required to attend weekly religious services. The only persons excused were the sick and those on duty.[22] This earned the regiment the nickname "McKean's Sunday School Boys."[23] Their chaplain, Reverend David E. Tully, was a talented clergyman. Ordained as a pastor in the Presbyterian Church, he had served at Princeton and Ballston Spa, New York. With the outbreak of the war, the church granted Tully a leave of absence for one year and he enlisted.

While the regiment was camped at Hill House in early January of 1862, an order came from the War Department to destroy the alcoholic beverages of any hotel or saloon selling such beverages to soldiers. Shortly after this order, an intoxicated soldier staggered back into camp. The drunken soldier was forced to show Captain Judson and two noncommissioned officers where he had imbibed. Warned that the proprietor could be violent, Judson instructed his men to carry their weapons in a threatening manner. The captain and his detail quickly entered the establishment. Surprising the proprietor, they ordered him to put his hands up. They kept him in that position until he was relieved of a heavy caliber pistol and all of his beverages had been emptied into the gutter outside.[24]

Unsanitary conditions and the lack of a clean water supply for drinking and bathing inevitably led to sickness and disease. Corporal Skinner mentioned in a letter that he had washed his hands only twice since leaving Saratoga. Some soldiers had not washed at all. He commented that "We are smoked almost black. Pull on my gloves when I eat and laugh at the other boys for having dirty hands."[25] By mid-January, the majority of the regiment was deemed unfit for duty with the morning sick call averaging between 150 and 200 men every day.[26] The 77th's surgeon, Dr. John L. Perry, overworked and in poor health, was discharged in early February. Fortunately a suitable replacement was quickly secured. Dr.

Augustus Campbell, from Gloversville, was mustered in as the regiment's new surgeon. Campbell had a quiet, easy manner that was comforting to patients.[27]

The regiment's health improved miraculously—if only for a day. On January 16, only those who could not walk remained on sick call. Everyone else turned out for inspection and mustered for pay. The 77th gave the appearance of being a much larger regiment. Soldiers were supposed to be paid every two months but were lucky to receive payment at four-month intervals. In the Union army the pay scale in a regiment ranged from privates at $13 per month to colonels at $212. For some, the long-awaited pay muster took on a different meaning as their purchases on trust had to be paid. "It was laughable when our suttler opened his stand some weeks ago. The boys had no money and he sold to them on trust. For some days he was overwhelmed. His stand was surrounded . . . now men are beginning to curse the suttler."[28]

A mud-splattered horse and rider galloped into camp and stopped at the regimental headquarters. Barely recognizable under a coating of mud, Lieutenant French dismounted and announced that the regiment had been ordered to pack up and march in the morning. They were to join Smith's division at Camp Griffin, located about eight miles outside of Washington in Virginia. Excitement surged through the camp and cheers spontaneously went up as the word spread. The 77th had been called before other regiments with longer service. Almost immediately the regiment's first camp breakdown began. The pounding and tearing of boards and shouting of men combined with the braying of the mules into one loud racket. Throughout Camp Hill House, using the light from over one hundred bonfires, the regiment worked through the night. By 7:00 a.m. the next morning, the men and 130 wagons loaded with the regimental baggage were ready to move out.

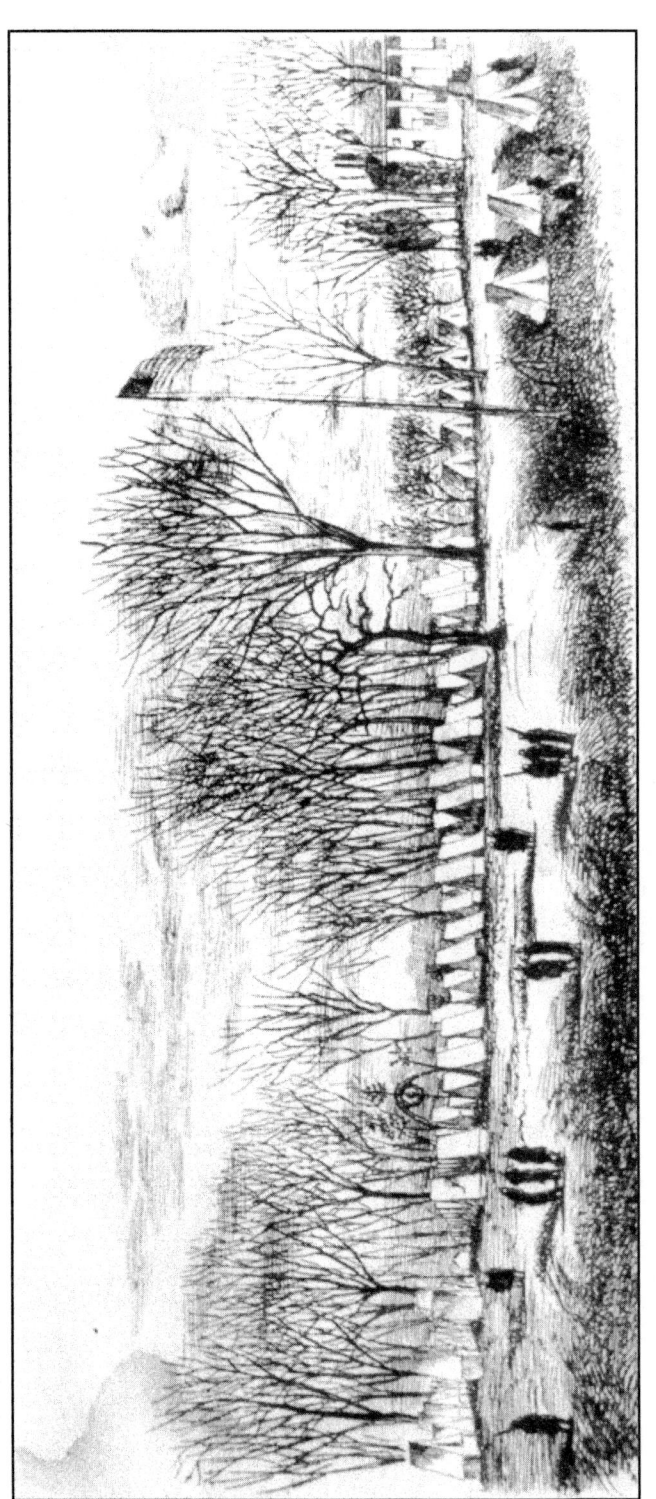

Sketch of Camp Hill House, on Meridian Hill overlooking Washington, D.C.

Courtesy of the Saratoga Springs Historical Society

**Chaplain David Tully,
77th New York State Volunteers**

He was the regiment's first chaplain.
Courtesy of the USAMHI and Military Order of the Loyal
Legions United States (MOLLUS)
Civil War Library & Museum

– 4 –

Hello Baldy
Camp Griffin
Winter 1862

My little Seventy-Seventh—It is a little regiment, but it is always in the right place.

—Brigadier General John W. Davidson

George T. Stevens, *Three Years in the Sixth Corps*

The 77th marched, or more accurately waded, through the mud while rain and sleet poured down on them for most of the day. Their wagons stretched from Camp Hill House all the way to the White House. Their route took them through Georgetown and over the Chain Bridge into Virginia. Colonel McKean sent Adjutant French and Quartermaster Sergeant Edward S. Armstrong ahead to select the best available campsite. About 3:00 p.m. the regiment arrived at Camp Griffin. The first order of business was to clear away the brush and snow. When darkness closed in, they were still pitching tents.

The first few days at Camp Griffin were spent getting their camp in order and making new friends. They were warmly welcomed into the Third Brigade by the 33rd New York under Colonel Robert F. Taylor, the 49th New York commanded by Colonel Daniel D. Bidwell, and the 7th Maine Regiment with Colonel Edwin C. Mason. Brigades were usually named after their commander, and although its name was changed often, the 77th was part of this unit for the balance of its service.[1] Their commander was born in Virginia, not far from Camp Griffin. Grandson of a general officer in the Revolution, John W. Davidson, like his father before him, was a West Point graduate. Captain at the start of the Civil War, Davidson cut all his family ties and remained loyal to his country. Davidson stated that as much as he loved his relatives, friends, and Virginia, he loved his country more. After initial duty in the defenses of Washington, he was appointed brigadier general of volunteers in February 1862.[2]

As at Camps Schuyler and Hill House, drill was still the order of the day at Camp Griffin. The soldiers practiced the full range of exercises by squad, company, regiment, brigade, and division. After extensive squad drilling in loading and firing, the regiment went target shooting. Private Aaron B. Quivey and Corporal John Hulburt proved to be among the best shots in Company C.[3] Each of the regiments were assigned their share of the picket duty.

Sickness and disease continued to plague the regiment. The regiment's sick, unable to walk, were left behind with a suitable number of nurses at Camp Hill House's hospital.[4] Before he passed away from sickness, Corporal James O. Green said that he "felt it was his duty to devote his life to the service of his country and died only regretting that he had no opportunity to show his bravery on the field of battle."[5] Corporal Skinner expressed similar feelings: "We expect to fight as soon as the weather will permit . . . My greatest fear is that I shall not be allowed to partake in the glorious work."[6]

Their orders arrived on Monday, February 24. Each soldier was issued 40 rounds of cartridges and three days of rations. Just after 1:00 a.m., the regiment tramped out of Camp Griffin to perform a reconnaissance behind enemy lines. They had a scout with a lantern to guide them as the regiment slogged through the night over roads covered knee-deep in mud toward Venice, Virginia. Many of the soldiers lost their boots in the mud and endured the trek in stocking feet. They went south for six miles, the last four of which were outside the Federal lines. By 4:00 a.m. they reached their destination without event. Companies C and B were thrown out as skirmishers while the main body of the regiment remained concealed in the woods beside the road. That evening, the regiment returned to Camp Griffin without incident. The boys felt that with more luck and less mud, they might have continued on to Richmond.[7]

During the early morning on March 9, the whole army was on the move with two days of rations in their haversacks. Early morning rainbows gave way to rain that did not let up all day. The army set up camp about one mile north of Fairfax Court House on Flint Hill. Arriving at 5:00 p.m., the Bemis Heights boys were drenched, tired, and hungry. Many accustomed to the spacious Sibley tents, did not appreciate the merits of the new shelter tents that were introduced. The shelter tents were carried on the soldiers' backs and forced the soldier to sleep directly on the ground. "Rains and a dog-tent are not conducive to the happiness of a soldier, and they are both combined to make me miserable. It rains and my tent leaks."[8]

Davidson's brigade combined with Hancock's and the Vermont Brigade to form General William F. Smith's division. Initially their division was part of the IV Corps commanded by General Erasmus D. Keyes. Smith's crack division was rated as one of the best, if not the best, division in the army.[9] William Farrar Smith was well respected and liked by his men, but his brash mouth often got him into trouble. A Vermonter, Smith was nicknamed "Baldy" at West Point because of his thinning hair. When the Civil War began, he was appointed colonel of the 3rd Vermont. At his suggestion the Vermont Brigade was formed. Never timid or hesitant, Smith continually volunteered to get his boys into the action.[10]

The army left Flint Hill on March 14, 1862. The weather turned to a steady rain that let up occasionally to a heavy mist.[11] The 77th stopped to camp in the woods along the road five miles outside of Alexandria. After dismissing the regiment, Colonel McKean told the boys to make themselves as comfortable as possible. Corporal William H. Wright took this comment too literally. After the camp had quieted down, he slipped out and went into the nearest town, where he enjoyed a hot supper. On his return to camp, the duty sergeant caught Wright and reported him for being absent. Wright was called up before Lieutenant Colonel Henderson, who ordered him to his quarters and chided him, "I will see if a ball and chain will keep you."[12]

Saturday, March 15, the regiment was about four miles west of Alexandria on the Leesburg Pike waiting for their turn to embark on the transports. Here the 77th experienced some of its worst nights in the service. One soldier "felt like sleeping but my clothes being wet I feared to lie down commenced to dry them piece by piece. Stockings first I pulled them off and stood barefoot in the mud. While holding them over the fire I grew quite sleepy—nodded—reeled—staggered—then bled, gathered up, awoke with my foot in the coals of the fire. Caught up my stockings wrung the water out of them and began to sing."[13] Camping on ground covered with ankle-deep water and no dry wood available for fires they named the place Camp Misery. Still residing at Camp Misery a week later on Saturday, March 22, the regiment spontaneously gave three hearty cheers when the order to move the following morning was read during dress parade. The morning air was filled with the music of one hundred bands. It was a grand sight to behold, as regiment after regiment paraded aboard the boats with their colors proudly waving. In Alexandria, the 77th was split up and boarded onto three different ships. The boys took in the sights as the ships took them down the Potomac River. They anchored in the Chesapeake Bay, and early the next morning, the fleet hoisted anchors and made way to Fortress Monroe.[14]

Brigadier General John W. Davidson

Davidson was a brigade commander.
Courtesy of the Arthur Marchand
Collection at the USAMHI

Sergeant William H. Wright, 77th New York State Volunteers, Company K

Wright was wounded at Spotsylvania. He claimed to be the first man over the wall at Petersburg.
Courtesy of the USAMHI and New York State Division of Military and Naval Affairs Adjutant General's Office Albany, N.Y.

– 5 –
Siege Yorktown
Peninsular Campaign
Spring 1862

They went out from us, because they were not of us.
— Surgeon George T. Stevens
Three Years in the Sixth Corps

The morning of March 25, 1862, found the Army of the Potomac anchored under the protective guns of Fortress Monroe with the USS *Monitor* nearby. Corporal Skinner described the vessel as a short piece of plank with a snuff box in the middle.[1] The transports weighed anchor at sunrise and headed west to the burned-out ruins of Hampton. The Virginia shoreline became a spectacle of sights and sounds as the Army of the Potomac disembarked. Thousands of men, animals, supplies, wagons, and cannons emptied from the steamers and regrouped along the shore. Major General George Brinton McClellan's Peninsular Campaign had begun. The strategy was to avoid the main Confederate army by taking an alternative route to Richmond. McClellan's army would be ferried around the tip of the Yorktown Peninsula, and once ashore, they would fight their way to Richmond.[2]

McClellan was a brilliant engineer, but he was overly cautious on the battlefield. Born in Philadelphia, McClellan attended the University of Pennsylvania and later the Military Academy. After nine years in the army, he resigned to take a position with the railroad. By the start of the Civil War, he was one of the nation's highest paid railroad executives. The governor of Ohio appointed him to major general. After the

Union defeat at Bull Run, Lincoln gave McClellan command of the Army of the Potomac. In letters to his wife, McClellan often referred to Lincoln as "nothing more than a well meaning baboon."[3]

Once ashore, Smith's division quickly sorted themselves out and marched. Halfway to Newport, they camped in a field beside the road. On March 27, Baldy's division led the way marching 15 miles along the left bank of the James River. Spotting the enemy, they quickly formed into a line of battle near Warwick. Ordered to advance, Smith's battle line swept forward through the woods and across a cleared field. Driven off by a shell from a Union Parrott cannon, the rebels skedaddled. Davidson's troops swept through the abandoned Southern encampment and bivouacked there for the night. The next morning they marched back, camping two miles outside Newport News. Along the way, the regiment was delayed when they stopped to investigate what appeared to be an enemy cannon overlooking the road. With each step toward the distant cannon, the men expected the gun to bark out a shower of lead. The gun stayed silent—fabricated from a large wooden grain mortar mounted on a cart, it was a Quaker. Continuing on, they were directed to set up camp along the banks of the James River. The watery grave of the USS *Cumberland*, sunk by the CSS *Merrimack,* was clearly visible out in the bay with only the tops of the ship's masts rising out of the water.[4]

On Monday morning, March 31, Assistant Surgeon George T. Stevens performed his daily rounds at the field hospital. To practice medicine Stevens, a talented surgeon, had earned degrees from both Castleton and Union College.[5] By mid-afternoon the surgeon finished his duties and was on his way back to camp. Stevens noticed a boat rapidly steaming down the river. Some men from the Vermont Brigade were down on the riverbank dredging for oysters. No one gave much thought to the approaching boat, until a puff of smoke burst from it, followed by a shrieking sound increasing in volume until it passed overhead and exploded with a loud bang farther inland. The Vermont boys quickly lost interest in the oysters and rapidly sought cover. The puff, shriek, and bang sequence was repeated a couple of times; then the CSS *Teaser*, commanded by Lieutenant Hunter Davidson, steamed back up the river. Ironically, this Davidson was their brigade commander's brother.[6]

Returning to the camp, Stevens found the brief bombardment had unnerved one of the officers. The man made a nosedive into the sand floor under his tent, screaming out, "Get into your tents, boys!"[7] Later that evening, Stevens rejected the officer's request for a certificate of disability. A few days later, the officer resigned and left the service. Stevens concluded, "It was too noisy along the banks of James River for a quiet citizen like him."[8] This and other recent activity intimidated some of the officers and men, triggering a weeding-out process. During the winter months, some of the officers and men established themselves with reputations for bravery by heralding their own praises. Discovering that the 77th and Smith's division were not going to be a safe haven for those with questionable courage, they found reasons to resign or managed to get sent to the rear. "They went out from us, because they were not of us."[9]

On April 2, General Davidson's brigade made a reconnaissance to drive back the rebel pickets, but by late afternoon they had marched 12 miles without encountering the enemy. April 4 was a clear and warm day, as the Army of the Potomac advanced along the James River toward Yorktown. As the day progressed, the soldiers' knapsacks got heavier and the straps cut deeper and deeper into each man's shoulders. Dropping out of the ranks, tired soldiers rifled through their knapsacks, judged what was worth carrying, and discarded the rest. "I have only one change of underclothes here and it is enough."[10] This process left the bushes and trees along the roadsides strewn with cast-off clothing, blankets, uniforms, and coats. The soldiers who followed, noticing that some of the discarded items were in better condition than their own, began to swap items.

On Saturday morning, April 5, Smith's division with Davidson's brigade in the lead resumed the advance toward Yorktown. After marching less than a mile, Davidson's troops came upon a recently abandoned enemy fort at Young's Mills. A violent thunderstorm enveloped the brigade as it advanced through the woods. Vivid streaks of lightning flashed and rolls of thunder boomed as the soldiers picked their way through the briars and thorny bushes. Scratched and bleeding the battle line emerged from the woods into a clearing. After cautiously making their way across a clearing and through a swampy section of woods, they were at the bank of Warwick Creek. The enemy entrenchments were positioned along the opposite side of the creek. Only Smith's division was up, the others waited on the road behind them. The enemy quickly acknowledged their presence with a barrage of shells crashing into the trees around them.[11] Federal cannon were brought into play and an artillery duel ensued that continued until that night. The boys of the 77th and their division spent the night without tents, and those without food in their packs went hungry. Positioned in the swamp at Lee's Mills, they were approximately three miles from Yorktown. On April 6, the artillery duel resumed. On the edge of a marshy stream, five companies of the 77th were assigned picket duty, approximately 150 yards from the Southern positions. "The second night, the boys all went to sleep on their posts. I could not keep them awake, nor myself either. We were so worn out with watching . . . My men were posted before night behind large trees and could not be relieved until after dark again. For if a man showed himself outside his tree, he was sure to get a rifle shot very near his head."[12]

A major came down the 77th's line checking and commenting on the contents of each soldier's cartridge box. Upon reaching Privates Dave Allen and George Percival, the major questioned why they were not firing. Private Allen replied that he was not there to waste ammunition, then he directed the major's attention to a mounted officer across the line. The major nodded and Allen quickly raised his rifle, aimed and fired. Seconds later the officer fell from his horse. The private commented: "Now you don't see him, Major."[13] Across the battlefield another officer mounted the same horse but cautiously stayed farther back. To prove their point, the privates directed the major's attention back to the mounted officer. Percival raised his rifle, aimed, and fired. However, the distant officer remained mounted, and the privates had made their point.[14] At Lee's Mills the Bemis Heights Boys returned just as many shots as they received in the regiment's baptism to fire. "We did not mind the rifle bullets much, but not so the grape shot and shells which they commenced throwing at us from the fort. One of the shells burst near us, a piece of which tore off the leg of Francis Jeffords, one of my company, or so mangled it that it had to be cut off below the knee."[15] His comrades rushed over to aid him and the resulting crowd drew the attention of a Confederate battery. Another shell burst overhead and grazed Lieutenant John Patterson, knocking him down.[16] "For three days and nights our troops have fought them . . . Four times we shot their flag down, and as many times they raised and cheered it."[17] With night approaching, those officers and men not lucky enough to have found a dry spot fabricated platforms of logs and bark to keep them out of the water. Even General Smith made his bed at the foot of a pine tree near the battle line with only his overcoat for warmth and shelter. Colonel McKean and Surgeon Stevens had been sharing blankets since landing at Fortress Monroe. They found a good dry spot just to the left of the regiment with a big pine stump for protection against the Southern shells. Stevens gathered some pieces of bark and built a pillow of sorts for their heads while their blankets were spread out with one blanket beneath and the other one drawn over them. The colonel and the surgeon had barely settled down for the night's rest when a full charge of shrapnel crashed into their stump. The noise of the impact was deafening and fragments of the stump were scattered in all directions. They arose and the colonel asked if they should relocate. Stevens replied that he had not seen two shells hit the same spot. They spent the balance of the night resting behind the remains of their stump.[18]

While at Lee's Mills, General Davidson issued strict orders that no one could fire their weapons without authorization from a superior officer. The enemy tried to wear them down with night firing for real or threatened actions. On one dark and rainy night, the 77th was ordered to fall in. The regiment was called out to support the pickets. Darkness made it necessary for every man to use his hands to feel for the next in line. In the confusion, one man fired his rifle just as Corporal David N. Wetherwax put his hand on the man's shoulder. Colonel McKean yelled out demanding to know who had fired. The man tried desperately to wiggle out of the corporal's grip and slip away into the darkness. But the corporal firmly held on to the soldier until the colonel and the general arrived and the soldier was escorted to Davidson's headquarters. Corporal Wetherwax was promoted to sergeant for his actions.[19]

On picket duty, it was Private Charles Blanchard's turn to be the number one with orders not to fire unless under attack. After establishing the picket line, Blanchard took up his position near the reserve. Close to the end of his watch, he heard the sounds of men approaching from the direction of the enemy lines. In a trembling whisper Blanchard said "halt" and all was quiet for a short time. When the noises resumed, the excited private drew up his rifle and fired in the direction of the noise. His number two also fired, then three, four, and so on right down to the camp. Before the last gun sounded, the whole VI Corps was on full alert and ready for action. The noise ceased, and at first light some of the boys went out to bring in the dead. The only body found belonged to a plump pig. Later that morning, Private Blanchard and his comrades dined on pork chops.[20]

On April 9, the 77th occupied a piece of woods within one half of a mile from the enemy batteries. Despite 48 hours of bombardment, the boys from Bemis Heights showed their mettle and all stuck it out. The fight began at 1:00 p.m. on Saturday and continued into the afternoon. Awakened at 10:00 p.m. from their beds on the ground, they stood in a line of battle for the remainder of the night. Half of the day on Sunday was spent formed up in a line of battle, and they continued to fight through Tuesday.

On April 16, McClellan ordered Smith to stop the Southerners from strengthening a weak spot at Dam No. 1 on the Warwick River near Lee's Mills. The 77th was ordered to form on the left with their right resting on the road. In the pouring rain the regiment advanced across a section of plowed field where their feet sunk and stuck in the ankle-deep mud. When Colonel McKean noticed that the colors were being carried in a black case, he ordered his men to "Unfurl those colors, it does not look well to have ones colors draped in mourning the first time they meet the enemy."[21] Baldy's artillery bombarded the Confederates across the millpond, while four companies of the 3rd Vermont gallantly charged, driving the rebels back to secure the line of rifle pits. The Vermonters held this line until reinforcements in gray arrived and compelled them to fall back. The 77th's brigade, held in reserve, suffered no losses in this engagement known as the Battle of Lee's Mills.

Heavy siege guns and the roads to put the guns in place were needed to break the Yorktown entrenchments. During the siege there was no reprieve in the daily routine of working and fighting. The brigade spent its days performing exhausting physical labor including building bridges, putting up earthworks, and building roads. The work was so grueling that a special whiskey ration was dealt out to the diggers.[22] Night attacks by the enemy occurred frequently. It was not out of the ordinary for the regiment to be called out at midnight and remain in arms until the morning. Adding to their misery, on two thirds of those days it rained and they were on a very limited diet. "Our diet consisted of hard-tack, pork and beans, varied only by leaving off the pork and beans for supper."[23] The duties imposed on Smith's division seemed too great for men to accomplish, but the men of the 77th would have resented being sent to the rear. Baldy remarked that he had spoken for a front seat for his boys and intended to keep it.[24]

The water from the marshy ponds on the peninsula was more lethal than the Confederates' bullets. As this was the only available drinking water, it was only a matter of time before typhoid broke out among the troops. A severe shortage of medical supplies did not help the situation. As one member of the 77th commented: "the names of those smitten down by that dreaded swamp fever, are too numerous to mention, the weeping families at home can tell the sad story, that they lost a soldier, brother, husband or friend at Yorktown; but how he came to die they will never know, only that it was caused by fever. Yet it is a soldier's death, and just as noble as though suffered on the battlefield."[25] During 1862, 119 men in the regiment died from disease and 225 men were discharged for disability, the majority afflicted by disease. Josh Billings, a well-known Yankee humorist, defined Military Strategy as "tryin' to reduce a swamp by ketchin' the billious fever out of it."[26]

On April 21, the 77th was positioned five miles from Yorktown and two miles from Lee's Mills on Mulberry Island. The regiment had moved twice and was two miles from their original position on the line. On Saturday evening, May 3, the Federal corduroy roads were complete and the siege guns were in place. That night, the Confederates abandoned the line of works at Yorktown, and retreated to nearby Williamsburg, Virginia. The following morning, the 77th was the second regiment to enter the evacuated fort near Lee's Mills. Before leaving, the rebels planted torpedoes, the first land mines, in the center of the main roads. Colonel McKean uncovered the first of these torpedoes upon entering the Confederate camp. His horse stepped on something covered by a piece of canvas that emitted a loud crack. Using his sword, McKean lifted up the canvas that covered the device. Fortunately for both the colonel and his men in the front ranks, the shell's primer had failed to ignite the shell. Many of these devices were discovered and removed by the men of the brigade without a single casualty.[27] Inside the enemy works, they found an extensive network of rifle pits that extended for miles. By mid-afternoon on May 4, the regiment was ordered to send their sick to the rear and prepare to march. Stationed since April 5 in that miserable swamp, the soldiers were only too happy to leave. Camp was quickly broken and Smith's division marched 14 miles up the road toward Williamsburg in pursuit of the rebels.[28]

Surgeon George T. Stevens, 77th New York State Volunteers

Stevens is the author of *Three Years in the Sixth Corps*.
Courtesy of the Edward A. Dowling Collection at the USAMHI

Confederate gunboat CSS *Teaser*

This gunboat bombarded the 77th's division on March 12, 1862.
Courtesy of the Library of Congress

– 6 –

Advance—Williamsburg & Mechanicsville
Peninsular Campaign
Late Spring 1862

Men of the 77th, now is the chance to cover yourselves with Glory, CHARGE!

—Colonel James B. McKean

"Report of the Thirty-Ninth Annual Reunion"

Smith's division spent the night in a line of battle, sleeping on their arms just outside of Williamsburg. The 77th took shelter under a rail fence, and on May 5, 1862, they awoke to rain splattering down upon their faces. Skirmishing began at first light in front of Fort Magruder, the rebels' earthworks on a rise overlooking the road into Williamsburg. General Joseph E. Johnston, commander of the Army of Northern Virginia, commanded the Confederate rearguard manning the fort.

McClellan remained at Yorktown, and command of the Federal troops at Williamsburg went to the senior officer, General Edwin V. Sumner. Major General Joseph Hooker's division did most of the fighting while Smith's division was held in reserve. As the morning wore on, the intensity of the battle increased, and Baldy Smith made repeated requests to get his division into the battle. Nevertheless, Sumner kept him in reserve. Later, Hooker, fearing his flank would be turned, requested reinforcements. Sumner allowed Smith to send one brigade to assist. General Davidson was on temporary absence for the day, and Smith selected Major General Winfield S. Hancock's brigade.[1] As the battle raged on their right, the regiment patiently waited off the Yorktown Road in a drenching rain from morning until the mid-afternoon. Late that afternoon, General McClellan arrived and ordered more reinforcements for Hooker and Hancock. The 77th gave three cheers and were off on the double-quick, 140 steps per minute.[2] Despite sodden uniforms and deep mud, they were the first of the rescue regiments to arrive on the field, just as the Union forces drove off the last of the Southerners. By dusk, the battle was over. The 77th had one casualty.[3] The Union had driven off the enemy rear guard, but the amount of time it took allowed the Confederate army to regroup. The rain continued through the night, turning the ground into a bed of liquid mud. Rather than making their beds in the mud, the men of the 77th's only option was to stand around shivering all night.[4] For the next two days, the regiment helped bury the dead and took care of the wounded. Many of the Confederates' wounded were in poor shape with shabby clothes and dirty bodies. Most of the soldiers in the rifle pits died from head wounds. These were the same rifle pits that had been used during the Revolutionary War, and one of the Bemis Heights boys found a piece of grape shot covered with 81 years of accumulated rust, which he presented to Colonel McKean.[5]

Corporal Robert H. Skinner and a squad of men took care of some of the wounded in Williamsburg. Skinner sent Private Frederick N. Perkins out in search of food for their patients. Returning from his foraging trip with a bag of uncooked barley, Perkins came upon an occupied house and knocked on the door. A few moments later, the door opened and a distinguished looking old man asked what he wanted. Private Perkins held out the bag and asked for someone to cook its contents.[6] While the man's wife cooked the barley, the two chatted. Ironically, the man had spent many of his past summers in Saratoga Springs. He was acquainted with Colonel McKean, Perkins' uncle, and his sister. After their conversation, at his new friend's request, Perkins nailed a small national flag onto the house. Private Perkins left with the man's good wishes and two tin buckets of cooked barley for the wounded.[7]

Chapter 6

During the early morning on May 9, the regiment took down their tents and marched 15 miles north. Reveille sounded at 3:00 a.m. the next morning, and they covered another eight miles before halting to enjoy the Sabbath. Tuesday, tents were struck at dawn and by dusk they were another six miles closer to Richmond. On May 14, Smith's division proceeded up the river four miles to camp at White House Plantation, the home of Robert E. Lee's son, Rooney. Located 22 miles below Richmond, it became the home for both Smith's and Franklin's divisions. The 77th bivouacked in a large field of fresh clover along the river. One of the soldiers wrote in a letter that it did not look like the same field when they left. The following day the rest of the army arrived.[8] On May 18, 1862, Smith's and Franklin's divisions were combined to form the VI Provisional Corps.

On Friday, May 23, at 2:30 a.m., Davidson's infantry brigade and Brigadier General George Stoneman's cavalry broke camp. The 77th led the brigade's advance toward Richmond. Ordered to leave their knapsacks and tents, a fight seemed to be in the works. About four miles out the 77th came upon the enemy's artillery, positioned across a swamp at New Bridge. The regiment was formed into a line of battle, and deployed as skirmishers along the edge of the swamp. Union batteries were brought up to drive back the rebels' artillery and control the crossing. The 77th's skirmish line was ordered to advance straight across the marsh, ten to eighteen feet wide and three to five feet deep. On the left wing, Adjutant French's horse got so mired in the mud that French had to dismount to allow her to get free. Surgeon Stevens joked about the boys becoming amphibians.[9] Reaching the other bank of the swamp, they found the enemy had retired to Mechanicsville. With darkness closing in, the men of the 77th, wet to the middle and cold, lay down in a wheat field. The regiment slept on their arms with two companies thrown out as pickets. The pickets traded shots with their rebel counterparts until 2:00 a.m. Two hours later night gave way to morning and it was time to start the new day.¹⁰

The regiment formed up and continued on, advancing until one-quarter of a mile outside of the village. The Southern artillery opened on them, a solid shot passing just above their heads. Guarded by four squadrons of cavalry, five artillery pieces, and two infantry regiments, the tiny village of Mechanicsville was five miles outside of Richmond. Ordered to take cover, the 77th filed off into a wheat field under the crest of a knoll. While making their way up the hill, the cannons barked again, sending canister and grape to kick up the dirt and gravel. The adjutant's horse spooked, rearing up and jumping, until she managed to break free. Fortunately, the doctor caught and calmed the beast. "Bang, bang she came again killing one private of Company I and slightly wounding five others of the regiment."¹¹ The colonel's horse rebelled, forcing him to dismount. When Colonel McKean yelled, "Down men,"¹² they took shelter in the wheat field lying flat on their faces. Wheeler's battery arrived to riddle the village with shot and shell, driving out the enemy sharpshooters, and causing the Confederate artillery to fall farther and farther back. General Davidson ordered the 77th and 33rd New York to advance into the village, and held the rest of the brigade in support. Prior to the charge, the 77th had seven wounded, one of whom died later.¹³

Out in front, Colonel McKean yelled, "Men of the 77th, now is the chance to cover yourselves with Glory, CHARGE!"¹⁴ The regiment responded with a deafening shout and charged down the road with fixed bayonets. Wheeler's 12-pound cannons gave covering fire as the 77th and the 33rd quickstepped it up the main road. With the 77th pressing down the road, the rebel artillery quickly limbered up and galloped away as fast as they could go. The 8th and 9th Georgians, drawn up in a line near the edge of a small grove, grabbed their muskets, and ran. "In we went, and out went the rebels without firing a shot. They left their knapsacks, canteens, blankets, flags, two or three dead horses, and one wounded soldier."[15] The boys were still yelling as they entered Mechanicsville. Private Allen McLain and a squad of three others from Company C entered a house whose occupants apparently had left in a great hurry to get away from those screaming Yankees. With a hot breakfast cooking on the fireplace and preserves in the pantry, the boys did not need a written invitation and they did not walk away hungry.[16] The regiment had no additional casualties during the charge. A wounded private from the 8th Georgia Regiment was found and taken prisoner. "Many trophies were secured by our men but my ambition rested on a copy of Davies Surveying taken from the knapsack of a Georgia soldier."[17] Private John E. Evans, a drummer, captured a battery flag that stated "VICTORY OR DEATH." Evans presented the flag to Captain Franklin Norton, who passed it on to Colonel McKean. The colonel in turn presented the flag to General Davidson.[18] The capture of Mechanicsville established the right flank for the Union army within sight of the spires of Richmond and earshot of the church bells.[19]

The next day, the enemy was found in considerable force at Hanover Court House located on the right and to the rear of the Army of the Potomac. Davidson's brigade was withdrawn from its position on Beaver Dam Creek. The brigade moved down the river about five miles and encamped with the rest of the VI Corps on Gaines Farm, one of the more charming places on the peninsula. Within easy range of the enemy guns, the pickets could easily observe their counterparts on the opposite shore. The regiment did picket duty and built both roads and bridges.

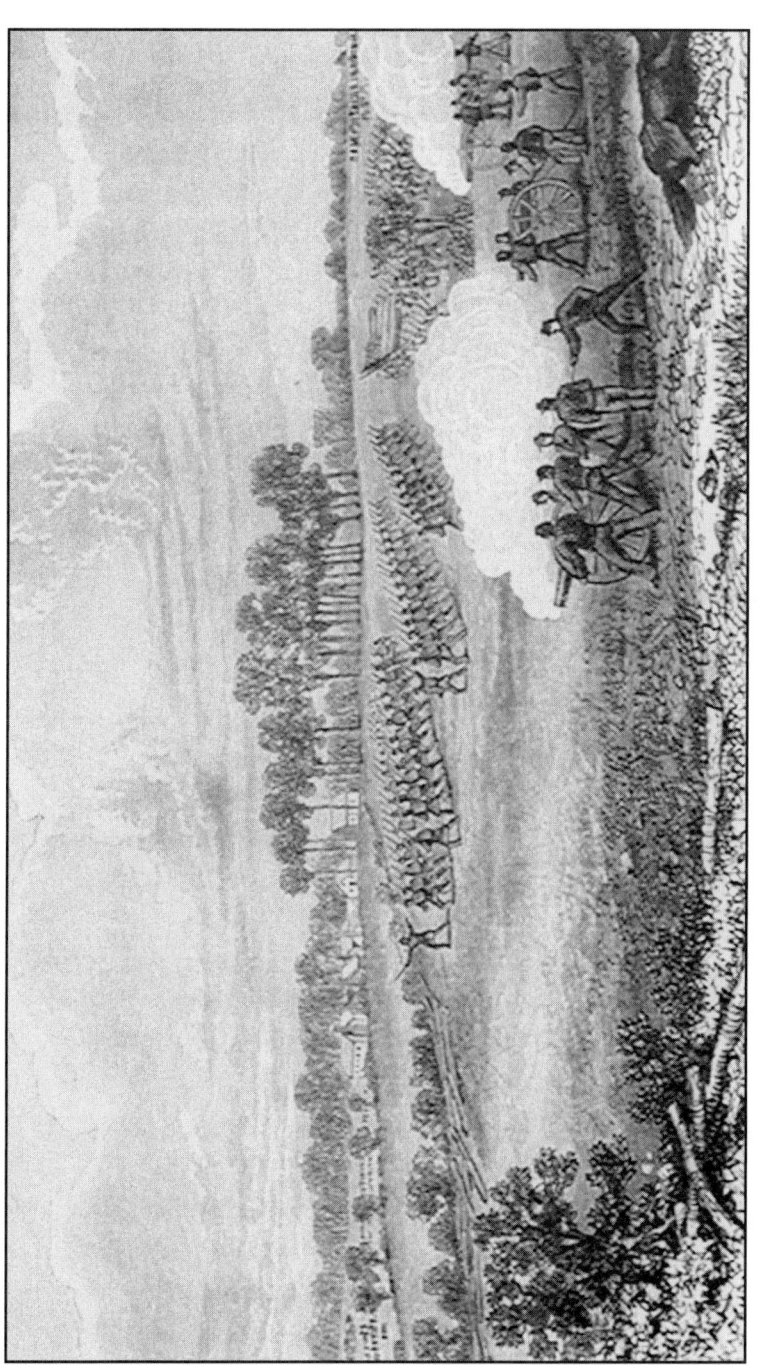

The 77th's charge at Mechanicsville, Va., on May 24, 1862

Courtesy of Stevens' Three Years in the Sixth Corps

Portrait of Colonel James B. McKean

Courtesy of Stevens' *Three Years in the Sixth Corps*

–7–
Seven Pines & Retreat—The Seven Days Battles
Peninsular Campaign
Early Summer 1862

They always got scorched when they pitched into old Baldy's division.
—Confederate Prisoners of War
"Letters and Extracts from Diary of Captain Martin Lennon"

In late May, numerous storms and the rapid surge of rising waters made the Chickahominy River too deep for crossing and there were no bridges in the immediate area. The majority of McClellan's army, including the 77th, were camped on the river's south bank. Taking advantage of the situation, General Joe Johnston attacked the smaller group of Union troops, Erasmus D. Keyes' IV Corps. Several valiant attempts to cross the river to aid their comrades were undertaken. McKean and the 77th armed themselves with all the axes they could find and began dropping the forest trees. Working the entire day in the waist-deep water, they tried to fashion a makeshift bridge. However, the rushing waters defeated all their ambitious efforts.[1] Keyes' corps, on the far bank, dug in and managed to hold off the rebel attacks, in what would be known as the Battle of Seven Pines. During the battle, a shell knocked General Johnston off his horse, severely injuring him. Shortly after the battle, Baldy Smith's division was sent to support Keyes. They marched along the bank of the Chickahominy to the closest bridge and returned on the opposite bank. The next three weeks, whether on picket duty or building earthworks, were spent within the range of the rebels' rifles.[2]

Shortly after the battle, Colonel McKean and many others came down with typhoid fever. The colonel, once a vibrant man, was hit hard by the sickness. Flat on his back, at times he had a high fever, shaking fits, and night sweats. With his life on the line, McKean was taken to a hospital in the rear. The medical director at Hampton sent the colonel home, where he would have the best chance for recovery. A father figure to his boys, the colonel was missed.

At this point the regiment was unable to muster more than one-third of the men for active service.[3] The soldiers were being asked to do more than men were capable of doing. Weakened by performing arduous tasks under a blistering sun day after day, night after night the soldiers were called to arms to fend off the attacks of the enemy. With clothing and tents sodden from the frequent rains, their only relief was to sleep in the mud. "Men who worked on the breastworks one day would be found in the hospital the next, burning with fever, tormented with insatiable thirst, racked with pains or with deliriums their parched lips, and teeth blackened with sordes, the hot breath and sunken eyes, the shallow skin and trembling pulse, all telling of the violent workings of the disease . . . At times one might sit in the door of his tent and see as many as six or seven funeral parties bearing comrades to their humble resting places."[4]

After McKean came down with the fever, leadership in the 77th shifted to a number of temporary commanders. These lieutenant colonels included Joseph Henderson from the 77th; John W. Corning, 33rd New York; Wheelock G. Veazey, 3rd Vermont; and Selden Connor, 7th Maine.[5] The governor also promoted Adjutant First Lieutenant Winsor B. French to major, and a cavalry captain, Samuel McKee, to lieutenant colonel. McKee was given command of the 77th, but he became ill with typhoid fever and was forced to decline.[6] Eventually, based on his brigade commander's recommendation, French was promoted to lieutenant colonel and given command of the 77th.

As ordered on June 9 at dawn, the regiment packed up, and continued on toward Richmond. By the end of the day, they were 14 miles closer to Richmond. The 20th New York joined Davidson's brigade. Composed entirely of German immigrants, they were nicknamed "the Turner Rifles." Turners, being popular German fraternal organizations, centered their programs on disciplined physical training. Their full ranks and unsoiled uniforms were in sharp contrast to the brigade's veteran regiments. Saber bayonets and high conical black hats made the Turners a sight to behold on the parade ground. Nevertheless, they would have to prove themselves on the battlefield. The next day, the brigade marched another eight miles before they encamped to enjoy the Sabbath.

When Johnston was injured at Seven Pines, Jefferson Davis appointed General Robert Edward Lee as commander of the Army of Northern Virginia. Lee was born in Virginia. Raised in genteel poverty, he had gladly accepted an appointment to the Military Academy. He graduated second in his West Point's Class of 1829 without a single demerit. At the start of the Civil War, Lee refused an offer to command the Union forces. His nicknames through the war ranged from "Granny Lee" to the "Ace of Spades."[7]

During June, General Lee began a series of battles designed to drive back McClellan's army from the gates of Richmond. Lee also brought Thomas J. "Stonewall" Jackson and his army up from the Shenandoah. McClellan was aware of Jackson's arrival near his flank and he believed that his rail supply line north of the Chickahominy River was threatened. He shifted his base to the James River on the south side of the peninsula. In the 1860s siege guns could only travel overland by rail, and there were no railroads along the James River, forcing McClellan to abandon his plan of capturing Richmond.

On June 25, Franklin's VI Corps was positioned on the army's right flank near Golding's Farm and was not directly involved in either the Battle of Oak Grove or the Battle at Beaver Dam Creek. These were the first two days of the Seven Days Battles. When the news of the second day's battle reached the VI Corps, spontaneous cheering erupted throughout all the camps. In celebration, the division's bands were allowed to play. The bands had been ordered silent for the past months, so as not to reveal the Union positions. They made up for lost time with a patriotic fervor and filled the camps with music. The men went happily to their beds that night, with each soldier expecting to move on toward Richmond in the morning. Unfortunately the following morning, the regiment was ordered to arms and told that their army was in retreat. Passed in whispers from camp to camp the orders came to "Leave your tents standing; save a few of your most valuable effects; destroy the balance; the army must retreat."[8] Before sunrise, they heard volleys of musketry off on their right, but no artillery. Later in the morning the reality of the situation hit home as they watched a long gray battle line advance into positions they had recently occupied across the river. The 77th was held in reserve and spent the day under arms. Called up during a battle, the boys formed up quickly and took only their arms and ammunition. Their brigade was exposed to artillery fire while deployed as support on the second line. First Lieutenant Winsor B. French recounted, "as I was forming the battalion a solid shot came close by me, and struck Isaac Boice and John Seeley. It was a spent shot, which came from Gaines Hill. I saw it as it came fluttering like a partridge and gave warning."[9] At the front the regiment lay in rifle pits with musket balls whistling over their heads. During the night, Davidson's brigade relieved Hancock and occupied the advance positions. Enemy activity kept them on alert until they were relieved. Early in the morning, General Davidson came and spoke to the adjutant. He instructed French to take a commissioned officer of each company and go to their camp and pack up a few articles of value, but only one wagon would be allowed per regiment.[10] French exclaimed, "My God, General, does the Army of the Potomac retreat?"[11] General Davidson responded to no questions, implying just to do it.

On Saturday, June 28, the 33rd New York held most of the picket line, but a detachment of the 77th was also deployed. The regiment's picket duty included manning a small advanced redoubt on Golding's farm. Private John Ham was stationed there with two other soldiers. Ham vowed to his comrades that he would not fall back in the face of the enemy. The rebels sent out two regiments, the 7th and 8th Georgia, as a skirmish line to push the Union pickets back. The two soldiers stationed with Private Ham fell back with the other advance pickets. The private, true to his pledge, stood his ground alone. Crouched down in his redoubt, Ham waited until the advancing line was within rifle range. Using the top log of his redoubt as a gun rest, Ham raised himself up, aimed his rifle at the chest of the nearest man in gray, and squeezed the trigger. Not waiting to see the impact of his shot, the 18 year old was already crouched down low and reloading his rifle. He repeated this process ten times, until the line of advancing Georgians overpowered him with bullets and bayonets.

Colonel Lucius M. Lamar's gray line continued to advance until they came upon the Federals' main line. Ordering a charge, the Confederate colonel and his men threw themselves at the entrenched 33rd and 77th New York regiments. They were met with staggering volleys of hot lead that brought the charge to a quick halt and left the ground littered with dead and wounded. Not quite convinced, Lamar regrouped his men and tried again. The results were the same, and the ground in front of the two New York regiments became more littered with over one hundred dead and wounded Southerners, including Lamar. Sergeant Isaac Bemis brought in the badly wounded Confederate colonel. Some of the other prisoners commented to Lieutenant Lennon that they always got scorched when they pitched into old Baldy's division.[12]

Later that day, a skirmish line from the 77th pushed the rebel pickets back and reclaimed the original line. At the advanced redoubt, they found Private Ham's body riddled both with shot and bayonet wounds. The Confederates paid a price to get past the man who would not retreat or surrender—four dead gray-clad bodies lay nearby. Returning to camp, they found it occupied by another division, who had appropriated their haversacks and blankets. The boys were given replacements and bore the loss patiently.[13] On Sunday, June 29, the Confederate artillery fire from new positions won the prior day, forced Franklin's corps to abandon their camps at Golding's Farm. Ordered to leave their tents standing, they cut the canvas into pieces and broke up everything that the enemy might use.

Assigned to the Army of the Potomac's rear guard, Smith's division quietly withdrew at 3:00 a.m. the following morning. Marching through Savage Station, they observed burning, house-sized piles of hardtack boxes. Hill-sized piles of barrels, full of supplies, burned nearby. The soldiers could pick and choose from huge boxes of clothing and shoes left along the road. Boxcarss loaded with munitions and set ablaze, filled the air with explosions as the cars passed on their downhill journey to the river. After a short rest in the woods near Savage Station, Smith's division resumed the trek south. However, they returned when they heard heavy firing in the rear. By 1:00 p.m., Davidson's brigade formed into a battle line, shielding the retreating army and wagon train. The oppressive heat and humidity of the day took a toll. In mid-afternoon General Davidson, overcome by severe sunstroke, fell from his horse. The general went to the rear in an ambulance and Colonel Taylor from the 33rd New York assumed temporary command.[14] Late in the afternoon, there was an artillery duel followed by a rebel assault. The 77th, held in reserve, watched their comrades check the Confederates. Nightfall ended the Battle of Savage Station.[15] Abandoning 2,500 sick and wounded men, the remaining Union forces pulled back toward White Oak Swamp.

The regiment began their trek southward about 10:00 p.m. and continued on through the night. "The boys would drop down by the side of the road completely exhausted. But we got across, the 77th bringing in more men than any other regiment of the Third Brigade, not excepting the 20th. The general highly complimented us."[16] The road was always full, but the retreating columns exhibited no haste or panic. Davidson's brigade marched southward a few miles, and halted to let other brigades pass. About 2:00 a.m., the brigade arrived at White Oak Swamp. After crossing the creek, they destroyed the bridge, and, exhausted, they flopped down into the grass on the hillside. The sun was high up on the horizon when the 77th awoke and were assigned to guard a road from the east. After replenishing their haversacks, they took up their position in the line of battle, intending to stay through the day and hold the enemy back until the baggage train was safely away. Forty Confederate cannons opened fire at 12:00 p.m. from the opposite bank, belching out sheets of flame and unleashing howling projectiles at those of Smith's division unlucky enough to be within range. Fortunately, the 77th was positioned out of range. The intense barrage kept Smith's batteries silent. Generals Smith and Davidson occupied a small wooden house that stood on the crest of the hill facing the bridge. The gunners in gray quickly found the range, and shells began to rain down upon the house. Baldy lost everything, including his pistols, watch, and horse. The 20th New York Regiment bolted in confusion, leaving the field strewn with their black conical hats. Teamsters cut loose their mules and ran for their lives. The infantry fell back and formed another line out of range of the enemy guns. This Battle of White Oak Swamp was the fifth of the Seven Days Battles. Moving south, the Third Brigade withdrew, with the 77th and General

Davidson in the lead.[17] During the night, they marched 12 miles to Malvern Hill.

Despite protective fire from the gunboats covering the Union position, Lee was determined to carry them with a direct assault. On the morning of July 1, the entire Confederate army rushed in an assault to gain the high ground. The VI Corps was assigned to hold the right side of the Union line and was not directly engaged in this battle. Bristling with bayonets, Baldy's three brigades looked quite formidable spread across the wheat field. With three lines of rebels on their front, the men of the 77th held their position all day, resting upon their arms while the battle of Malvern Hill raged off to their side. On July 2 at 2:00 a.m., the Bemis Heights regiment and General Davidson led the brigade on the march in one of the worst rainstorms. Every soldier was wet and muddy from head to toe.

The retreat or change of base was accomplished without panic or haste. The men endured these long marches through enemy country, not in a demoralized manner, but ready and able to fight at a moment's notice.[18] The regiment had been under fire during six of the last seven rearguard engagements from Savage Station to Malvern Hill. The general complimented the 77th on their conduct. Later these battles were tied together and named the Seven Days Battles.

Chaplain David E. Tully resigned after the army reached the James River. True to his word, Tully returned to his home in Ballston Spa, honoring the promise that he had made to his congregation before he left for the war. The manner in which Chaplain Tully performed his duties endeared him to both the officers and men of the regiment. The demands placed on him were severe because of the number of sick and dying men he ministered to.

Brigadier General William "Baldy" Smith

Smith was an outspoken division and later corps commander.

Courtesy of the Gil Barrett Collection at USAMHI

Seven Days Battle, White Oak Swamp, June 30, 1862 (Alfred Waud)

Courtesy of the Library of Congress

— 8 —

The 77th Needs a Few Good Men
Harrison's Landing & Bull Run
Summer 1862

I have finally come to the conclusion that a good set of bowels is worth more to a man than any quantity of wisdom.
—Josh Billings, Yankee Humorist
Donald Day, *Uncle Sam's Uncle Josh*

Brigadier General Davidson sat tall in his saddle and looked back with pride at his brigade as they marched almost unbroken into Harrison's Landing.[1] Harrison's Landing was a vast plantation, strategically located on a bend in the river that enabled the gunboats to cover the army's flanks and rear. Setting up their camps, the boys began to carry off the nearby fence rails. Furious, Davidson rode up and demanded to know their regiment. The closest soldier answered, "20th New York." The general swore and ordered them to put down the rails. Spurring his horse up to the next group of soldiers he asked the same question. A private replied, "The 77th New York," and Davidson responded: "All right, boys, go ahead."[2] The general had a special affection for the 77th and often referred to the regiment as "my little Seventy-Seventh."[3]

Major Selden Hetzel had not been with the regiment since Alexandria, when Colonel McKean brought him up on charges and the major was discharged. Hetzel's influential friends pressured the New York governor to get him reappointed. While the 77th was at Harrison's Landing, he returned and tried to take control of the regiment. However, all the regiment's officers judged him to be unworthy, and threatened mass resignation if

Hetzel were reinstated. On General Davidson's recommendations Major French was promoted to lieutenant colonel.[4]

Death's shadow never strayed very far from the 77th, even during the six monotonous weeks spent in the relative safety of Harrison's Landing. Recovered from typhoid, Lieutenant Halsey Bowe returned to the regiment. On July 19, a group of the officers got together to chat in one of their tents. A pistol accidentally discharged, fatally wounding Lieutenant Bowe. Immediately after he learned of the accident, Bowe's father went to aid his son. Seeking better care, he took his son to the Cooper Shop Hospital in Philadelphia. Despite these efforts, young Bowe died several days later.[5]

In mid-July, the VI Provisional Corps became the VI Corps.[6] During July, on the recommendations of the brigade surgeon, General Davidson left for his home in St. Louis on sick leave to regain his health. In August, Davidson was reassigned and given command of a cavalry division. Despite his occasional confusion with the capabilities of men versus horses and the severity of his discipline, the men liked Davidson.

By early August, of the nearly one thousand strong and healthy men who had left from Saratoga Springs on Thanksgiving Day in 1861, only about one-quarter of them remained fit for duty. With the regiment's ranks devastated by sickness, Major French and Lieutenant David J. Caw returned home to Saratoga Springs, New York, on a recruiting mission. The recruiting detail consisted of the two officers and one soldier from each of the regiment's companies.[7] Lieutenant Caw refused a promotion to major in a new regiment. He responded that he would rather be a second lieutenant in the 77th than a colonel in a new regiment.[8] He was not the only one who felt like this. In mid-August, John Rockwell and Bill Fursman recruited a full company of men from Schuylerville, New York and the surrounding areas. One of the new regiments had designs on Rockwell's company, but Rockwell wanted to enlist in the 77th. One soldier in an old regiment was worth two soldiers in a new regiment. After meeting Major French at a recruiting station, Rockwell, Fursman, and French went to call upon the governor in Albany, who agreed and issued the necessary paperwork. Rockwell was made captain of the new company and Furman became the first lieutenant. Joseph H. Loveland and John W. Belding assisted Stephen S. Hastings in the signing of 60 additional recruits.[9]

A war meeting was held on Sunday evening, August 31, 1862, at the Pavilion Spring grounds in Saratoga Springs. A speaker's platform was erected and the seating for several hundred consisted of planks resting on spring water boxes. By mid-afternoon the seating was filled, and the meeting was called to order. Several church officials took their turns on the platform. Next, Major French gave an inspiring speech on the wickedness of the rebellion and the benefits of enlisting over waiting to be drafted. A gold chain and 20 dollars were needed to entice the first recruit. The crowd heartily cheered for both the gift and the volunteer. With the ice broken, the night's work now began in earnest. The audience was worked up and freely parted with money and jewels to entice the volunteers. Three hearty cheers were given for each gift or volunteer for the 77th. There was no letup in the crowd's excitement and enthusiasm. Laboring men emptied their pockets, two cows were donated for prizes, and a little girl donated her entire life's savings. An older woman, with a young man by her side, stood up and said: "I am a widow; I have no money to give; I have no fine jewelry to give; but I want to aid in this cause and I give my only son. John, go up and sign the enlistment papers."[10] The meeting ended just after midnight. Over the next month War Meetings for the regiment were held throughout the county.[11] Late in August William A. Baker, whose large hands were better suited for holding the reins of a plow team or the stock of a rifle, awkwardly maneuvered a pencil and made his mark on the enlistment papers as Major French watched over him. Baker became a private in Company H of the 77th.

During their stay at Harrison's Landing, the 77th and their brigade worked on the construction of an extensive fort with mounts for several heavy guns. Worn down by the labors and demands put upon them, they became very susceptible to sickness and disease. The soldiers in their time on the peninsula had not developed any fondness for the heat and swamplands. On Saturday, August 16, orders were given to the regiments to pack up their knapsacks and be ready to move. Even the scorching midday sun couldn't diminish the soldiers' enthusiasm to leave Harrison's Landing. After the Army of the Potomac encampment, the land that had been blanketed with corn and wheat was now covered in mud.

That afternoon the column moved rapidly on a hot and dusty march. The foraging was good; there were plenty of chickens, green corn, fresh meat, sweet potatoes, plums, and peaches. At the end of the day, they had to make their way over an enormous two-thousand-foot-long pontoon bridge composed of 90 boats. Once across, the VI Corps bivouacked for the night on the eastern bank of the Chickahominy River. The next day would bring another equally hard trek to Williamsburg. On the third day, their journey down the Peninsula brought them to Yorktown. The next day Smith's division continued on to Big Bethel. On the fifth day the 77th and its division arrived in Hampton, where the transports were waiting.[12] On Sunday, August 24, 1862, the embarkation and passage was a somber one. The once invincible army was now facing the reality that many of their comrades were no longer with them and that the war was going to take much longer than originally thought. The regiment had lost almost half of its men, most due to sickness not bullets. The total Union loss in the Peninsular Campaign was 15,849 men, and rebel flags were still flying in the skies above Richmond. Those who survived the campaign were veteran soldiers. The glory of the quick capture of Richmond had given way to the reality of a botched campaign. The regiment disembarked at Alexandria, Virginia, and camped nearby.

In late August, General John Pope's army was fighting at Bull Run, and the VI Corps was ordered to support Pope. Due to some delays, they did not arrive on the field in time to take part in the battle. When they arrived at Fairfax Court House, the popcornlike sounds of distant gunfire were audible. Ordered to proceed two miles to Cub Run, they came upon a small bridge. The bridge was crowded with the walking wounded and stragglers moving toward Centerville. Captain Seth W. Deyoe, a tough soldier who worked his way up from the ranks, sat calmly on the bridge filling his pipe. A frightened captain without a sword was hurriedly making his way by dodging around slower, wounded soldiers. The man's zigzagging course brought him face to face with Deyoe. Striking him on the shoulder for emphasis the frightened captain told Deyoe not to be afraid.[13] Glaring directly into the man's eyes with a look of pure contempt, Captain Deyoe replied: "Well, Who the d___ is afraid? Oh, yes, I see, you are. Well, you had better get away from here then!"[14] Later that day the Third Brigade was sent to the rear of Centerville to stop stragglers. Drawn up in a line across the turnpike until the following morning, the brigade turned back hundreds of stragglers with the points of their bayonets.[15]

Two months after leaving the regiment, Colonel McKean was barely recovered but anxious to return to his boys. Against the advice of his doctors and friends, the colonel buckled on his sword and pistol, vowing to return to his regiment. In late August, McKean, barely able to walk, caught up with the 77th near Bull Run. General Smith took one look at him and ordered him to go to Washington to take care of his health.[16] In Washington, the colonel suffered an ulceration of his bowels that forced him to return to Saratoga Springs, New York. When a year later his health had not improved, James B. McKean gave up his hope of rejoining the regiment.

Four officers from the 77th New York State Volunteers—all killed in battle

Captain Luther Wheeler, *seated left*, killed at Marye's Heights on May 3, 1863; Captain Orrin Rugg, *seated*, killed at Spotsylvania on May 12, 1864; Captain Martin Lennon, *standing*, killed at Cedar Creek on October 19, 1864; and Lieutenant John Belding, *standing*, killed at Cedar Creek on October 19, 1864.

Courtesy of the International Museum of Photography and Film; George Eastman House

**Lieutenant Joseph H. Loveland,
77th New York State Volunteers, Company B**

Courtesy of Joseph Covais

– 9 –
Baldy Ordered Them to Fall Back
Antietam
Fall 1862

The damned rebels, not satisfied with the steak in my haversack, they have taken a steak off my round.
—Lieutenant Stephen S. Horton
Edward H. Fuller, *Battles of the Seventy-Seventh New York State Foot Volunteers*

When Lee and his army crossed the Potomac, Lincoln ordered McClellan to drive them back. By mid-September, the Army of the Potomac was bearing down on the Confederate army. Lee fell back to Sharpsburg, Maryland, an excellent defensive position with Antietam Creek's steep banks and deep bottom. Camped near Alexandria, Virginia, the VI Corps' assignment was to push through Crampton's Pass, Maryland.[1] As they marched into Maryland, the citizens turned out to greet the boys in blue with cheers and food to show their appreciation.

When the army reorganized on May 18, 1862, William Buell Franklin was promoted to major general and given command of the newly formed VI Corps.[2] Pennsylvania-born Franklin was a West Point graduate. When the Civil War began, he was promoted to colonel and three days later to brigadier general. Baldy Smith was in command of the 77th's division, and Colonel William Howard Irwin was temporarily in charge of the brigade. Irwin, a prewar attorney, had fought in the Mexican War.[3] In the 77th Regiment Major French was on a recruiting mission, and the senior captain, Nathan S. Babcock, was in command of the regiment. Born in New York

State, Babcock had prior experience in the New York Militia. He was employed as a glove cutter when the war started. Babcock, who enlisted as a private, was voted captain of Fulton County's Company K.[4]

Arriving at Crampton's Pass, Smith's division, including the 77th, formed into a battle line. Held in support they stood ready for action for over an hour, while Slocum's First Division drove the rebels out of the pass. Finally, with darkness closing the day, Captain Babcock came down their line and told them to lie down and rest, but no fires. Private Milton F. Sweet awoke the following morning and found that in the darkness he slept between two dead men, one clad in blue and the other in gray.[5] At 6:00 a.m. on Wednesday, September 17, 1862, Baldy's division left Crampton's Pass and began marching to Sharpsburg.[6]

The morning's quiet hold over the surrounding hills and valleys was broken by the harsh sounds of distant cannons—an indication of the coming day. Tramp, tramp from every front the Union's troops came. Still closer they could now hear distant bugles luring them to the contested field.[7] With each step closer the battle sounds intensified. An hour out from the battlefield, hundreds of the walking wounded moved away from the fury, as fast as Smith's quickstepping column moved toward it. The suffocating dust off the road engulfed the columns and limited the visibility to the next regiment.[8]

Baldy Smith arrived before his troops about 10:00 a.m. and sought out their orders. He caught up with McClellan on a nearby hilltop. Smith's division was the first of Franklin's corps to arrive on the field, and Smith's orders were to wait until directed right or left as the situation warranted. Halted alongside the road for one-half hour, they waited in the sweltering heat. While they waited, the picket detail caught up with the 77th Regiment, bringing them up to full strength of 175 officers and men.[9]

At 11:00 a.m. McClellan sent orders for Smith to go to the right to assist Sumner. Smith led his troops away on the double-quick, plunging into the knee-deep water at Pry's Ford. Their progress to the east woods was slowed by the number of wounded men filling the roads as they staggered to the rear. They entered a field covered with gray- and blue-clad bodies. The roar of musketry rolled up and down the battlefield.[10] Reporting to Major General Edwin Sumner, Baldy was ordered to close his division en masse and face them in the direction of the enemy.[11] Deploying his troops, Smith ordered Colonel William H. Irwin to have his brigade take a holding position beyond the Mumma farm to prevent another counterattack along the Hagerstown Pike and Sunken Road near Dunker Church.[12]

Rather than just tying in with Hancock's troops to shore up the Union line, Colonel Irwin elected to go for the glory and sent three of his regiments charging straight for the Dunker Church.[13] Irwin was alleged to have been intoxicated. In his defense, Colonel Bidwell of the 49th New York said that Smith had given hurried orders.[14] Irwin did not take the extra time to assemble his whole brigade and allow them to charge in force. Instead as they entered the field he had each regiment charge independently.[15]

He deployed the 77th as skirmishers on the right. The boys emerged from the east woods, with Smoketown Road on their left, proceeding straight into the field toward the Hagerstown Pike. The 20th New York, eight hundred strong, charged through the cornfield and drew most of the enemy's fire.[16] While the Turners were getting shot up, the 77th and 33rd advanced with bayonets gleaming, slightly behind them and off on the right toward Dunker Church.

Captain Babcock and his regiment picked their way through the field littered with the bodies of dead horses and men. Irwin sent the 77th careening, by the left flank, by files, down the Hagerstown Pike toward Dunker Church. The men of the regiment ran southward down the Pike with their rifles slung on their shoulders, trying to catch up with the 33rd

New York. Approaching the church, the 77th was slipping into position on the 33rd's right when they came in contact with the 49th North Carolina. Commanded by Colonel Matthew W. Ransom, the Confederates were well positioned in the woods alongside of the Pike. Captain Babcock stated that they were so close that he could see the whites of their eyes.[17] One of the first casualties, color bearer Corporal Joseph Meurer, was killed instantly when a bullet pierced his head. Collapsing to the ground, the corporal dropped the colors. They barely hit the ground before another brave soldier gathered them up to flaunt in the face of the enemy and rally the regiment.[18] The North Carolinian troops poured a merciless fire into the 77th's exposed ranks.[19] Both the 33rd and the 77th pulled back in confusion from the intense flank fire.[20] The boys returned fire with some well-placed volleys of their own. Babcock theorized that the rebels disappeared so quickly into the woods because of the devastating effect of their volleys.[21] Wounded, Lieutenant Stephen S. Horton yelled out: "The damned rebels, not satisfied with the steak in my haversack, they have taken a steak off my round."[22] Babcock's high-water mark was located approximately three hundred feet away from the bullet-riddled Dunker Church building.[23] Far in advance of the other regiments, the 77th stood firm, returning fire with spirit, and holding its ground despite murderous fire from the woods.[24]

A Southern battery opened on the 77th, at less than twenty yards from the regiment's left front, raking the regiment with both canister and solid shot.[25] "The enemy now had us under cross fire—front & left—it went well with me until they flanked me! They played upon our left with artillery. A shell burst on the left of us and fairly ploughed our ranks about center & left a tremendous punch as if the Steed of Balaam had kicked me with all his feet at once."[26] Lieutenant Robert Skinner was mowed down, and Private Gideon M. Rowley was mortally shot through the head.

Riding along the battle line, General Smith observed the 77th fighting far in advance of the other regiments in an exposed position. Smith exclaimed: "There's a regiment gone! Call it back!"[27] Receiving the orders to fall back from Smith's aide, the regiment faced by the rear rank, suffering heavily before they fell back over the crest of the hill. While Irwin's brigade had been unable to take the woods, they had flushed out the rebels in Mumma's Swale. By about 1:00 p.m., they had done what was requested of them. Five or six batteries were dueling over their heads at a similar number of the enemy's batteries near the Dunker Church.[28] Private Davis Green from Company E was killed by grapeshot while lying on the ground. Sergeant Henry Allen was wounded in the shoulder.[29] For the balance of the battle, the brigade was subjected to both heavy artillery and sharpshooter fire. "With the exception of a little fighting which Colonel Irwin took upon himself to do . . . the remainder of the day was spent in artillery fighting."[30] The advance of the brigade had carried them so far forward that they were abreast of Dunker Church.

As night set in, Baldy Smith's division was holding their line, which extended along the Sunken Road, through the intersection, and down the Hagerstown Pike almost to Dunker Church. Hancock's division was on their right, and their left flank was open, with Slocum's division positioned well behind them in the cornfield. The musketry died down with the increasing darkness, but the battlefield was not still or quiet. New sounds came forth with the moans of the wounded replacing the noise of the guns. Lanterns winked in the darkened fields as medical orderlies and stretcher-bearers searched for the wounded.[31]

First Sergeant Carlos W. Rowe and Private Sam Dodge went out to look for their friend Private George Huntington, a color guard. While backtracking over the regiment's movements, they heard a faint voice calling out. They found two men lying side by side, one wounded and the other dead. The wounded man asked them to "take the blanket off of my brother and put it over me. I'm so cold."[32] After covering the wounded man, they fetched him a canteen of water. Rowe and Dodge continued to search until they found Huntington. With a bullet in his head, the two men found solace in that their comrade had died instantly without suffering. At dawn, the two soldiers returned and carried Private George Huntington's body to a cemetery near Sharpsburg. They wrapped him in a blanket and buried him.[33]

Despite heavy artillery and sharpshooter fire, the 77th's brigade held their position until relieved by Brigadier General John Cochrane's brigade of Major General Darius N. Couch's division at noontime on September 18. That evening Lee began withdrawing his forces across the Potomac River. The Battle for Antietam was the most bloody single-day battle of the Civil War with 12,410 Union and 10,700 Confederate casualties. The regiment suffered 6 men killed and 32 wounded. After the battle, Major Babcock became quite ill and Lieutenant Colonel Selden Connor, 7th Maine, was in temporary command of the 77th.

Lieutenant Colonel French left Saratoga Springs with 360 new men for the regiment. They traveled by train on their journey to catch up with the 77th in the field. In New Jersey, Private Edward Fuller had fallen asleep with his head resting against the open window. He instantly awoke when he felt the cap slip off his head. Still in dreamland, Fuller watched as his cap fell out of the window. The private sprang from his seat, ran to the car door, and stepped off the moving train. He landed and rolled a couple of times but fortunately Fuller was not injured by his stunt. After he had retrieved his hat, the train was nowhere insight. Fuller found some rail workers who agreed to transport him to the next station for five dollars. Arriving too late to catch his train, Fuller boarded the first train going toward Washington. He fell asleep on the train and woke up to find that someone had stolen his cap. In Philadelphia Private Fuller purchased a new cap for two dollars and caught up with the group.[34] On September 23, the recruits visited the Cooper Shop Volunteer Refreshment Saloon and availed themselves of the excellent fare and hospitality there.

After the battle of Antietam the regiment went into camp at Williamsport, Pennsylvania. Colonel French, Lieutenant Caw, and the new recruits joined up with the regiment while they were camped here. Late September the regiment packed up and moved on to Bakersville and then to Hagerstown where they camped. At Hagerstown, 92 new recruits under Captain John R. Rockwell, First Lieutenant William H. Fursman, and Second Lieutenant Cyrus F. Rich joined the regiment. One of the new lieutenants, who had brought his bed and mattress, was very unhappy to find that he would have to transport his household furniture on his back. Rockwell's company became the new Company K, and the men from the original Company K were consolidated into Company F.[35] The veteran soldiers taunted the new recruits who signed up for bounty money, calling them two hundred dollar sons of bitches.

Major Nathan S. Babcock, 77th New York State Volunteers, Company K

Babcock was Company K's first captain. He commanded the regiment at Antietam and the Wilderness.

Courtesy of the Roger D. Hunt Collection at USAMHI

Sergeant Henry Allen, 77th New York State Volunteers, Company K, and daughter

Allen died of wounds from Antietam.

Courtesy of the Gloversville Free Library

– 10 –

Good Generals Are Hard to Find
Fredericksburg & the Mud March
Winter 1862–1863

Never take the Bull by the horns, young man, but take him by the tail; then you can let go when you want to.
—Josh Billings, Yankee Humorist
Cyril Clemens, *Josh Billings—Yankee Humorist*

On Thanksgiving Day, November 27, 1862, the VI Corps was camped near Aquia Creek, Virginia. The 77th, as well as the rest of the corps, anticipated just another march in the rain, with rations of pork and hard bread. After the brigade inspection the regiments marched back to their respective camps, pleasantly surprised to find dinner smoking by the cook's tents. Fresh sheep pelts were hanging in profusion, and the odor of roasting meats filled the camp. The bill of fare for the Field and Staff of the 77th included vermicelli soup, roast beef and lamb, baked and fried potatoes, carrots, plum pudding, peaches, black walnut loaf cake, and whiskey and coffee. Lieutenant Colonel French, Captain Jessie White, Dr. Campbell, Dr. Stevens, Assistant Surgeon John W. Fay, Quartermaster First Lieutenant Jacob F. Hayward, and Adjutant First Lieutenant David Caw dined together. After the banquet their toasts included "Thanksgiving,—may we celebrate it at home next year" and "The girls we left behind."[1]

Thanksgiving was also the anniversary of the regiment's departure for the war. Lieutenant Colonel French assembled the 77th at the sunset dress parade, and gave a brief account of the past year. A year spent with four months in

Washington, five months on the peninsula, two in Maryland, and the balance in Virginia. Of the original 38 officers, 24 were no longer with the regiment. Three had died, 17 had resigned, three were dismissed, and one was transferred. Captain Franklin Norton was transferred to the 123rd New York and promoted to lieutenant colonel.[2]

On the Saturday following Thanksgiving, the roads became too bad to get a wagon over, so each regiment detailed soldiers to fetch rations on their backs from their last camp. "It was some way to fetch rations, I started at noon and got back about 7:00 p.m. with 25 pounds of coffee."[3] That night six men, two of them from the 77th, died in the ambulances.[4] On Sunday, November 30, the day was intensely cold and they marched six miles with great difficulty to the rear of Falmouth Station, opposite Fredericksburg.

During November, changes took place in the leadership of the Army of the Potomac. Lincoln relieved McClellan and placed Burnside in command of the army. Ambrose Evert Burnside was born and raised in Indiana. At the end of his first year at West Point, Burnside was ranked at 207 out of 211 cadets for conduct.[5] Somehow, he managed to graduate. When the war began, Burnside organized the 1st Rhode Island. At Bull Run he commanded a brigade, and after a mission in North Carolina he was appointed as a major general of volunteers. He had refused the command of the Army of the Potomac twice before, but influenced by generals who wanted to block Hooker, Burnside reluctantly accepted. By his own admission, he was not well suited for the command of an army.[6] Other changes included Baldy Smith's promotion to VI Corps commander. General Albion Paris Howe replaced Smith as division commander. Howe was born in Maine. Nicknamed "Pop" at West Point, Howe commanded an artillery brigade during the Peninsular Campaign.[7] Shortly after Antietam, Colonel Irwin was removed as brigade commander. Colonel Ernest Von Vegesack of the 20th New York filled in as the temporary brigade commander, until Francis Laurens Vinton was promoted to brigadier general and given the command of the brigade. Vinton was praised for his ability and coolness under fire. Born in Maine, he had attended West Point.[8] Vinton's Third Brigade was composed of the 7th Maine, the 21st New Jersey, plus the 20th, 33rd, 49th, and the 77th New York regiments.

On December 12, Howe's division crossed the bridge without incident. The bridge and the river were covered with playing cards, as the soldiers, sensing a battle, did not want to risk meeting their maker with gambling devices in their pockets.[9] Once across, they lay down and waited for the signal to advance. "Every moment we were expecting to see death hurled among us from the enemy on the hills."[10]

On the first line, they were exposed to both artillery and musket fire. About 9:00 a.m., General Vinton was at the front directing the advance of his line of skirmishers when he was wounded by a rebel sharpshooter's minie ball. The wound in Vinton's abdomen was serious and required cutting out through his back. Colonel Robert F. Taylor of the 33rd New York temporarily assumed command of the Third Brigade. Taylor was relieved at noon on the same day by General Thomas H. Neill.[11]

Gentlemanly Brigadier General Thomas Hewson Neill was considerate, intelligent, and an experienced officer.[12] Born in Philadelphia, Neill attended the University of Pennsylvania for two years. Appointed to West Point, he graduated in the Class of 1847. A man with highly cultivated tastes and manners, he acquired the nickname "Beau Neill" in the regular army. With the war, Neill served as a general's adjutant, then he was appointed colonel of the 23rd Pennsylvania.[13]

Later that day, December 13, the regiment, positioned along the river, had grandstand seats to view the battle. Hooker and Sumner's troops chewed themselves up in frontal assaults against Lee's well-entrenched forces on Marye's Heights. "Oh! What a cruel sight to see men cut down so rapidly on both sides.

It made my heart ache to see our lines advance. Such firing as there was on both sides, I never saw before."[14] Captain Lennon observed five full regiments go into the woods, but only two colors with only a company of men behind each managed to come out.[15] The rebel fire from behind the wall was so destructive that none of the Union soldiers had been able to come within 25 yards of the wall. No troops ever showed greater valor than the Federal troops displayed at Fredericksburg. After 14 unsuccessful frontal assaults, Burnside stopped only because they ran out of daylight. He still had not realized the futility of his actions, and he planned to lead the first assault the next morning to ease his troubled conscience. Total Union casualties were roughly eleven thousand men killed, wounded or missing, and the Confederate casualties were about half of that amount. The 77th lost only one man, Private Paul A. Brown of Company H.

In the moonlight, the 77th relieved the 121st New York on the front line.[16] The explosions and crack of muskets that had dominated the sounds of the day gave way to the moaning sounds from the nearby battlefield. The cries for water, loved ones, and God's mercy mixed with the groans of thousands of dying soldiers, and blended into a deep, many-voiced moan. The temperature dropped well below freezing, with a stiff wind blowing across the battlefield, and men began to die from exposure as well as bleeding to death.

Some newspapers called the Battle of Fredericksburg a reconnaissance in force. Yet the gut feeling was that their army had been badly whipped.[17] Lincoln referred to the Fredericksburg campaign as snatching defeat from the jaws of victory. The privates in the Army of the Potomac were very quick to learn that when the men of the Army of Northern Virginia were dug in at a location of their choice, it could be extremely difficult to move them.[18] This proved to be a very tough lesson for some of the Northern generals to learn.

The next day the 77th was on picket duty near Fredericksburg. After trading some shots with the rebels, both sides realized that if they did not shoot, their counterparts stopped shooting also. "They came pretty close to killing one of our boys. Hit him in the breast. Bullet struck him on his breast plate and turned him."[19] The next day under a white flag agreement there was no firing on the picket line. Private T. Scott Fuller wrote that "the picket lines talked to each other, and the rebels wanted to know how we liked Burnside."[20] The men settled in for the winter around Falmouth. The regiment had its camp at White Oak Church, Virginia. The men built huts and made themselves as comfortable as possible. The regiments were nestled closely together on low ground that some considered too wet for good camping.[21] From December of 1862 through March of 1863, the VI Corps was stationed near White Oak Church, Virginia. The Third Brigade even planted trees along the company streets to provide shade and make the upcoming hot months of summer easier to tolerate.[22]

On January 16, 1863, orders came down to have three days of cooked rations on hand and sixty rounds of cartridges and be ready to march with a moment's notice. On January 20, Major General Ambrose Burnside launched his infamous Mud March. Burnside's plan was to cross the river at Banks' Ford and to assault Lee's left flank. On a bright and balmy day, the army marched at noon and moved several miles up the river. In the thick woods near Banks' Ford, they bivouacked out of sight of the rebels. That evening just before midnight the rain started. The intensity of the rain increased through the night and by the following morning everything was flooded. The ground on which they had slept was soaked, and their wet wool blankets and coats did little to protect them from the pelting storm. The roads were over knee-deep in mud and quickly became blocked with hopelessly stuck pontoons, wagons, and cannons. Manpower replaced horsepower, but nevertheless even one hundred soldiers could not pull a pontoon through that quagmire. The 77th was "laying in a gorge which protects us from the wind but not the rain."[23] General Burnside and two staff officers rode through the Second Division's camp in the afternoon offering encouragement to the wet soldiers. Both the general and his horse were completely covered with mud. The rebels were alerted to Burnside's intentions, and that evening it was decided to abandon the operation. The next morning the 77th and the rest of the Army of the Potomac began to slog back to their old camps at Falmouth. The road back was littered with a multitude of dead mules, horses, cannons, pontoons, and wagons—all stuck in the waist deep mud. The efforts of the cannoneers and teamsters were futile as they lifted and tugged with rails and poles to free a wagon or cannon from the mud's grip. "The mud was deep, the day was gloomy, and the men were discouraged. They straggled badly. Regiments could not be distinguished. The whole column became an unorganized crowd."[24] The rebels were greatly amused by all of this and put up taunting signs in Fredericksburg to greet the returning Union troops. At the end of January, General Burnside resigned and Major General Hooker assumed command of the Army of the Potomac. Also during the last days of January 1863, Baldy Smith was relieved of his command. On February 5, Major General John Sedgwick was assigned as the commander of the VI Corps.

General John Sedgwick, known as "Uncle John" to his men, was considered one of the most beloved officers in the army because of his kind nature and genuine concern for his men. One of the best Northern generals, Sedgwick was born in Connecticut and a West Point graduate. Perhaps the most battle-experienced officer, Sedgwick had served against the Seminoles, Cherokees, Kiowas, Cheyennes, Comanches, and Mexicans. After being wounded three times at Antietam, Sedgwick recovered and was given command of the largest Union corps.[25]

Major General John Sedgwick

Sedgwick, the corps commander, was killed by a sharpshooter at Spotsylvania.
Courtesy of Stevens' *Three Years in the Sixth Corps*

The Stone Wall at Marye's Heights Above Fredericksburg on May 3, 1863 (Andrew J. Russell)

Courtesy of the Library of Congress

– 11 –

Legend of the Greek Cross Begins
Marye's Heights to Banks' Ford
Spring 1863

Noble Seventy-Seventh, you have covered yourselves with glory.
—Brigadier General Albion Howe
George T. Stevens, *Three Years in the Sixth Corps*

    A spirited and aggressive soldier, Joseph Hooker looked like a general. Hooker was credited with bringing spirit, discipline, and sanitation to the army. His personal courage warranted his nickname, but "Fighting Joe" actually evolved from the consolidation of a newspaper headline. Born and raised in Hadley, Massachusetts, he graduated from West Point. With the advent of the Civil War, Hooker rose quickly through the ranks, but his biting tongue, drinking, gambling, and womanizing took the luster off his star.[1]

    During March of 1863, Joe Hooker initiated several policies to raise the morale in his army. He got the troops paid, allowed leaves home, and made sure that the men were well fed and clothed.[2] Hooker's greatest contribution to the army was the institution of corps badges. For purposes of identification and morale, he assigned each corps a different symbol, and each division had a different color. The VI Corps symbol was the Greek cross (✚) with white signifying the Second Division. "Every member of the corps felt an exulting pride in his relation to it, and regarded his badge as a mark of great honor."[3]

    Hooker's plan was to split his force and attack Lee from two directions. In April of 1863, Hooker took most of his army, and circled north and then westward to attack the Confederates from the rear. Sedgwick's corps was left to occupy Lee's attention at Fredericksburg. However, Lee anticipated Hooker's tactics and divided his forces, with the main part of his army firmly entrenched in the densely forested wildernesslike terrain near Chancellorsville. Hooker's advance bogged down against Lee's lines.

On May 1, 1863, to demonstrate their presence for the rebels, the VI Corps mustered for pay in the afternoon parading back and forth.[4] Late evening on Saturday May 2, Hooker's orders arrived, and Sedgwick's corps broke camp to march through the night. Their first objective was to capture the heights above Fredericksburg. Sedgwick proposed to attack both flanks to capture the heights, rather than straight on in the Burnside manner.

"On the first Sabbath in May, God called upon the regiment to ascend Marye's Heights and worship him, not with psalm and thanksgiving, but with the musket."[5] Before sunrise on Sunday May 3, 1863, Howe's division crossed the river. The first light found them formed in a line of battle opposite Fredericksburg, protecting their batteries. Howe positioned his three batteries of Parrott guns to allow simultaneous fire upon the enemy works and the advance of his storming columns.

Lee placed Major General Jubal Early in command of the forces defending Marye's Heights. Early's command included the Washington Artillery Battalion of New Orleans and Barksdale's Mississippi Brigade.[6] The charismatic General William Barksdale was born in Tennessee and studied law. Elected to congress in Mississippi, Barksdale resigned at the start of the war to become a colonel in the 13th Mississippi.[7]

Howe's assignment was to advance from the left side of Hazel Run and turn the rebels' right flank. The 77th was employed as a skirmish line preceding the division's storming columns. Skirmishing was only assigned to disciplined, fast-thinking soldiers who were good with their rifles. Such being the case, it was an honor for a regiment to be selected as skirmishers. Howe paired off his inexperienced units with the veteran regiments from his division, dividing them into three lines commanded by General Neill, Colonel Lewis A. Grant, and Colonel Joel J. Seaver.

At 8:00 a.m. Major Babcock with Companies A, G, and F formed a skirmish line, rose up, and quickly advanced on the rifle pits in the middle of the plain. After a brief exchange of fire, Babcock and his three companies pushed the Confederates back, and took their rifle pits with minimal loss. Holding these positions for two hours, they were ordered to advance to the second line of rifle pits. Colonel French brought up the regiment's reserves and deployed them along the line. Fearlessly, French rode his old white-faced bay horse up and down the regiment's line. The men of the Bemis Heights regiment stood ready to take on any foe. The signal was given and French, with his sword slicing through the air above his head, yelled, "Come on boys."[8] With bayonets fixed, the men of the 77th advanced onto the exposed plain adjacent to Hazel Run. The rebel batteries opened on them. Despite musket and artillery fire the regiment continued on unhesitatingly. The barrage was so intense that Major Babcock felt that he "occupied the only place that was not struck by a shell or grape!"[9] The boys took the second line of earthworks and waited for their support to join them. Alone up to this point, the 33rd New York was brought up to support the 77th and lengthen the skirmish line. The New Orleans Artillery continued taking a heavy toll. Nevertheless the skirmish line never wavered; when one fell, he was quickly replaced by another soldier.

The colonel frequently looked back, waving and beckoning with his sword and enthusiastically yelling, "Steady boys! Come on boys, come on."[10] French tried to throw off the aim of the artillery gunners by ordering a double-quick right oblique followed a few moments later with a double-quick left oblique, zigzagging them across the wide plain. Out in front, the colonel's horse pranced happily along and seemed to be enjoying the melee. The regiment crossed the plain in splendid style. Their line was perfect, and the men could not have performed better if they were drilling.

The Confederate guns on the heights raked the plain with grape and shell. One shell exploded in the midst of Company B, stunning Captain Horton. Presuming him mortally wounded, Horton's comrades carried him from the field.[11] Grape and canister whizzed past them and made holes in the ground that feet occupied only seconds before. Another shell burst tore a man into pieces; still the 77th pressed on.[12] As the skirmish line approached the railroad bed along the base of the heights, a number of gray-clad soldiers rose up from behind this protective cover and opened fire. Corporal William Deyoe fell and Private Edward Fuller felt a sharp pain behind his right ear, then nothing as his body collapsed onto the plain. Captain Andrew Cowan's 1st New York Battery swept the railroad bed with enfilade fire, driving the Confederates back. French's line seized the work and pushed on.

Crossing the plain, the left side of the skirmish line veered off toward Telegraph or Lee's Hill, while the right side of the line went on toward Marye's Heights. On any given day most people, even without the weight of a musket, would find the climb up the heights difficult. Ignoring the bombardment around them, the blue line started up the slope. Leading his company, Captain Luther Wheeler, the regiment's senior captain, urged his boys on. Standing tall on the exposed plain, Wheeler felt an intense pain burning its way into his stomach. Dropping his weapon, the captain clutched his stomach before he staggered and fell. Yelling like madmen, Captain Rugg's company charged up the hill while carrying on a brisk fire with the retreating rebels.[13] Stunned by a shell burst and wounded in the foot, Corporal William W. Finch fell to the ground.

Farther up the hill a dense cloud of smoke, flickering with numerous muzzle flashes, enveloped the stone wall. The skirmishers on the right moved up the heights past the wall. Crossing Hazel Run Creek, they emerged from the wooded bank and flanked the wall. With bayonets gleaming, the Bemis Heights boys flanked the wall at the same instant the 7th Massachusetts and 36th New York approached head-on. With the Yankees pouring in from two directions, the 18th Mississippi fought like tigers. Some fought with stones, others clubbed with their guns, while others fought hand-to-hand.[14] During the mayhem, Corporal Michael Lamey seized the 18th Mississippi's color. The boys in blue, using bayonets and rifle butts, quickly outnumbered and overpowered the rebels.[15] Captain Martin Lennon's company captured over one hundred prisoners, more men than he had in his company. One of his men alone had captured eight prisoners.[16] Most of the prisoners, including Lieutenant Colonel William H. Luse, were from the 18th Mississippi.

Observing that their objective was already taken, General Neill redirected his attack to the batteries on their left. After catching their breath for a moment, Rugg's company pushed forward with the rebs falling back before them. The boys from the 77th made their way through a deep hollow.[17] Using the ravine to conceal their presence, the 77th assaulted the works near the brick schoolhouse, manned by the Washington Artillery's 1st Company. Coming up from the rear, they surprised the artillery men busy at their guns.[18] Lieutenant Colonel French was a model of bravery as he rode at the head of his regiment. "Colonel French and General Neill riding up the hill to see who would reach the cannon first; and I see the flash of Colonel French's sword as he tapped the cannon first."[19] General Neill told French to "write your name on it! You have won it! It is yours!"[20]

The 77th captured two pieces of artillery and the associated limbers, two wheeled carts used to carry ammunition and tow the cannon, as well as a pair of horses.[21] General Howe rode up while Colonel French was standing on one of the captured cannons. Howe exclaimed: "Noble Seventy-Seventh, you have covered your selves with glory."[22] A few minutes later, one of the reb cannons that had evaded capture by taking early flight, opened on them from a distant hill. Lieutenant Thurber and William Caw were forced to seek protection behind a nearby stump. One shell killed Private Benjamin H. Day, took a leg from Private Branch, as well as an arm from Private McNaughton, and mutilated the regiment's colors.

Private Charles H. McNaughton from Company A was struck in the elbow by a piece of shell that severed most of his arm. With a bone sticking out, his lower arm hung by a piece of flesh. As the private walked, the weight of his lower arm caused it to swing around, twisting itself up until it unwound. The sight of McNaughton's wound was enough to make most men faint, but the young private was in good spirits. As the blue line surged up the hill, he swung his good arm above his head, laughed, and shouted out, "Hurrah boys, we are whipping them! We are driving them back!"[23] Chaplain Norman Fox helped McNaughton get out of the line of fire. Later Chaplain Fox assisted in transporting the wounded private to the hospital. When it was McNaughton's turn to have his arm amputated, the boy acted as calmly as if he was sitting in a barber's chair for a haircut.[24]

Private Erskin Branch's leg was blown off below the knee by a 12-pound shell. Two men carried him on a stretcher to Fredericksburg. While en route to the hospital, another shell passed over them, prompting Branch to give three cheers for the flag and commence singing the red white and blue.[25] At the field hospital Private Branch argued with the surgeon on duty to save his knee joint. With the timely arrival of Surgeon Stevens and a German doctor from the 20th New York, Private Branch got his wish and they amputated his leg four inches below the knee.

At the top of the heights, with no more entrenchments to storm and the rebels fleeing toward Chancellorsville, a great cheer spontaneously erupted from the victorious soldiers, before they sank down exhausted, trying to catch their breath. Captain Wheeler lay on the hillside mortally wounded. Nearby was Major Thomas C. Kendall, 21st New Jersey, missing a leg. When they heard cheering from the heights above them, Wheeler asked the major what was happening. Kendall replied that the 77th had captured the battery and planted their flag. Captain Wheeler sighed and said: "Ah Major, you and I helped place it there."[26] Shot in the stomach, Wheeler died later that day surrounded by his friends in an old barn, on the road to Fredericksburg.

Private Edward H. Fuller regained his consciousness and found himself alone on the battlefield with a bullet wound in his head. Fuller managed to get up, and began his journey to seek medical help. He zigzagged back and forth across the field as he reeled toward the rear. After covering a good distance, Fuller encountered some Union soldiers. When asked if he was wounded, Fuller turned his head and displayed his bullet wound. The soldiers helped him to the medical station, where Assistant Surgeon DeLong removed a rifle ball from Private Fuller's head. He lost the hearing in his right ear and was later reassigned to do clerical duty in the War Department in Washington.[27]

Corporal William W. Finch waited until night, then he managed to crawl to safety behind the Union lines. Wounded earlier that day, Finch had lain on the battlefield while both armies passed over him. When the rebels returned, he crawled into a ravine and hid under some laurel bushes. He remained undetected as they passed nearby on both sides of his hiding spot.

On May 3, 1863, the ground leading up to Marye's Heights was covered with hundreds of wounded and dead bodies. The dead were left as they had died on the field in whatever position they had fallen.

After capturing the heights, the VI Corps needed a couple of hours to sort things out. Mid-afternoon, with the First Division in the lead, followed by Howe's Division, they advanced toward Chancellorsville. The reinforced rebels elected to make a stand, a short distance down the road at Salem Church. After enduring substantial casualties, the Union advance was checked. While not actively involved in this battle, the 77th and their brigade were assigned a support position on the left flank.

All through the night the Confederates massed their forces and continued to do so during the following day, May 4, 1863. With Lee's troops almost surrounding him, Sedgwick had his corps positioned in a rough horseshoe shape protecting Banks' Ford. The ford was their only means for getting back across the river. Around 9:00 a.m. the following morning, the rebels opened fire on them from the same heights that they had taken the prior day. This confirmed that rebel reinforcements had arrived and the VI Corps was almost surrounded. One of Sedgwick's younger staff officers stated that the outlook appeared to be very bleak. Sedgwick smiled and responded, "It has somewhat that appearance, I will tell you a secret; there will be no surrendering."[28] The VI Corps would have to fight for survival. Neill's brigade was positioned as the toe of the horseshoe along the crest of an open field, supporting an artillery battery.[29]

After a day of skirmishing, around 5:00 p.m., Longstreet's corps attacked Neill's brigade on the right front. The 77th occupied a little height on the left and was only partially engaged. During the attack, Colonel Ernest Mattais Peter Von Vegesack was mortally wounded, causing his regiment, the 20th New York, to break and run to the rear. This forced Neill's brigade to fall back. "They came upon us with such a tremendous force that we were driven back about a mile, but we didn't run, but fell back with our faces to the enemy, fighting as hard as men could fight."[30] General Neill seemed to be everywhere on the battlefield encouraging his men, especially where the fighting was the thickest. Neill's horse was shot and killed from under him. The badly bruised general was carried from the field and command of the Third Brigade transferred to Colonel Robert F. Taylor of the 33rd New

York. With the Confederates closing in on three sides, the Union artillery's volleys of grape shot were closely followed by the infantry's musketry. This staggered the rebel advance, allowing the Union forces to fall back. "The rebs had our regiment fairly flanked once with a whole brigade but we fell back through a piece of wood and formed a new line and held it until about 9:00 p.m. when we fell back."[31]

Except for the 20th, the other regiments in Neill's brigade stood their ground nobly under a murderous fire, and their stubborn resistance enabled the VI Corps to cross at Banks' Ford that night.[32] Darkness ended the fight and covered their retreat.[33] The boys from Bemis Heights regiment paid dearly for their part in these battles: 7 men were killed in action, 5 died from wounds, 40 were wounded, and another 30 men were missing.

Captain Luther Miller Wheeler's body and the news of his death arrived simultaneously in Saratoga Springs. The result was as profound a feeling of sorrow as had ever been experienced by this community. All remembered his manly bearing, fine form, and noble presence. By the age of 22 years, he had quickly risen to command a company. Indeed, he was the 77th's senior captain. He had proven his courage on a dozen battlefields. He was the idol of his men and the pride of his regiment. It was not unusual for the loss of such a man to produce such sorrow. On Sunday afternoon, the funeral procession was formed on Broadway. The quarter-mile-long procession proceeded to Wheeler's father's house where the remains were taken in charge and conveyed to the Baptist Church. Both sides of the streets were lined with spectators as the entire village and a large number of county residents turned out. The church service had three reverends, including former Chaplain Tully.[34] Former Captain B. F. Judson was a pallbearer and Colonel McKean was among the mourners. Following the service the procession was reformed and proceeded to Greenridge Cemetery.

Corporal Altus Jewel, *left*, wounded at Marye's Heights, and Private William Deyoe, killed at Marye's Heights
Both were 77th New York State Volunteers.
Courtesy of the Warren K. Tice Collection at the USAMHI

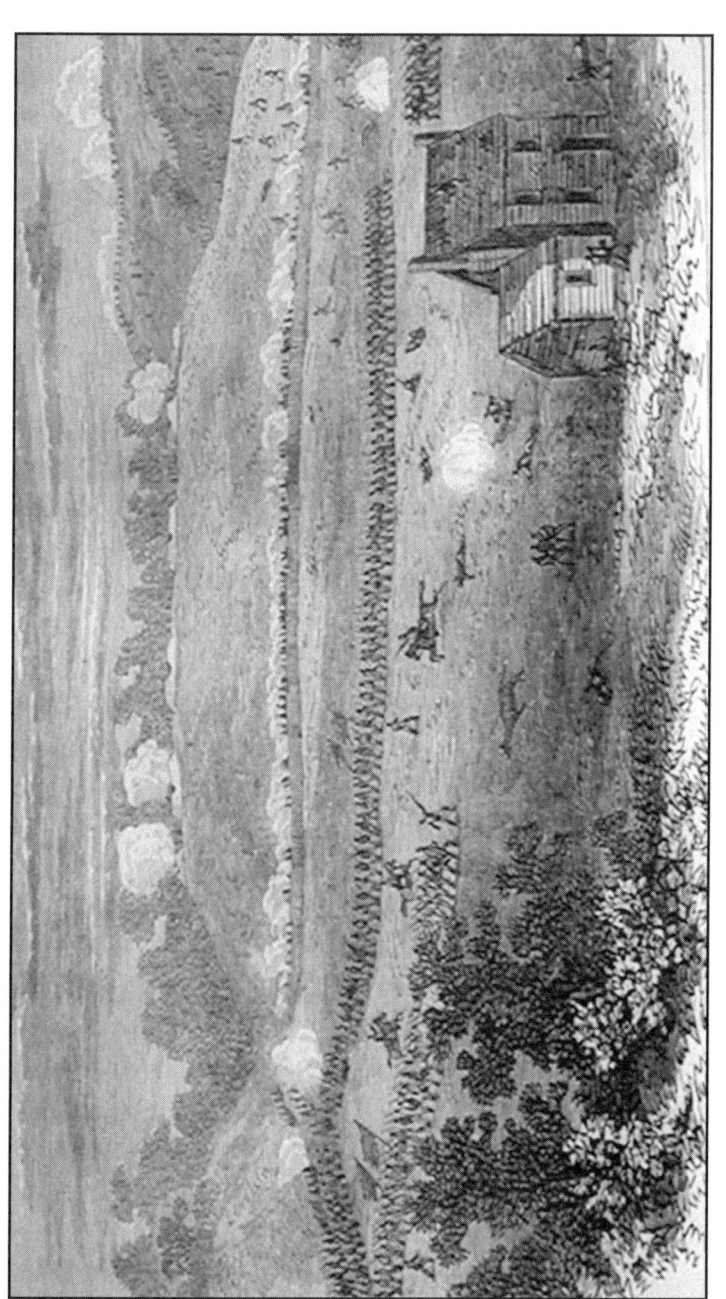

77th's charge of Marye's Heights on May 3, 1863

Courtesy of George T. Stevens' Three Years in the Sixth Corps

– 12 –

Chasing Bobby Lee
The March to Gettysburg
Summer–Fall 1863

Sedgwick's Foot Cavalry on the March

On June 5, 1863, the 77th helped the 50th New York Engineers set up a pontoon bridge at Franklin's Crossing, the same spot they used during the Fredericksburg campaign. Ordered not to shoot unless fired upon, Private Terrance Gray stated, "A good order, have to wait until one is dead before he can fire his gun."[1] Half of the regiment assisted on the pontoons, while the other half held the guns and covered those on the pontoons. The rebels on the opposite bank opened fire. A Confederate bullet gave Sergeant Wash Sherman a close call, tearing into his coat under his arm and ending up in his knapsack.[2] Five Union batteries were brought up and the plain across the river became a sheet of flames and dust from the bursting shells. The rebels persisted, thrusting their guns above their rifle pits to fire at the workers on the bridge. The 26th New Jersey and the 5th Vermont got the assignment to cross the river in boats and capture the rifle pits. Before darkness fell, the 77th suffered five casualties. Sergeant Rex Havens, one of the best soldiers in the regiment, was shot through the head and killed instantly.

The next day, Saturday, the regiment crossed the river at about noon and lay in a line of battle for the remainder of the day and Sunday. Formed in a semicircle the Union picket line radiated off from the pontoon bridge extending almost to the railroad. The rebels formed their own line. In some places the two lines were within a few yards of one another. By mutual consent an informal truce came into existence between the two picket lines. Being so close, the boys began to recognize their counterparts and soon after trading began. Those in blue traded newspapers or coffee for tobacco from the men in gray, until forbidden by division headquarters. On Monday, June 8, Howe's division was relieved, and they pulled back to the north side of the river.

Saturday, June 13, the VI Corps left their winter camps at Fredericksburg and began a series of grueling marches. The Army of the Potomac was on the move and the VI Corps was assigned rear guard duty. They began at 10:00 p.m. in the dark during a violent thunderstorm. The rain came down in torrents and the resulting mud made marching tedious. Negotiating corduroy roads constructed of various-sized logs proved challenging even in daylight. In darkness, with the logs wet and slippery from the rain, men were falling and breaking arms or legs. The men, top heavy with full packs and rifles, were prone to stumbling and losing their balance. Some tumbled off the sides and rolled down the steep embankments. When this occurred, one of their comrades would shout down: "Have you got a pass to be down there?"[3]

The next day the corps rested at Potomac Creek, and waited for the army to pass. While waiting, they watched the spectacle of the Army of the Potomac in motion. All that day, wagon trains streamed by, four or five wagons abreast with the drivers shouting and lashing their animals up to top speed. It was calculated that if put into a single line, the wagon train of the Army of the Potomac including artillery would extend for 70 miles. The regiment's quartermaster, quartermaster sergeant, and commissary sergeant were considered non-combatants. They went with the wagon train carrying the regimental supplies and books. A line captain or lieutenant was allowed only a small valise for his clothes. His company books were to be carried on the wagon train. Staff officers were allowed a slightly larger valise. The regimental books were red in color and roughly twelve inches wide, eighteen inches long, by one to two inches thick. They contained various records from general orders to daily strength reports.

At sunset, the regiment gathered for prayers led by Chaplain Norman Fox under the shade of a large tree by the colonel's headquarters. "Truly precious is the recollection of these army gatherings for religious worship. Sometimes we assembled in the beauty of groves, which were God's first temples, and sometimes we met around the campfire in rain and storm and bodily discomfort; but still our hearts were warm."[4] Norman Fox, with a perpetual smile on his face, was beloved by all. He was born in Glens Falls, New York. Fox graduated from the University of Rochester, and like his father and grandfather before him, he became a Baptist preacher. When duty called, Fox volunteered his services as a comforter and counselor of soldiers rather than carrying a gun. After dark they formed up, joined the rear of the column, and marched north through the night.[5]

The VI Corps continued their trek on Monday, June 15, one of the warmest days of the season. The intense heat made this one of the severest marches that the regiment would endure. "Company D had but one man besides the captain, and there were not over 40 or fifty men in all. The rest had fell out. . . . There were a great many sun-struck that day, and I heard of two or three that died."[6] Moving along normally one moment, the next moment the soldier would stagger and fall as if shot, having suffered a sunstroke. In some instances death followed shortly after. The victims' faces turned purple and their skin was dry and hot. Others became dizzy and fell with perspiration streaming down their faces. In either case, these men could march no farther and sought relief any place they could find it, even in the shade of a rail fence. Regiments soon became companies, and then the companies lost their identities. Men died along the roadsides, and still the corps marched on. At mid afternoon they halted, but very early the following morning, the call to fall in was passed up and down the line. There was no time for coffee as the regiments rolled up their blankets and fell into line. They marched until mid-afternoon when a halt was called at Occoquan Creek. Ordered to go swimming, they skinny-dipped on a grand scale. Multitudes of pale, bare bodies splashed about in the cool water. Revitalized, the men marched the last hour as if it were their first, before halting at Fairfax Court House.

After a few more days of marching day and night in the rain, the corps waited at Edwards Ferry for their turn to cross the pontoon bridge over the river into Maryland. After crossing the river, they marched until halted for dinner. The tired men in the 77th had barely dropped their knapsacks when they were startled to hear a church bell. Hidden by the surrounding trees, a small church was ringing its bell for Sunday services. With the endless marching most of the men had lost track of the days and were surprised that it was Sunday. A number of them attended the service.[7] That morning, they learned that Fighting Joe Hooker had been relieved of his command and his replacement was George Gordon Meade. A West Point graduate, Meade was born in Spain. A captain before the war started, he was made a brigadier general of volunteers at the insistence of the governor of Pennsylvania. The general's abrasive personality and sharp tongue earned him the nickname of "the old snapping turtle."[8]

With Lee's army on the march, the Army of the Potomac was spread out. Positioned farthest to the east, the VI Corps camped along both sides of the Baltimore Pike near Manchester, Maryland. Most soldiers spent the day resting and stayed in the shade. The camp had settled in for the night, when Meade's order to assemble the Army of the Potomac at Gettysburg arrived. Bugle calls sounded, the camp bristled with activity, and by 11:00 p.m. Sedgwick's Corps began their march west.

They marched silently in the darkness until a band near the head of the column began to play. Soon the men were marching in cadence to the distant music. The band played "Old John Brown's Battle Hymn" and when they reached the chorus, a few voices began to sing out. Soon a few more strong voices joined in and the sound began to gain power in the darkness. The sound amplified from a few scattered voices to whole companies, then entire regiments, brigades, and divisions belting out the lyrics. When the song ended, the entire corps had joined in with thousands of voices. The music continued on through the night, alternating between the bands or the shrill fifes with rattling drums as they marched toward Gettysburg.

The next morning, Thursday, July 2, they halted only once for coffee. During the stop, Sedgwick ate nothing but passed continually among the men, making his presence felt until marching resumed. Late morning there was no music, as men tested the limits of their endurance and marched on. Perspiration was running down their faces in little rivulets, and the intense heat made their woolen uniforms sticky and uncomfortable.[9] Along the Baltimore Pike the residents fetched buckets of water out to the roadside so that the passing soldiers could fill their canteens. "The day was bright and the sun poured scalding rays from a cloudless sky. The weight of knapsack, gun, and accoutrements bore heavily but the men strove hard to keep in ranks for few in that corps were willing to be left behind if there was a good prospect of a fight."[10] Knowing the importance of this battle, Sedgwick frequently encouraged his men to make haste as he rode alongside or watched the passing column. Often the men would shout quips like: "We'll wait for you, Uncle John," and "We're in no hurry, Uncle John."[11] They joked that the general only called a halt when his horse, named Cornwall, gave out. The soldiers began to call themselves "Sedgwick's Cavalry" and joked that "they were kept on the gallop."[12]

At 4:00 p.m. a fast-moving dust cloud was spotted over the Baltimore Pike, alarming Meade's staff. Initial speculation had J.E.B. Stuart's cavalry attacking the Union rear, until a sharp-eyed staff officer identified the column emerging from the dust as the VI Corps.[13] General Albion Paris Howe's Second Division brought up the rear of the column and arrived at 6:00 p.m. The men were turned into a field beside the road and took a short break. Having gone without food since their morning coffee, they quickly went to work frying up pork and boiling coffee, unconcerned that a major battle was unfolding over the next hill. Just another day at work, if sojering was your business.[14] While the men cooked, curiosity got the best of Surgeon Stevens and Adjutant First Lieutenant William H. Fursman. Determined to see what was happening over the hill separating them from the battlefield, they mounted horses, crossed the creek, and rode up the hill. Passing through the ranks of a brigade, they found themselves on the north side of Little Round Top. From their vantage point the entire battlefield was spread out before them. The two officers watched the vast spectacle in amazement. Satisfied, Stevens and Fursman galloped back to the regiment, arriving just as Neill's brigade was forming up.

General Meade used the VI Corps as a reserve manpower pool, plugging in Sedgwick's brigades where and when they were needed as gaps or situations developed along the Union line. With all of his brigades parceled out to other officers, Sedgwick commented that he might as well go home. The 77th was temporarily transferred to Major General Henry Warner Slocum. Born in New York's Onondaga County, Henry Slocum was Phil Sheridan's roommate at the Military Academy. He proved to be one of the army's toughest fighters.[15] Slocum assigned the 77th to support his artillery. The next day, July 3, the XII Corps Batteries sounded their version of reveille, ending the slumber of both Confederates and Federals. Positioned along Powers Hill they lay in front of the batteries overlooking the Baltimore Pike.[16] The boys from Bemis Heights found it difficult to guard cannons while their comrades went into battle.[17] Prior to Pickett's Charge, Lee opened with every cannon he had. During the bombardment, the shells that came in the 77th's direction passed overhead doing little damage. Private Sanford Campbell in the rear of the regiment's ranks witnessed a shell take off the under jaw of a horse and the fore legs of two others before it plowed up the ground, sending stones flying.[18] In less than five minutes scores of horses and mules attached to the ammunition wagons in the grove behind them were lying dead.[19] Listening to the intensity of both the bombardment and Pickett's Charge from the 77th's position on the flank, Chaplain Fox became worried about his two brothers serving in the 107th New York near the Union center. After the battle he was given permission to check on his brothers.

General Neill was placed in charge of a flying division with orders to follow and harass Lee's retreating army. Neill's new division was composed of Neill's brigade, Colonel McIntosh's cavalry brigade, and two light batteries. Nipping at Lee's heels, on July 6, Neill's column descended into the beautiful Cumberland Valley. The small army camped just outside the village of Waynesboro. The 77th was assigned picket duty a mile away from the main body, extending over a two-mile section along the banks of Antietam Creek.

Picket duty along the Antietam proved to be so enjoyable that the regiment quickly petitioned General Neill to allow them to remain on picket duty until the army moved. The general approved their request. It was harvest time and the inhabitants were more than happy to welcome the soldiers into their homes. The farmers provided the soldiers with home-cooked delicacies, and the soldiers gladly pitched in to help with the harvest. Soon after their arrival in Waynesboro, they were joined by a division of militia under the command of William "Baldy" Smith. Undisciplined and not accustomed to the rigors of a soldier's life, the militia in their new uniforms thought themselves above eating hardtack. They took to plundering from the neighboring citizens, the same citizens the 77th were assigned to guard. Dreading the approach of any soldiers with new blue uniforms, the citizens soon began to look upon the 77th as both friends and protectors.[20] After a few encounters, Baldy's militia quickly learned why the VI Corps was referred to as the Fighting VI Corps. They soon came to respect the men in the faded uniforms with the white crosses on their hats.

Major Babcock was in charge of the left wing of the regiment's picket line. He and the line officers set up their headquarters in the miller's house. Located in a pleasant grove by the river, the miller's house offered a strategic location, comfortable rooms, a well-stocked larder—plus the miller's three charming daughters. The entire regiment was soon aware of the major's good fortunes, the chaplain referring to it as flirting with the Pennsylvanians. An excuse to visit Major Babcock was soon formulated by Colonel French, Surgeon Stevens, and Colonel Connor from the 7th Maine. The visiting trio found their comrades in exceptional spirits. The miller's wife and daughters brought out their best wine and largest apples for the new guests to sample. The wine loosened up the officers' spirits, bringing out laughter, jokes, and songs. The good picket duty lasted until July 11, when the pickets were drawn in and the brigade continued to shadow Lee.[21]

During mid-July the main army caught up with Neill's brigade and General Lee at Beaver Creek. Lee occupied a strong position, and apparently intended to make a stand. The Vermont Brigade was deployed as skirmishers in a section of woods and the rest of the division was massed and held in support. The Confederates' main line advanced, but the hot steady fire from the Vermonters' skirmish line repulsed them twice, after which Lee's forces withdrew from Beaver Creek and took up position near Funkstown. The brigade marched until darkness and camped near Williamsport. On July 15, Neill's brigade made a fast-paced march that left the Vermonters in the dust. They joked that Neill's brigade after association with the cavalry was now a flying brigade.

In mid-July, the regiment was camped in Virginia about five miles from the Hazel River, which was rumored to be full of fish. A regimental fishing expedition was organized. Provisions were gathered for the expedition, including several boxes of sardines from the suttler and canteens filled with a beverage that was referred to as commissary. Charley Benedict, Tom White, and some of the boys departed at sunrise one morning. They returned just after sunset with empty canteens and no fish. Some of them seemed to be experiencing difficulty walking and standing up. When questioned about the absence of fish, Tom White rummaged through his haversack and produced some sardines from an opened box. Making better use of the river, Chaplain Fox baptized eleven men from the 77th.[22]

Late in July 25, the VI Corps camped for three weeks at Stone Mountain. Confirmation of French's commission arrived, and the regiment's line officers decided to honor him. W. T. King was dispatched to New York City to secure the gift. Made to order by Tiffany & Co. of New York, the sword was an elegant piece of craftsmanship, engraved with the Greek inscription "He fights for his country."[23] The colonel was surprised when the brigade band appeared at regimental headquarters one afternoon. A large number of officers from both the regiment and the brigade gathered for the event. With an appropriate speech, the regiment's senior captain, George S. Orr, presented the sword to Colonel Winsor French on behalf of the officers.[24]

The 77th Regiment suffered no casualties in the mid-October engagement at Chantilly, Virginia. Late in October the temperature was "cold enough to freeze the devil . . . So cold that the Chaplain preached with gloves on, and a short sermon at that."[25] During early November, the VI Corps engagement at Rappahannock Station was brilliantly executed. The enemy occupied a fortified position on the north side of the river accessible by two small bridges. Sedgwick's corps broke camp at Warrenton on November 7 and marched the twelve miles to Rappahannock Station. By 2:00 p.m. the corps assembled in a line of battle near the station. First Division positioned front left, Second Division in the center with the 77th deployed as skirmishers, and the Third Division positioned on the right rear.[26] Artillery opened about mid-afternoon and continued until dusk, softening up the rebel positions. Two regiments from the First Division charged the enemy works using their bayonets and got possession of the two access bridges. Cut off with no way to escape or be reinforced, the rebels trapped on the north bank surrendered. The 77th, positioned in support, suffered no casualties. General Neill ordered Colonel Bidwell to charge the rebs and drive them into the river, taking the 61st Pennsylvania for support.[27] Colonel Bidwell, 49th New York, rode up to the general, taking his hat in hand, and inquired as to what regiment he had said. To which Neill replied: "Colonel, put on your hat. I know what regiment you want. You want McKean's Sunday School boys."[28] Bidwell responded that was exactly what he wanted, and with the 77th he could drive the Johnnies to Richmond if ordered to![29]

Early morning, Thanksgiving, November 26, 1863, the Mine Run campaign began. The 77th and their corps marched until 10:00 p.m. when they halted for coffee. General Thomas Neill broke open a piece of hardtack that he intended to eat, and found it to be full of frozen occupants. Neill asked his servant, "Jim, give us one that hasn't so many worms in it."[30] Distant cannonading was heard for most of the morning. The next day after lunch they formed up and were off on the double-quick toward the sounds of distant musketry. The VI Corps was held in reserve and not heavily engaged. They started again on the following morning. "We hadn't gone far when our skirmishes was driving the rebs at a pretty good rate. The rebs kept falling back until they got into their rifle pits and across their swamps and a creek, now they are alright and want us to follow them, but our Generals knew a little better."[31] That night, to survive the cold without fires, the men had to beat their arms and stamp their feet to stay warm.

"Here we had the privilege of lying down, but oh dear, talk about sleeping, it was easier to freeze . . . one man died with the cold . . . all that we could do was to keep walking to be the least comfortable."[32]

**Lieutenant Sidney Cromack,
77th New York State Volunteers, Company B**

Cromack was captured at the Wilderness.

Courtesy of Joseph Covais

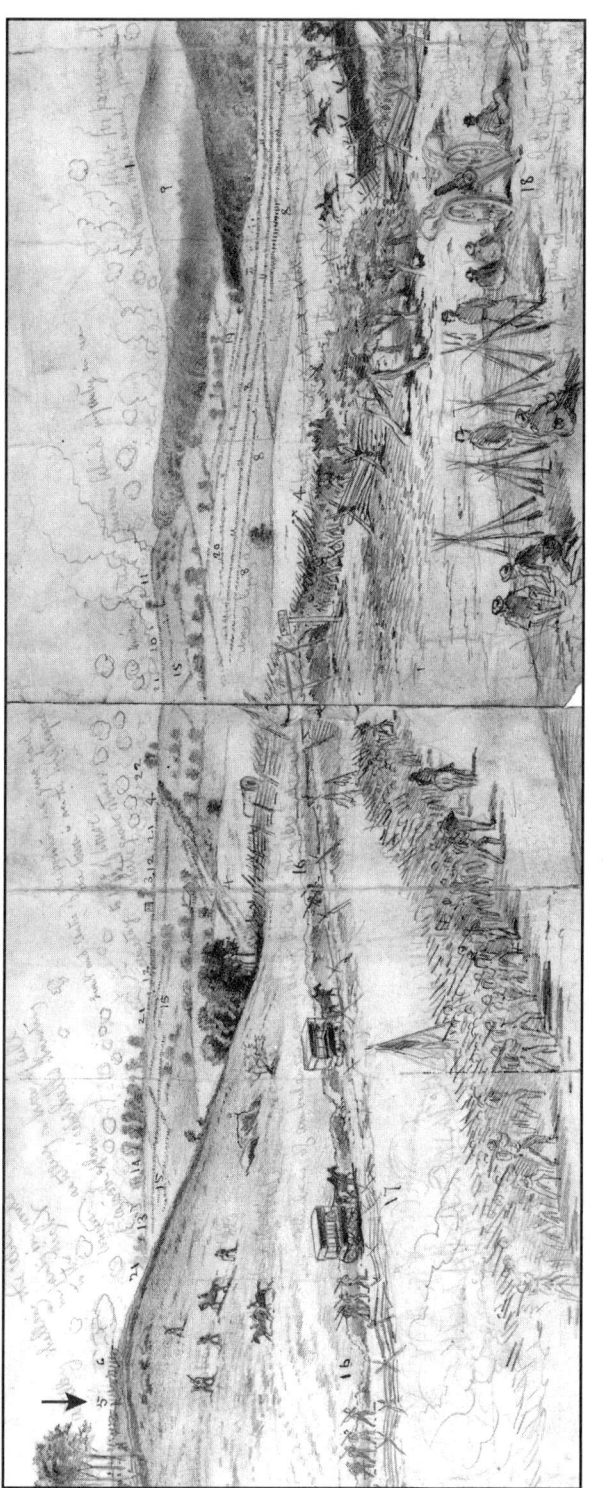

Gettysburg, July 3, 1863, 77th on Powers Hill (position #5 on sketch) (Edwin Forbes)

Courtesy of the Library of Congress

– 13 –

Besides Sojering
Winter Camp
Winter 1863–1864

Crop predictions for 1864, although the ground at present is dry and hard, a good crop of mud is expected for the year.
—*Saratogian* 1864

John Minor Botts once boasted that he had six hundred miles of fence. One week after Howe's division of the VI Corps went into winter camp on his land, if half of Mister Botts' fence was still standing then he was a lucky man. It is unlikely that Botts had any of his fence by the time the division moved out in the spring. Encamped about two miles from Brandy Station in a fine forest of prime trees, Howe's men used them to build comfortable houses and for heat.[1] "Not that living in a tent or shanty is as cozy as being at home . . . but with blankets and good fire places to our tents we keep warm."[2] They soon settled into a daily routine that started with reveille, sick call, afternoon drill, dress parade, and ended with taps. Fighting was only a small portion of a soldier's life. An anonymous soldier in the Army of the Potomac wrote that soldiering was 99% boredom and 1% of sheer terror. Regular duties such as the picket line, drill practice, reviews, gathering firewood, foraging, and other chores filled up a great deal of their time. "You must not think a soldier is entirely without enjoyment! We often get together and enjoy ourselves in any way, which the opportunity suggest."[3] In camp they boxed, played practical jokes, wrestled, and did whatever to cope with their situations, wagering on the outcomes of many if not all of these events. "After drilling all day, at sundown we had a footrace in our regiment. Bill MaCall and Sam Kidd. The latter beat by the odds."[4]

Foraging supplemented the soldier's standard diet of hardtack and salt pork. Early in the war it was frowned upon on the Union side and orders were in place forbidding the Northern troops from foraging. As the war dragged on, Union politicians were less concerned about the South's feelings after the war and more concerned with shortening the war.[5] "By this time we had got into a country where we could get green corn and potatoes, peaches, and watermelons, no mortal power could restrain the men from foraging."[6] As resourceful soldiers, the boys of the 77th sharpened their foraging skills during the Peninsular campaign. They feasted on oysters from the nearby tidal pools, gray squirrels filled their stew pots, and the hogs that roamed the woods found their way to the regiment's cooking fires. "It was amusing to see the men as they passed along the road. A crowd would rush around the house, some into the pig pen, and some into the hen-coop, and others would take the field. Before the column would get by, there would be mighty little left for the man to live upon who owned the place."[7] As part of a ration detail, Private Dennis B. Smith was one of a squad of soldiers who visited a Southern farmer's house. There they put in claims for apples, potatoes, and bacon and then opened up the rails on a pen so the hogs that were inside could escape and come over to the Union camp for protection.[8] Based on many accounts, the 77th's picket line provided a fairly steady flow of meat for the regiment. The nervous soldiers on picket duty never seemed to miss, even on the darkest nights, when various rebel deer, cows, and pigs attacked them.

In late February, they endured four days of very cold weather. During this period very little outdoor duty was performed and the priority of the soldiers was just trying to keep warm. The closest firewood for the regiment at this point was two miles away.[9] "An average one trip a day will get us wood enough to last all day. We generally keep enough ahead to stand us if a storm appears so we do not have to go out in the storm."[10] The landscape of the countryside near the winter camps had been swept clean of all wood in the army's quest for firewood. They had taken the timber, the rail-fences, next the groves of trees, and finally the smaller building on the nearby plantations.

The Christian Commission offered to loan each brigade a large canvas tarpaulin to be used as a roof for a chapel. Chaplain Fox took advantage of the offer and Lieutenant Lyon was assigned to oversee building the chapel. Some of the officers joked that with the lieutenant in charge there might be more swearing during the construction phase of this endeavor than Chaplain Fox's preaching would offset afterwards.[11] Fox felt that the influence of an army chaplain could not be measured with certainty and that all he could do was to keep firing shots.[12] "Last Sunday I preached to the boys on swearing, the shot struck a good many."[13] He regarded the winter season as the time when a chaplain could do the most good. Their chapel was constructed of logs, with slabs for seating, and walls that were plastered with mud. Utilized by the 77th and the other regiments of the Third Brigade, the structure accommodated two to three hundred. Chaplain Fox held divine services twice on Sundays and once or twice during the week. The structure was also used for spelling school, arithmetic classes, debating school, and a literary discussion group. The energetic Fox procured enough reading materials to stock a reading room.[14] On Washington's Birthday, the men spent the day preparing the chapel for an evening celebration. The Second Division's officers filled the chapel, and outside a large gathering assembled of men from the 77th's and the Vermont Brigade. At 6:00 p.m. the band played their first tune, and they continued playing until taps.

Drill and parades continued to be a large part of the 77th's itinerary. On December 15, 1863, "Our corps was reviewed by

General Meade and the Russian Naval Officers the day before yesterday if there is any corps to be shown to foreign officers, it has to be the VI but I suppose that the general wants to show off the best troops he has under his command."[15] On Tuesday, February 23, General Sedgwick reviewed his corps. A number of ladies were present to witness the review and to see the Fighting VI Corps. The president was expected but did not make it. In late April the men expressed their confidence in Grant as they prepared for the next campaign. He had reviewed the corps a few days earlier. Sick and feverous, Private Fountain accidentally put a bayonet through his hand when preparing for a dress parade.[16] On Saturday, April 16, the corps review was rained out, but an unsanctioned prizefight between two of the 61st Pennsylvania boys was not affected by the weather.[17] When target practice was added to the required drills, the boys indulged themselves with some fancy shooting. The 77th Regiment had some excellent marksmen who could shoot with deadly accuracy at three to five hundred yards' distance.[18]

Perhaps the most common leisure time activity for Union soldiers, including the 77th, was letter writing. At any point in time one could walk through a Civil War encampment and find off-duty soldiers writing letters. The typical Civil War letter consisted of four written pages. Approximately one third of the letter was usually devoted to "I received your letter, did you get mine" type of information. The next third was in most cases devoted to describing or complaining about the weather. The last portion was the meat of the document, describing either life as a soldier or a recent battle. Penmanship as well as eloquence in the letters ranged from very good to very bad. The average number of letters received per day was 45,000 at the Washington Post Office, with an equal number being returned.[19]

The prior year the 77th were spectators when the Vermonters squared off against the 26th New Jersey in a regimental-sized snowball fight. When the New Jersey center broke in confusion, the retreating Jersey men were closely chased by both the Vermonters and the spectators. Acting on the principle of kicking a man when he is down, the spectators pitched into them unmercifully.[20] During late March of 1863 a storm dropped a sizeable amount of snow. A day or two later, with the top layers melting, the snow soon became a packable consistency. This was reason enough for the playful boys of the 77th to bombard the neighboring 61st Pennsylvanians' camp with snowballs. The Pittsburghers quickly turned out in mass, and the air was soon filled with non-lethal projectiles composed of Virginia snow. The other regiments of their brigade turned out as spectators, their cheers intensifying the melee. The hard-throwing boys of the Bemis Heights Regiment drove back the Pennsylvanians and took possession of their camp, calling the 61st "shad-bellies." The snowball fight lasted for about an hour. The prisoners captured by both sides during the melee were exchanged and affairs returned to normal. Quite a few of the participants sported black eyes the next day.[21]

Baseball had become the passion of the Army of the Potomac. Every regiment had its ball players, including the 77th's Sergeant Oped Coleman, an underhanded hurler with a fast delivery, one of the regiment's key players. The sound of a bat striking a ball became a familiar background noise during the daylight hours in camp. The men took advantage of the fine weather in mid-February and got their exercise playing baseball. During early March the 77th played the 49th and got beat badly.[22] On April 18, the two regiments played again, a grand game on the parade ground before a spirited crowd. The 2nd New Jersey, a championship caliber team, played a challenge from the 77th New York Infantry.[23] For the 77th to be playing outside of their division, they had to have been one of the better teams in the army.

Some of the boys of the 77th were performing on a horizontal bar that had been set up in camp. They were closely observed by one of the Maine boys. After watching for quite awhile the fellow offered to bet five dollars that there wasn't a man in the regiment who could jump up, catch the bar with one hand, and pull himself up three times. Sergeant Leonard Fletcher took the bet and brought out Sergeant Thomas M. White. A lightweight, White went to the bar and proceeded to easily do five or six one-armed pull-ups. After he had looked Tom over carefully, the man who made the wager turned and said to Fletcher, "The money is yours, but I will swear that that man did not pull up anything but his clothes."[24]

One spring day found the Bemis Heights boys a bit restless. A fellow came riding up on an old crow bait horse. Before he realized what was happening, both he and his horse were lifted on fence rails by the boys and treated to a ride.[25] Another regimental favorite was blanket tossing. A dozen or so muscular fellows took hold around the edges of a single blanket. The victim was placed in the center of the blanket and with a one, two, on three count the blanket was tightened and snapped, sending the victim flying up in the air, only to come down head first into the blanket and be launched again.[26]

In the spring of 1864 just prior to breaking up the winter camp, Major Babcock was in command of the regiment, with Colonel French away on a temporary leave. Orders were issued from regimental headquarters, including one that prohibited soldiers to go outside the camp limits without a pass. Since the latrine area was well outside of the camp limits, this order met with resistance from the men. They decided a late-night demonstration was the appropriate means for expressing their grievances to the major. A rifle barrel was loaded to the brim with black gunpowder and put into a length of stovepipe. After taps most of the men were deep in sleep; the only sounds were the footsteps of the pickets. The makeshift cannon was positioned as close to the major's tent as possible before the gunner lit the short fuse and escaped into the darkness. A few seconds later the device exploded with a loud ba-boom! The major and a squad of soldiers quickly turned out to meet the attack, but they found no one, only the smoking remnants of the device. The rest of the brigade, including their brigade commander, had also experienced the blast and were not amused. The general threatened to place the whole regiment under arrest if there was any more noise.[27] "The major placed a guard in our street to keep the boy(s) from raising the devil with him in the night."[28]

Chaplain Norman Fox Jr., 77th New York State Volunteers

Courtesy of the International Museum of Photography and Film; George Eastman House

Private James Daivenson, 77th New York State Volunteers, Company I

Daivenson was killed at Spotsylvania.

Courtesy of John Parsley

– 14 –

Fighting in the Wilderness
Overland Campaign
Spring 1864

It all went back until it came to our regiment.
—Lieutenant Charles E. Stevens
"Report of the Thirty-Ninth Annual Reunion"

After his victories in the West, on March 1, 1864, Lincoln promoted Ulysses S. Grant to lieutenant general and gave him command of all Union forces.[1] Grant was the second person (George Washington was the first) to hold this rank in the United States Army. Grant planned to flank Lee on the left in the Wilderness in a battle named the Overland campaign. This maneuver was intended to place the Union army between Lee and Richmond, forcing Lee to take on Grant in the open. Ulysses Simpson Grant was born in Ohio. Known to his classmates as "Sam," he graduated from West Point. At the start of the war, Grant was employed as a clerk in his brother's store in Illinois. Initially he was appointed colonel in an Illinois regiment. In his victories at Forts Henry and Donaldson, Grant did not allow any terms in the surrender agreements, which earned him the nickname "Unconditional Surrender." Lincoln's description of Grant was simply "He fights."[2]

Both the officers and men of Sedgwick's corps were in good spirits. A number of the officers' wives, including Surgeon Stevens' wife, had been allowed to spend the winter months with their husbands.[3] The rank and file troops contented themselves with making it through a relatively mild

Fighting in the Wilderness

winter. Throughout the ranks of the Army of the Potomac the feeling prevailed that this would be their last campaign.

In May 1864, Lee's army was one of the worst fed and clothed armies ever mustered into service. Uniformed in what had now become an assortment of patched rags, thousands of his men were barefoot. The standard daily ration for both private and general in the Army of Northern Virginia was one quarter of a pound of pork fat with a little meal or flour. Lee interpreted the sounds of laughter and singing by his troops in their entrenchments as a positive indication of their morale.[4]

On May 4, 1864, at 2:00 a.m. reveille sounded throughout the VI Corps' winter camps at Brandy Station. Later the steady voices of the sergeants called out the rolls and men dropped into the ranks. The dark groups closed into a line, and the lines formed companies, then regiments, and ultimately brigades. Soon they were ready to march. The 77th's brigade led the VI Corps column down the road toward Germanna Ford. The V Corps was supposed to be out in front, but they were delayed and for most of the trek they marched alongside the VI Corps. Grant and his staff passed along the marching columns riding toward the river.

On the march, most of the veteran soldiers abandoned their haversacks. They wore, over the head and on one shoulder, what was known as a horse collar. The collar consisted of one-half of a pup tent, a wool blanket, and a rubber blanket. These were rolled tightly together with the rubber blanket on the outside and the ends tied off with twine. Any extra clothing was rolled up inside, along with the soldiers' rations.[5] Each of the infantrymen also carried 50 rounds of ammunition.[6] The day was bright and clear with cooler than average temperatures—an excellent day for marching.

At the ford, Sedgwick's troops were held up until late afternoon waiting to cross the pontoon bridge. With Neill's brigade at the head, they resumed marching down the road until bivouacking for the night. Although the sounds of skirmishing could already be heard off in the distance, they enjoyed a quiet night. The night's silence was broken only by the sounds of an owl or a whip-poor-will. Dawn found the 77th's brigade deployed along the road leading from Robertson's Tavern to the Germanna Plank Road.[7]

The Wilderness measured about 12 miles across in any direction. Its terrain was a gentle rolling tract of low ridges alternating with swampy marshlands. There were few clearings and even fewer roads. Most of the area was covered with a dense second growth of small pines, mixed with oak, ash, and walnut trees. In some places the thick and matted underbrush was deemed impenetrable. Daylight was a stranger to most places within these gloomy woods.[8] The heavy population of smaller pines and underbrush filled in the areas between the big trees. The undergrowth was so thick in some parts that visibility was limited to less than five yards.[9]

On May 5, 1863, the corps probed deeper into the Wilderness. The 77th were deployed as skirmishers and immediately began exchanging shots with rebels from Ewell's Corps.[10] Colonel French was on sick leave, and Major Nathan S. Babcock was in command of the regiment.[11] Later that morning, their brigade, Neill's, was detached from Getty's division and temporarily assigned to Wright's division.[12] They marched down the Wilderness plank road until 11:00 a.m., then the corps faced to the front and advanced into the tangled maze of vines and brush. Intent on delaying the Union troops, rebel skirmishers lay on the ground and covered themselves with leaves, utilizing the underbrush for concealment. Lying in wait, they would then rise up and deliver a volley into the oncoming blue line before retiring into the brush. Neill's and the New Jersey brigades led Wright's advance. It took them four hours to cover one and one-half miles; under average conditions this advance would have taken them less than an hour.

After driving the enemy back for two miles, they came upon a well entrenched rebel line with supporting artillery. Two 12-pound Napoleons opened on them from the opposite side of the swale, sending shells screaming over their heads. A rebel brigade tried to turn their flank and made a desperate series of charges. The charges were fended off by two of Neill's regiments.[13] The Union and Confederate lines were on the two opposite slopes of a ravine, with a strip of marshy ground running through the middle. The woods echoed with the sounds of rebel axes, as the Confederates strengthened their positions. While the battle raged up and down the line, "the rattle of musketry would swell into a continuous roar as the simultaneous discharge of ten thousand guns mingled in one grand concert . . . then would be heard the wild yells which always told of a rebel charge, and again the volleys would become more terrible and the broken crashing tones would swell into one continuous roll of sound."[14]

Just after sunset, several brigades from the V and the VI Corps, including Neill's, made a joint attack to retake Saunder's Field and the wooded ground north of the field. Neill's unit was formed up with the first line composed of the 49th New York and the 7th Maine, followed by the 61st Pennsylvania, and supported by the 43rd and 77th New York Regiments. Advancing cautiously up to the wooded ridge that ran south into the swale toward the V Corps, the rebels crouched down in their earthworks and allowed the boys in blue to get within 40 yards before rising up to rake them with lead. The first line suffered high casualties and Neill's three supporting regiments were quickly brought into action. Subjected to intense pressure, the 61st, 77th, and 43rd withdrew stubbornly from the action, but not before they expended a great deal of ammunition. Private William G. Watson considered himself to be one of the lucky ones. He put his trust in the Lord, who he believed saved his life by altering the course of a rebel's bullet that passed through him.[15] Along the

Germanna Road, Captain Albert Nickerson, 7th Maine, awoke from his wound-induced sleep, as warm burning whiskey made its way down his throat followed by warm water splashing onto his face. Opening his eyes Nickerson focused on Chaplain Norman Fox bending down over him with a canteen in each of his hands. Moments later Nickerson was placed on a stretcher and loaded into a nearby ambulance.[16]

General Neill reported that late in the day several attempts to advance his lines failed, due to the strength of the enemy's position.[17] Unable to maneuver in the dense underbrush, the cavalry and artillery had been used very sparingly—this was to be an infantry battle. Night fell with both rebels and Yankees entrenched on opposite sides of the ravine.[18] Chopping sounds, the crash of falling trees, as well as the sounds of troop movement continued throughout the night. The following morning, on May 7, Sedgwick's and Hancock's corps were preparing to attack at 5:00 a.m., but Ewell beat them to the punch. At 4:45 a.m. his troops poured out of their entrenchments and charged Sedgwick's line. Uncle John joked that Ewell's watch must be running fast. The rebel attack was easily checked.

The muzzle flashes of the muskets ignited the dry leaves that blanketed the ground, and before long Sedgwick's whole front was ablaze.[19] "Volleys of musketry echoed and reechoed through the forest like peals of thunder and the battle surged to and fro . . . leaving the ground covered with dead and wounded."[20] The wounded, who were incapable of crawling or limping away, perished in the fires. Their screams and groans were audible to their comrades. Most of the VI Corps front was so fire-swept that it was judged impassable and the units remained pinned down under intense fire.[21] Neill's brigade and the others on the north end of Sedgwick's line tried to breach Ewell's line. Crashing through the brush toward an unseen enemy, they found themselves slogging through a marsh heavily laced with prickly brush. Strategically located on the other side of the bog, the Confederates' entrenched lines were positioned along a slight ridge that enabled their sharpshooters to fire down into the bog with deadly accuracy.[22] As the charge lost its momentum, the wounded began to trickle back to the rear. Lieutenant William Worden, shot through the thigh, was making his way back to the aid station. As Worden limped along a narrow path through the woods, he passed directly under the nose of General Sedgwick's horse. Mounted on Cornwall, the general noticed Worden's wound and asked if he was in much pain. Before the lieutenant could answer, Sedgwick turned to his staff and asked for whiskey.[23] A staff officer handed a small flask to the general, who in turn passed it down to the lieutenant. Uncle John possessed such a kind heart and genuine concern for his troops' welfare that every man in his corps loved him.[24] By 10:00 a.m. on May 6, Sedgwick's front had quieted down and stayed that way until late afternoon.[25] When General Getty was wounded, General Neill assumed command of the VI's Corps Second Division, and Colonel Bidwell of the 49th New York took over Neill's brigade.[26]

With supplies robbed from the pockets and bedrolls of the prisoners and the dead men in blue, Gordon's troops were well supplied with the best the Union had to offer. That morning, squatting down behind their breastworks, they feasted on hard crackers, salt pork, and coffee sweetened with sugar. During the late afternoon as the rebels formed up for their assault, General John Brown Gordon rode alongside one of his six Georgian regiments and imparted: "This is the VI Corps we are going to attack, the same fellows we fought at Marye's Heights; those that we didn't get then, we want now."[27] Gordon was born in Georgia. He attended the University of Georgia and became a lawyer. With no prior military experience, Gordon was elected captain of a company. One of his soldiers said, "He's the most prettiest thing you ever did see on a field of fight. It'ud put fight into a whipped chicken just to look at him."[28]

At 7:00 p.m. on May 6, Confederate Generals Richard S. Ewell and John Brown Gordon began a coordinated attack on Sedgwick's corps. Ewell attacked along Sedgwick's entire front, while Gordon and his brigade of Georgians swept down upon the corps' right flank. Flanked and surprised, Shaler's brigade gave way after offering only slight resistance. After the door was opened, Gordon's troops smashed through it upon Seymour's brigade. Shaler's and Seymour's brigades made up the VI Corps' recently acquired Third Division.[29] General Sedgwick arrived on the field just as Seymour's last line of breastworks gave way. Gordon's troops were pouring through the breach in the line, led by a man on a black horse. The rider leveled his pistol at Sedgwick, calling him a "Yankee son of a bitch." Before the man could pull the trigger, a New York soldier shot him down dead. Muttering something like "damn rebels" or "devils," Sedgwick rode off looking for reinforcements. Ewell's artillery had the range, and shells whistled down among the Union troops. Sedgwick bolted toward a line forming along a nearby wagon track.[30]

Receiving fire from three directions, Colonel Bidwell sat mounted on his horse coolly directing his brigade, oblivious to the swarm of bullets humming by him. He sat like an iron man among the bullets, an inspiration and a comfort to his soldiers. Subject to an intense crossfire, Bidwell's troops hopped over their breastworks and returned fire from the opposite side. Heeding the increasing volume of the impending battle on his right side, Bidwell reformed his second line, deploying them at a right angle along a nearby wagon track. The 77th and 43rd New York Regiments fixed bayonets and dashed for the road, where they changed front to rear.[31] They had formed only seconds earlier when small bands of disorganized soldiers from routed brigades poured out of the brush, disrupting the Union line in their haste to flee from the Georgians. General Sedgwick rode up, hatless and swinging his sword, trying to rally the fleeing soldiers. Sedgwick reassured the men, saying, "Boys, don't run. I will stay here with you and get you out."[32]

In simple words: "It all went back until it came to our regiment."[33] The 77th was positioned just to the left of the Pennsylvanians, whose commander yelled out for his soldiers to shoot or bayonet their fleeing comrades. Major Nathan Babcock stood with drawn sword urging his boys to hold their ground and trying to rally the fleeing soldiers from the Third Division. In the fighting, the 77th's courageous colorbearer, Sergeant Michael McWilliams, was killed. One ball shattered the flagstaff he was carrying and five others pierced him.[34] Major Babcock "seized the colors himself, and told the men never to desert them, and they rallied around him like good fellows."[35] Lieutenant Stevens' aide was wounded and making his way to a hospital station. The wounded sergeant had gone a short distance when he came upon General Sedgwick traveling with only a single aide. The wounded sergeant from the 77th asked the general where the rear was. The general replied, "Stay right where you are. I haven't any right now, but will soon have one."[36]

Major John W. Daniel, one of General Early's aides, called out, "Follow me, boys,"[37] and two Virginia regiments, the 31st and 58th, fell in behind him. They stumbled up the hill toward the 77th and 43rd New York regiments. The Union skirmishers spotted the advancing rebels and quickly darted up the hill to warn the main line. Private Jacob Heater, 31st Virginia, said that at less than thirty paces, a voice had boomed out in the darkness and yelled, "Boys, here we are."[38] With the Virginians almost close enough to spit at, the boys of the 77th and the 43rd rose to their feet behind their entrenchments along the crest of the hill and delivered a volley like a sheet of flame into the faces of the advancing Confederates. Major Daniel and many others went down, as the gray advance was stopped dead in its tracks. All those who still had the power to move turned and ran back down the hill. One rebel recounted: "We got within fifteen feet of the Yankees before we saw them. They poured a shower of balls at us."[39]

The Union right flank was secure in the trustworthy hands of Bidwell's veteran brigade, formerly Neill's brigade.[40] The regiments were positioned with the 61st Pennsylvania at a right angle to the end of the line, which was manned by the 77th New York.[41] Along the Union's line, the veterans lay, silently waiting, alert for unfamiliar night sounds. Since more assaults were anticipated, the men were not allowed to spread their blankets or make fires. Instead each man slept on his arms with thumbs resting on the hammers of their rifles.[42] About 10:00 p.m. the Pennsylvanians checked a rebel advance on their front, and an hour later, the rebels tested the 77th. The night birds and insects became strangely quiet, the night sounds replaced by low tones urging men forward. Sharp eyes distinguished a dark line moving toward their position. As the dark shadows loomed closer, the hairs on the back of the men's necks bristled to attention, and Bidwell's boys fought to control the pressure being exerted by their trigger fingers. Their rifle barrels, aimed slightly above waist high, were hidden by the brush and branches piled along the line. The dark line was almost upon them, and they could make out the silhouettes of the advancing rebels. The command to fire rang out followed by the almost simultaneous cracks of the New Yorkers' rifles. The dark line's advance staggered and stopped as those who could still walk abandoned the wounded and made tracks back into the darkness.

The brigade had once more proved its steadiness under fire, and the threat posed by Gordon's attack had been repulsed through the bravery of the officers and men. The 77th had performed splendidly and maintained the regiment's reputation as a fighting regiment. At midnight the VI Corps fell back to an area where the old gold mine had been. Quickly they entrenched, remaining there without incident for the next couple of days.[43] Private Issac Lobdell, working at the hospital, stated that the number of wounded and killed was not known due to the number of missing men. "Those that have

Fighting in the Wilderness

been found are wounded in every imaginable manner—some with both legs shot off, some with arms shot off, and some with eyes shot out."[44] One of the 77th's wounded, Private James G. Scott, required the amputation of both his legs, one above the knee and the other below the knee. As the boys bid him an affectionate farewell, he responded, "I know what you fellows think, but by God, I will fool you. I will live."[45]

Late morning on May 7, Grant noticed through the thickets that heavy guns had been positioned along Lee's line of breastworks. He had no desire to test them. In the two days of almost continuous fighting, Grant's first meeting with Lee cost the Union 17,000 men, 66 of them from the 77th. Many expected Grant to fall back and lick his wounds; however, he broke off the battle and marched his columns deeper into Virginia. His soldiers knew things would be different, not easier, but now they had a general who would go the distance at whatever cost and end the war.[46]

The movement forced the Union to leave behind a number of their wounded. Assistant Surgeon Justin Thompson from the 77th and another doctor from the Vermont Brigade were assigned to stay and care for them. After weeks of caring for soldiers in both blue and grey, Thompson learned that the Southerners considered him a prisoner of war. Faced with being sent to prison camp the next day, after dark, Thompson and two comrades escaped and found their way back to the Union lines.

Brigadier General Daniel Bidwell

Bidwell was the Third Brigade commander.

Courtesy of the Massachusetts Commandery of MOLLUS at the USAMHI

Assistant Surgeon Justin Thompson, 77th New York State Volunteers

Courtesy of USAMHI and New York State Division of Military & Naval Affairs Adjutant General's Office Albany, N.Y.

– 15 –

Good-bye Uncle John
Overland Campaign, Spotsylvania
Late Spring 1864

Experience has the same effect on most people that age has on a goose, it makes them tuffer.
—Josh Billings, Yankee Humorist
Henry W. Shaw, *The Complete Works of Josh Billings*

Grant's decision to break off the engagement at the Wilderness and drive on toward Richmond made the crossroads at Spotsylvania into the war's next piece of key real estate. The Confederates arrived first and set up a line of fortifications in a rough loop shape around the small town. The bend in the center of the line was initially called the Mule Shoe; later it became known as the Bloody Angle. The breastworks were constructed of heavy logs with a slightly raised head log, enabling the defender to fire in relative safety. The Union lines were opposite the Confederate positions but in a wider crescent shape. After marching all night, Sedgwick's corps arrived late in the morning on May 8, 1864, and took their place in the line.[1]

The 77th were positioned on lower ground 50 yards in front of Colonel Andrew Cowan's First New York Independent Battery. The regiment lay behind a breastwork, with their national color planted on top. Cowan's battery, dueling with an enemy battery, was firing directly over the 77th. Deployed on the extreme right of the Union line, their brigade was ordered to advance when signaled. On the signal, they advanced and managed to break through the enemy line.

They found themselves in a very exposed position when the brigade on their right failed to advance; with darkness falling, they were forced to retire and retrench at their former position.[2]

The intensity of fighting reached a higher level at the Bloody Angle. Fighting side by side, the Vermonters and Bidwell's brigade occupied the ditch for the enemy works and stayed in this position. Separated only by the width of a log "Our men would reach this partition and discharge their muskets in the face of the enemy, and in return would receive the fire of the rebels at the same close range."[3] Private Fred Keenholtz fired 285 rounds before his boldness cost him his life. He climbed up on top of the breastworks to have loaded guns handed up him to fire.[4] Others held their rifles over their heads and fired over the breastwork without aiming. Some tried chiseling out holes between the logs so they could shoot through the parapet. Locked in battle for over an hour, the combatants clubbed and bayoneted one another over the logs that topped the breastworks, and the dead fell like cordwood in the trenches.[5]

Almost opposite the Bloody Angle at Spotsylvania, General Sedgwick was setting up an artillery battery. A New Hampshire regiment began to file past their rear on their way up to relieve the regiment manning the front line breastwork. A shot from the sharpshooter whizzed by, and one of the New Hampshire sergeants, obviously frightened, crouched down as low as he could go without actually getting down on his hands and knees. This seemed to bother Sedgwick, who told the sergeant not to worry and said, "They can't hit an elephant at this distance."[6] The words had barely gotten past his lips when a bullet hit him near his left eye. The death of their beloved commander, John Sedgwick, was a loss that was deeply felt by the 77th, the VI Corps, and the whole Union army.[7] Killed by a Whitworth rifle at a distance of more than five hundred yards on May 9, 1864, Major General John Sedgwick was the highest-ranking Northern officer to die on a Civil War battlefield.

Sedgwick's death had left some big shoes to fill. Brigadier General Horatio G. Wright, First Division Commander, was Sedgwick's designated replacement. The perfect subordinate, Wright was a capable soldier and a respected officer, but he lacked the dash of a Sheridan or Sedgwick. Wright was born and raised in Clinton, Connecticut. He attended Norwich University in Vermont and later he graduated from West Point. All of his duties prior to the Civil War were connected with engineering projects. In September of 1861, he led an expedition against the Florida coast.[8] An exceedingly careful officer, Wright was described as being competent rather than brilliant.[9]

Colonel Emory Upton had been expounding on his opinion of how to break through the Confederate lines. Grant decided to give the young officer a chance to prove his method. Orders were passed down and General Russell selected 12 of the VI Corps' finest regiments. Russell handed the list of the regiments to Upton and asked for his opinion. The young colonel responded that they were the best in the army. Informed that if he carried the rebel works he would get his stars, Upton responded he would carry them or he would not return.[10] The young colonel divided his command into four lines, the third line made up of the 43rd New York, the 77th New York, and the 119th Pennsylvania.

Courageous to the point of recklessness, Emory Upton was always at the head of any column under his command, leading it into battle. Born on a farm near Batavia, New York, at the age of 15 Upton with his brother left home to attend Oberlin College in Ohio. The boys worked afternoons in a sash factory for eight cents an hour to pay for their board.[11] After two seasons, Upton got an appointment to West Point and graduated in the academy's class of 1861. Deeply religious and a dedicated abolitionist, Upton never drank liquor, used profanity, or smoked. He seldom smiled, as humor was not a part of him. Wounded in the first battle of Bull Run, he was promoted to colonel commanding the 121st New York Volunteer Regiment. Upton was a whirlwind in battle, and troops under his command often used their bayonets.[12]

Late afternoon on May 10, the 77th and 11 other regiments stripped off everything except their guns, straps, and canteens and fixed their bayonets.[13] On command the four lines rose as one and moved without noise to the edge of the wood. With the enemy only about two hundred feet away, no talking was allowed and orders were whispered. Taking their places the regiments lay flat on the ground. Across the field, behind two lines of breastworks and in flanking rifle pits the Georgians from George Pierce Dole's brigade waited.[14]

At 6:32 p.m. Colonel Upton in resonant tones called out: "ATTENTION! BATTALIONS FORWARD! DOUBLE-QUICK CHARGE!"[15] With a wild cheer, the 12 regiments jumped up and charged, yelling like crazy men. The rebels quickly responded, meeting Upton's force with heavy canister and rifle fire from both the front and flank. Reaching the first parapet, a deadly hand-to-hand conflict ensued. The Georgians refused to give up the ground. The first Union men to mount the works fell back, their bodies riddled with musket balls. Dole's men sat with their bayonets fixed, ready to impale anyone who might try to leap over. Witnessing the fate of their more adventurous comrades, others held their pieces out at arm's length and fired downwards. Still others poised their pieces vertically, with the bayonet fixed, and hurled them down upon the enemy, pinning them to the ground. With an overall length of 73 inches and weighing about 9.2 pounds, an Enfield rifle with bayonet attached made a lethal spear.[16] The assault force quickly killed any resisters and sent those who surrendered to the rear. Upton's men pressed forward, expanding to both the right and the left. With the staff of the 77th colors in his hand, a Minié ball ripped into Corporal Edward Jennings' hand. Another rebel bullet smashed into Sergeant Fountain's rifle stock, knocking the gun out of his hands.[17] While reloading his rifle, Private Albert Snyder winced as a ball tore through his left arm near his shoulder.[18]

Next, the second line of entrenchments and a battery fell to Upton's brigade. One unidentified soldier of the 77th was among those who jumped over the second line of works and found that the assault had diminished to a skirmish line. Anxious soldiers took flight back to the first line where they found the troops exposed to a severe fire from their left flank. The man was about to resume his flight to safety, when a mounted officer rode up and used the flat side of his sword to show him the direction in which his duty lay.[19] Lieutenant Carlos Rowe helped to capture the last entrenchment, but he failed to notice when the Union troops began falling back. Rowe was one of those taken prisoner and held for a couple of days. Lieutenant Rowe seized his opportunity, escaped, and made his way back to the Union lines a few days later.

At this point Upton's column had accomplished its task: the Confederate lines had been broken and an opening was made for the supporting troops to capitalize upon. Unfortunately, General Mott and his division failed to arrive. The rebel reinforcements arrived in great force. Upton's men held the captured entrenchments until ordered to retire. Private Frank Stillwell was shot in the enemy's breastworks. Despite both of his legs being broken, Stillwell managed to crawl 20 feet, because he did not want to die within the rebels' works. Ignoring the heavy firing, Private John E. Evans crawled out on his hands and knees to help Stillwell. While lying on his stomach, he pulled Frank onto his back and brought him back to the Union line. Laying Stillwell on his back, Evans took off his blouse and put it under Stillwell's head to make him comfortable. Exhausted, Evans lay down next to his comrade and was soon asleep. He awoke finding that both Stillwell and his blouse were gone. To justify replacing his blouse with one taken off a dead soldier at the angle, Evans said, "everything is fair in love and war."[20]

Upton's charge captured 1,200 prisoners and a couple of stands of colors, but it also carried a high price. The 77th's portion of that price was 5 captured, 7 killed, 13 missing, and 37 men wounded. After the assault, as the survivors made their way back to their camp, one of the Bemis Heights boys felt hungry and reached back for some hardtack in his haversack. He was surprised to discover that his haversack had been shot off his back, his bayonet sheath was hanging by a thread, and the left side of his coat had been riddled by shot.[21]

Among the wounded brought to the Union rear was a young rebel, Private Thomas J. Reilly of the 12th Georgia. Shot in the groin, a surgeon diagnosed the boy's wounds as fatal. He was lifted from the ambulance and placed upon a blanket on the grass. Blue or gray, the color of a dying man's coat did not matter to the chaplain, as he lay down next to the boy to comfort him. Speaking softly, Chaplain Norman Fox told the boy of courage and hope in his final hour. Cheerful despite his situation, the young soldier told Fox about his friends and relatives at home. The private asked for a drink of water. As the chaplain raised him up, the young soldier's head sagged, and he died peacefully in the chaplain's arms. They gave the boy a soldier's burial and prayed over his grave. Chaplain Fox prayed that the "God of all comfort would tenderly support those far away who would wait in vain the return of the boy of their love and hopes."[22]

On May 12, the morning weather was foggy and misty, with occasional rain showers. Shortly after 6:30 a.m. the fighting began. Later that morning, Bidwell was ordered to move up to support Edward's brigade at the Bloody Angle. Colonel Bidwell deployed his regiments about one hundred yards behind Edwards along the edge of the trees.[23] He selected the 49th and 77th New York Regiments to charge the enemy works at the Bloody Angle. Major Babcock was in command of the 77th, which numbered less than one hundred men. The two New York regiments were driven back from the rebel entrenchments but took possession of the crest that commanded the position. Hard fighting ensued and Major Ellis of the 49th was shot through the chest with a rebel's ramrod. The spurts of dirt caused by bullets hitting into the ground were similar to a rain shower, while the swish and hum of the bullets passing over their heads sounded like a swarm of bees.[24] The 77th and 49th held the crest until they were relieved. The troops that relieved them were driven off the crest by the intense musketry. Joined by some Vermont troops, once again the 49th and 77th formed up and took the crest.[25]

A correspondent of the *Tribune* wrote that on Thursday, May 12, Bidwell's brigade on the extreme right of the VI Corps received "the brunt of the fight."[26] They were engaged for 14 hours from 6:00 a.m. until 8:00 p.m. and words can't do justice to the intensity of the fighting there. Upton's, Bidwell's, and Grant's brigades generated the heaviest Federal fire that day, cutting down large trees. The rebels threw in every man that they could spare. Periodically the rain came down in torrents, saturating everything except the blazing muskets. Captain Orin Rugg was shot in the breast. He died while the stretcher-bearers were taking him to the field hospital and was buried on the battlefield. Sometime before 3:00 a.m. on Friday, May 13, the Southerners withdrew from the Salient. The wounded lay where they fell in the field and the dead rebels were piled three deep.[27] It rained all day, covering the ground with a mix of rainwater and blood that collected in the low spots.[28]

Late in the day on May 17, Colonel French caught up with the regiment. The colonel's presence seemed to infuse a sense of security into the minds of his boys, who greeted him with numerous cheers.[29] During March, French, sick with the fever, had gone home to Wilton, New York. After a few weeks his health was greatly improved, but his departure was delayed due to a relapse. The following day, the 77th and their brigade returned to the area of Upton's Charge. They found it disturbing to see comrades still lying where they had died eight days ago. They found the enemy to be too strong for an attack. The regiment was exposed to heavy artillery fire and suffered a number of casualties before they returned to camp. "We have truly had terrible fighting since this campaign commenced—when we say good bye to a friend now we hardly think of seeing him again. Every regiment is trimmed out the same. Every day has its battle."[30]

The wounded were taken by ambulance over 15 miles of rough roads to Fredericksburg. The wounded quickly filled the churches, warehouses, stores, and the private homes. On May 5, Private Hermanus A. Bowers was wounded through the chest and taken into Fredericksburg.

As soon as the news of young Bowers reached his father, a resident of Albany, New York, he immediately set out to help his son. Bowers arrived in Fredericksburg but was unable to locate his son. He enlisted the aid of the 77th's quartermaster, who assured him that Private Bowers was placed onto an ambulance and offered to help. To handle thousands of casualties, almost every building in the city of Fredericksburg housed the wounded. After two days of searching, they had not been able to locate Private Bowers. On May 19, the father received a note that his son might be at a certain church. Mr. Bowers hastened to the church, only to learn that his son had expired a half an hour before.[31]

On May 21, Private Aaron B. Quivey was on picket duty. An informal truce was being observed, with a no firing agreement between the blue and gray picket lines. From the gray line a shot rang out and Private Quivey went down with a bullet through his breast. The private died a few minutes later. This was the second time that Aaron Quivey gave all he had to the 77th New York. Worn out and near death from fever and sickness, Quivey had been honorably discharged for disability on February 8, 1863. He returned to his home in upstate New York. With God's blessings, Quivey, a soldier of the

Lord, regained his health in about a year's time. Feeling that he was still needed in the field, he reenlisted in the 77th.[32]

**Lieutenant Thomas H. Fowler,
77th New York State Volunteers, Company D**

Fowler was wounded in action at Spotsylvania.
Courtesy of Joseph Covais

Struggle for the Salient at Spotsylvania, May 12, 1864 (Alfred Waud)

Courtesy of the Library of Congress

– 16 –
Three One-Legged Jims
Overland Campaign, Cold Harbor & Petersburg
Early Summer 1864

Opinions are worth just about as much as turnips are, when there is a big crop of turnips.

—Josh Billings, Yankee Humorist

Donald Day, *Uncle Sam's Uncle Josh*

During the early afternoon on June 1, 1864, the VI Corps trudged into Cold Harbor. Their uniforms were so caked with dust and dirt that one couldn't tell whether they were Yanks or rebels. Many of the tired soldiers just dropped in their tracks and fell asleep along the roadside. To support Sheridan's troops holding on at Cold Harbor, Wright's VI Corps left the trenches at Spotsylvania and marched through the night. Located five miles northeast of Richmond, the name "Cold Harbor" did not seem appropriate since there was no harbor, and temperatures at that time of year were in the nineties. Brigadier General Neill was temporarily in command of the Second Division and Colonel Bidwell was the Third Brigade's commander. Colonel French was in command of the 77th Regiment.[1]

Late that afternoon, a concentrated assault began along the East-West Road with the VI Corps on the left and Smith's troops on the right. The artillery prepared the way for the infantry, and at 4:30 p.m. they were ordered to charge. The blue lines dashed across the open plowed fields toward the distant enemy works. The Federal advance halted 30 yards in front of the enemy line, encountering an abatis barrier composed of felled trees and sharpened sticks. A volley, like hell turned sideways, burst from the Confederate line. On the left, the 77th and Neill's division encountered strong resistance, but managed to drive the enemy back.[2] "The whole line thundered with incessant volleys of musketry, and the shot and shell of the artillery shrieked and howled."[3] Advancing just as far as the other divisions, the unfavorable nature of the ground forced Neill's troops to swing back. Only the Third Division managed to keep all that they had gained. As night settled in, the fighting died down and the Northern troops began to dig in.

Early the next morning on June 3, the assault began. With bugles blaring, 60,000 men in blue left their trenches, and moved toward the rebel lines. Wright's VI Corps was formed in two lines of battle with Ricketts on the right, Russell in the center, and Neill's division in support. The long blue lines moved across the open plain toward an unseen enemy. In the gray light of early morning opposite the VI Corps Kershaw's and Hoke's divisions watched and waited behind their breastworks. The previous night's rain turned the dust into mud. The contours of the land made it difficult to synchronize their movements with the other corps. Their advance funneled them into a semicircle of rebel trenches, exposing them to a deadly crossfire. Men fell so rapidly that the troops were ordered to lie down, putting many of them at the mercy of the rebel sharpshooters. In the first eight minutes of battle eight thousand men became casualties. The rebels' entrenchments proved to be so good, one Confederate general commented that firing at the Union troops seemed more like murder than war.[4] By 7:30 a.m. the fighting ceased, and the 77th moved up to the front line, captured from the Southerners.

At 8:00 a.m. the rebels launched a counterattack. Leaping out of their trenches, the Southerners advanced toward the Union line. This delighted the Northern troops, who were often asked to assault entrenched positions, but seldom got a chance to retaliate. The gray- and butternut-clad rebels came on yelling and with determination, but a series of well-aimed volleys and supporting artillery quickly crippled Lee's advance. The wounded rebels stayed where they had fallen between the lines.

The battle on June 3 was the last at Cold Harbor; however, the sharpshooters continued to take a toll on the Northerners. On June 4 just after darkness set in, Sergeant George Bolton left his trench to light his pipe from one of the campfires. As Sergeant Bolton approached the campfire, his form was outlined in the darkness by the fire's light. The silence of the night was broken by the crack of a musket when the sergeant was killed instantly by a single shot from one of Lee's sharpshooters.[5] Constantly exposed to sharpshooters, the men dug in and spent their days unpleasantly in rifle pits. "These rifle-pits are a little like the meanest place a man was ever put into. I have not straightened myself all day."[6] Looking at the dug up plain, Surgeon Stevens was reminded of the colonies of prairie dogs with their burrows and mounds.[7] Heavy rains and darkness did not improve conditions. With no break in the fighting or truce in place, the wounded and the dead from the earlier fighting lay where they fell. The groans from the wounded lying out in the broiling sun were very audible. The sharpshooters made any attempt to rescue a comrade suicidal. Lee took an excessive amount of time in response to Grant's request for a truce. After a couple of days in the warm sun, the obnoxious odors reeking from the dead filled the entire battlefield. By the time medical and burial details were allowed onto the field on June 7, the groaning had stopped and most of the wounded were dead.

Private Barnard Van Anden's hunger won out in the battle over his fear of sharpshooters. The private cautiously made his way over to a nearby battery to use their cooking fire. Sitting on his heels, with his back to the downhill side, Private Van Anden held his frying pan filled with melted salt pork over the hot fire. Recent rains left the trees wet, and a large drop of water fell from one of the overhead branches into the private's pan. Hitting the hot grease, the cold droplet exploded. Thinking he had been shot, Van Anden immediately jumped up. Off balance, he stumbled over backwards and proceeded to tumble down the hill. His comrades in Company D of the 77th had a good laugh over the incident.[8]

Knocked from a tree limb by an exploding shell, Private William A. Baker injured his head. Carried off on a stretcher, the private was loaded into the back of an ambulance. The horses, harnessed to Baker's ambulance, appeared to be anxious. With a close shell burst, the horses bolted, taking Private Baker on a wild ride. Banging about in the back of the ambulance, he sustained injuries to his back.[9]

The Union losses at Cold Harbor made it one of the bloodiest engagements of the war. The 77th lost five men killed and seven wounded. Grant decided to alter his strategy and postpone Richmond. On the night of June 12, his columns began to pull out from Cold Harbor, all happy to leave that stinking hole.[10] Grant directed his army south to Petersburg. Lee misjudged Grant and sent most of his forces to Richmond. Baldy Smith and his corps were the first Union forces to reach Petersburg on June 15. However, Baldy was slow and cautious in making his assault. Many believed if Smith had pressed harder and faster that the siege might not have been necessary. Lee was quick to make corrections, and his reinforcements soon arrived. In just eight hours, Union engineers built a 2,100-foot-long pontoon bridge across the James River. Grant changed his base from White House to the James River without losing as much as a box of crackers. Lee's army was in such a weakened state that he did not dare to engage Grant in the open.[11]

Although disheartened by the sacrifices made at Cold Harbor, the hard fighting and marching of this campaign had not dulled the patriotic spirit that burned within the volunteer soldiers. The feeling throughout the army was that with Grant to direct them the rebellion would be defeated. In simple terms: "Mr. Lee has his hands full while wrestling with General Grant."[12] On June 14 there was no fighting. However, there was a large turnout for foraging, and without a doubt the people from this area would remember for a long time the visits by the VI Corps. The next day was not a busy one. Captain Lennon passed the time cutting down a bee tree and drinking Doctor DeLong's whiskey.[13] On June 16, Neill's division stayed with the Army of the Potomac during the advance upon Petersburg. As darkness turned into night, the steady drumming of the VI Corps feet on the pontoons was audible up to three-quarters of a mile away. The next day, they arrived at Petersburg too late to participate in the assaults.

Badly mauled during the prior weeks of battles, the regiment played a supporting role in the June 18 assault against the Petersburg defenses. However, the 77th was subjected to heavy artillery fire.[14] Early afternoon on June 21, Bidwell's brigade occupied the front lines on the right side outside Petersburg. The Confederates had been shelling them for several hours: "bullets and shells are bursting and flying about us like hornets when their nest has been poked with a sharpened stick."[15] A group of the boys from the regiment were standing behind their breastwork enjoying the warm sunshine. The boys passed the time trading jokes and telling stories as they watched the enemy barrage. A 32-pound mortar shell shrieked through the air and descended in the direction of Company A. The big shell burrowed into the ground before it exploded, throwing bodies in all directions and turning limbs into jelly. Sergeant Jim Barnes was thrown to the left, Corporal Jim Lawrence was hurled to the right, and the blast lifted Private Jim Allen to the top of the breastworks. The three Jims were all rendered unconscious by the explosion. Sergeant Jim Barnes was the first to come to his senses, followed closely by Private Allen. Both men had lost a leg. Allen's teeth were locked in a death grip on his pipe. Thinking that he had been spared, Corporal Lawrence awoke. But as he tried to rise to help his comrades, he realized to his horror that his left leg was also missing from the knee down.[16] Colonel French ordered stretchers. The three were taken to the field hospital where Surgeon Stevens gave each man a glass of brandy before administering the chloroform. In less than 30 minutes, Stevens amputated three limbs, and dressed the stumps. The three Jims were placed in ambulances and taken to City Point Hospital. Assigned to adjacent beds, they drew a lot of interest. Afterwards they were moved to Washington, where the novelty of the situation again drew a great deal of attention. Thereafter they were referred to as the Three One Legged Jims. Although overshadowed by the others' injuries, Private Moses Tatro was also wounded in the hand by a fragment from the same shell.[17] The regiment remained in this exposed position until dark.[18]

On June 26, it was a fine day to be wearing a wool uniform with the temperature at 108 degrees in the shade. Major Babcock was profusely perspiring, wearing only his trousers and shirt, and wished he could dispense with these articles of clothing.[19] On July 8, Captain Lennon reported: "The weather is dreadful hot. Corps officers of the day found us with swords, coats, and belts off, and myself mixing a whiskey punch."[20]

On June 29 and 30, they moved down to the railroad to support the cavalry. After going into camp west of the railroad, the troops were given little rest between tearing up the track and building rifle pits.[21] "We have dug our way so near the enemy rifle pits and forts that we can almost throw a stone over into them. We have charged upon the enemy and tried to drive him out, but his works are too strong, and I think Grant has concluded to 'dig him out.' This we can do."[22]

During the early summer of 1864, Sergeant Albert J. Reid got permission to visit his brother, Jim, in the 115th New York. Reid had not seen his brother since Thanksgiving Day in 1861. He easily found the 115th and his brother about four and a half miles down the line. His brother's captain suggested they visit in the cook's quarters. The two spent the rest of the day catching up, and they arranged a reciprocal visit for three days later. The Reid brothers said their good-byes, each hoping to see the other again.[23]

On July 4, the ladies of Saratoga Springs presented a beautiful silk National Flag to the regiment. With the sutler out of whiskey and firecrackers, the day was far more peaceful than if they had been at home in Saratoga Springs. However, that evening the officers of the 77th and other officers of the Third Brigade assembled at their headquarters to celebrate the fourth with champagne and cigars. On July 5, Captain Lennon reported that a dead horse was buried too closely behind his tent. On July 6, the 77th moved their camp. Captain Lennon was happy to move and wished luck to the next man who camped by the horse.[24]

Private William A. Baker, 77th New York State Volunteers, Company H
(Charcoal Sketch)
Courtesy of the Author

Union Generals: David A. Russell, Thomas H. Neill, and John H. Martindale, June 20, 1864 (Brady & Co., Plate # 9421)
Courtesy of Massachusetts MOLLUS

– 17 –

Pursuing Old Jube
Battle at Fort Stevens
Summer 1864

Next to Shakespeare, Josh Billings was the greatest judge of human nature the world has ever seen.

—President Abraham Lincoln

Cyril Clemens, *Josh Billings—Yankee Humorist*

Prior to moving south with the Army of the Potomac, General Grant stripped Washington of all veteran troops. He left the capital defended by nine thousand poorly trained reserves. Rebel spies relayed this information to General Lee. To relieve the pressure on his besieged forces at Petersburg, Lee dispatched Lieutenant General Jubal Early with an army of twenty thousand to attack Washington. Victories at New Market, Piedmont, Lynchburg, and Monocacy brought "Old Jube" and his troops closer and closer to the capital. Each victory intensified the fear of the residents. The untested Sunday soldiers in the forts and trenches around Washington were judged to be incapable of defending the city.

Grant countered this threat by sending his best, the VI Corps, to save Washington. The Third Division had already been transferred to Washington. On Saturday night, July 9, the First and Second Divisions were ordered to break camp and march to City Point.[1] The men were happy to leave the flies and pestilent air quality at Petersburg. On Sunday, July 10, 1864, they marched all night. Reaching City Point about one hour before sunup, the two divisions boarded steamers. The 77th was split up and assigned to two steamers, the

Escort and the *Alla Knight*.[2] The two-night voyage was basically uneventful. A choppy sea made things uncomfortable for most of the soldiers.[3]

Nicknamed Old Jube, the Confederate general was respected by everyone but liked by no one. Stragglers under his command said many Confederates would shoot him "just as quick as they would a damn Yankee."[4] Born in Virginia, Jubal Anderson Early attended West Point. A classmate was so provoked by Early that he broke a dinner plate over his head during an argument. Early resigned from the army to study and practice law. In 1861, he voted against secession, but later he entered the Confederate service as a colonel. He was gruff, irreverent, and profane, and Lee referred to him as "my bad old man."[5] Old Jube's record was second only to Stonewall Jackson's.[6]

On July 11, Early and his army camped near Rockville, Maryland, just 12 miles outside of Washington. The majority of Old Jube's shoeless army wrapped their feet in rags and tied them with twine. Ragged pants, tattered shirts, and threadbare jackets made up their uniforms. Many wearing straw hats, they hung a haversack over one shoulder while balancing a Springfield or Enfield rifle on their other shoulder. Early's troops captured a train with former corps commander Major General William B. Franklin on board. Surgeon Stevens quipped that he had heard no one express any grief about it.[7] By late morning, the Southerners were probing the city's defenses around Fort Stevens.

President Lincoln greeted the VI Corps at the wharf with a quip: "You can't be late if you want to get Early."[8] Lincoln nibbled on a piece of hardtack while he chatted with the disembarking troops.[9] Bidwell's brigade, consisting of the 7th Maine, 61st Pennsylvania, 43rd, 49th, 77th, and 122nd New York Regiments, filed out onto the road followed by the Vermonters. "Stalwart forms! rugged, swarthy faces, tanned by many a hot sun and blackened by many a battle smoke, their 'baggage' tied up in their blankets rolled round their shoulders, dusty haversacks, old canteens, battered cartridge boxes filled until the covers would not shut down, bright rifles at right or left shoulder shift, their socks pulled up over their trouser legs and their stout shoes sounding a steady 'tramp, tramp, tramp' to the beat of the drums."[10]

Bidwell's veterans were a comforting sight to the frightened citizens of Washington. The soldiers overheard the civilians say: "Them's no clerks, them's fighters!"[11] Appreciative citizens gave water and ginger beer to the passing soldiers.[12] "God bress Massa Lincum for the Six Co."[13] It was a great day for Bidwell and his invincible brigade to lead the column.[14] "They say that they are regular devils!"[15] As the First and Second Divisions made their way through the hot and crowded streets of Washington, the heat took a heavy toll and a few fell victim to sunstroke.[16] The streets contained numerous pubs, which proved to be too inviting for some soldiers with a taste for something stronger. Making their way up Seventh Street, past the Post Office and Patent Office buildings, the troops headed north. They marched to a small wooded grove near Fort Stevens and bivouacked for the night.[17]

Daniel Davidson Bidwell earned General Sedgwick's praise at the Wilderness. Sedgwick reported that Bidwell's steadfastness saved the Union.[18] Born in the Black Rock section of Buffalo, New York, Bidwell was elected to justice of the peace. Enlisting in the 65th Regiment of State Militia, he earned promotions to lieutenant, captain, and brigade inspector. At the start of the Civil War, he was appointed colonel in the 49th New York.[19] Bidwell was a man who said, "come" and then showed you the way. Whether he was sitting on his horse in a parade or directing troops in a battle with shot and shell filling the air around him, his steady voice and calm composure never varied. The man was a rock.[20]

Eight hundred seven cannons and 98 mortars were mounted in the 68 forts that formed a 37-mile circle of defenses around Washington. Situated between Fort DeRussy on the west and Fort Slocum on the east, Fort Stevens, located about four miles from the White House, protected the main approach into Washington. Originally called Fort Massachusetts for the soldiers who had built it, the fort was renamed to honor Brigadier General Isaac Ingalls Stevens. The ground in front of the fort sloped down for one-half mile to a small stream, then it rose for a mile and one-half toward Silver Spring. The area between the fort and the stream had been cleared except for some tree stumps. Beyond the stream on the north side were some farms, a wooden mansion with a cupola, and the chimney of a house that had been burned out just the day before. On the northeast was a field of corn, a peach orchard, and an open field with a few large trees, the stream, and a bridle path that wound up from Seventh Street through a field of brush up a hill to a house encircled by a large meadow and cultivated grounds.[21]

General Early and his subordinates occupied the house of Postmaster General Francis P. Blair about two miles from the fort on Seventh Street. Not content to just avail themselves of all that was found in the wine cellar, they also ransacked Blair's papers and made obscene drawings on the mansion's walls. After his busy night, Old Jube, possibly suffering from overindulgence on foraged wine, rode out at sunrise the next morning to examine the Federal lines near Fort Stevens. When he saw that the rifle pits were full of men in blue uniforms, Early concluded that reinforcements had arrived. Abandoning his plan to capture Washington, Old Jube decided to keep up the threat for another day to make the Yankees sweat. With daylight the Southern skirmishers began a sporadic fire that continued throughout the day. Their sharpshooters were positioned in the trenches within six hundred yards of Fort Stevens.[22] No one was visible in the bushy field between the house and the brook, yet musket smoke seemed to be coming from every square inch of that field. The majority of the Southerners spent the day lounging, resting, smoking, and playing cards.[23]

The quantity and attitude of the citizens who came out to watch them fight angered Surgeon Stevens. His feelings were that they should be armed with Enfields and pressed into the ranks. "I would like to see their white linen coats dusted and the curls taken out of their hair."[24] The president and Mrs. Lincoln also came out to Fort Stevens.[25] After their group visited the fort's hospital, Mrs. Lincoln returned to their carriage. The president went up on the parapet with General Wright. The batteries at both Fort Stevens and Slocum were busy firing volleys of shells at Early's picket line. The enemy line kept up a hot fire on the fort.[26] Bidwell's brigade marched by in perfect order, and Lincoln doffed his stovepipe hat to the boys.

The brigade's job was to drive in the rebels' skirmish line and to occupy the two wooded hills in front of the fort. The boys in the 77th were in good spirits and all they wanted was to be let go at the rebels. Veteran soldiers were not usually anxious for a fight. Perhaps the spectacle of performing outside Washington acted like a home field advantage, where the players are inspired to perform their best.[27] Bidwell used the cover of a ravine outside the fort to maneuver his troops, without detection, up to the Union skirmish line. Wheaton's brigade manned the skirmish line. Bidwell selected three of his best regiments, the 7th Maine, the 49th and the 77th New York, for the first assault line. Colonel French was to be in command of the first line and Bidwell the second line.[28] In the field below the fort, Bidwell's troops were exposed to withering fire, and most of the men hit the ground for protection. The Sunday soldiers in the trenches around the fort were amazed at the boldness displayed by these veterans going out before the breastworks.[29]

With his troops in position, French instructed Color Sergeant Benjamin "Alonzo" Briggs to dip and wave the regiment's virgin National flag for all he was worth, signaling that they were ready. This was to be the flag's baptism to fire. The ladies of Saratoga Springs presented the flag to the regiment on

July 4. Back on the parapet, General Wright observed the signal and started the engagement. The 32-pound cannons from Fort Stevens, DeRussy, and Slocum opened fire. The long-throated guns sent their projectiles howling overhead, and two houses along the pike disappeared amidst the resulting explosions. Grey-clad soldiers could be seen jumping out the upstairs windows as the remains of the houses caught fire and began to burn.

From their front row, ground level observation post, the 77th and the rest of their brigade watched and waited for their turn. After 36 shots were fired the bombardment stopped, and Colonel Bidwell yelled "Forward!, Double Quick, MARCH!"[30] With bayonets fixed, the brave soldiers eagerly rose up and sprang forward past the skirmishers, advancing quickly up the slope. "In magnificent order with light steps they ran forward, up the ascent, through the orchard, through the little grove on the right over the rail fence, up to the road, making straight for the first objective point, the frame house in front. The rebels at first stood their ground then gave way to the impetuous charge."[31]

The fort's parapet had become a dangerous place. The air was full of bullets zinging by, and the surgeon standing beside the president was wounded in the ankle.[32] Captain Oliver Wendell Holmes, apparently without recognition of whom he was speaking to, called out to the man on the parapet, "Get down, you damn fool, before you get shot!"[33] As the battle heated up with more and more bullets flying by, General Wright ordered the president to get down. As he made his way down from the parapet, Lincoln responded to General Wright that he always obeyed orders.[34]

Private William J. Lattimore was the first man in the 77th to go down, hit squarely in the chest by a rifle ball. Leading the advance, Colonel French was struck on the thigh by a spent ball. His injury was not sufficient to force him from the field. "Soon another falls; it is Dowan of H Company, not to rise again. And there goes Morey of old K Company, to be followed by Mattot of G Company, neither of the three to rise again until the day when we are taught all will arise."³⁵ The battle, although it lasted but a short time, was a hot one. Corporal Milton Sweet had three balls pass through the well house while he was getting water.³⁶ After the initial surprise of the assault, the Confederate resistance stiffened. Bidwell quickly deployed his reserves. Aldice Walker, of the Vermont Brigade, commented, "our brave men charged handsomely, for they meant business and knew how it was done."³⁷ One-half mile in front of the fort, the Southerners were well entrenched and the struggle became costly. A number of the dead and wounded fell in this area.³⁸ Private Matthew Love was among the wounded; he died two days later in a Washington hospital. With the president watching, they fought with a bit more passion than usual. After offering a stubborn resistance for more than a mile, the rebels gave way and Bidwell's boys were in command of the field. Darkness stopped the fight, allowing Early's men to slip away. At midnight, the Vermonters relieved Bidwell's brigade.

Four of the six regimental commanders in Bidwell's brigade were killed or died from wounds in this engagement. Almost one-quarter of the brigade became casualties, and six of the 40 soldiers killed in this action were from the 77th. On July 13, they buried their dead comrades in the field where they had fallen. "None of those high in authority, who came to see them give up their lives for their country, were present to pay the last honors to the dead heroes. No officer of state, no ladies of wealth, no citizen of Washington was there, but we laid them in their graves within sight of the capitol without coffins, with only their gory garments and their blankets around them. With the rude tenderness of soldiers, we covered them in earth; we marked their names with our pencils on the little headboard of pine, and turned sadly away to other scenes."³⁹

Supposedly when Old Jube saw the Greek Crosses on the flags at Fort Stevens, he gave up all hope of capturing

Washington. "We haven't taken Washington, but we've scared Abe Lincoln like hell!"[40] One of the rebel prisoners, surprised to find the VI Corps in Washington, asked, "How the Devil did you Catholic fellows get here?"[41] Withdrawing, the rebels followed Union example, seizing and burning all the tangible goods that they could find and drinking up the contents of any wine cellars they encountered.

Early withdrew that night and crossed the Potomac River at White's Ford. Two days later on July 15, General Wright and his corps were ordered to pursue him. They began at 6:30 a.m. and marched all that day in hot dry weather on dusty roads clogged with obstructions left by Early's rear guard. After crossing the river without pontoons at White's Crossing, on Monday, July 18, the corps entered the Shenandoah Valley at Snickers Gap, following the rebels' trail. There they joined up with Hunter's forces and the men got their first look at the beautiful Shenandoah Valley. On Wednesday, July 20, Wright's forces were forced to backtrack, based on reports that Early's army was marching to Washington.

After several encounters with the Union cavalry, Early withdrew from Winchester to the security of Fisher's Hill. On Saturday, July 23, the VI Corps marched past Camp Griffin, crossed the Chain Bridge, and went into camp. About four miles outside of Washington, a number of soldiers took French leaves to wander around the capital's streets in the rain. With 450 registered bawdy houses and 163 gambling establishments, Washington was a lively place, a place where a soldier and his pay soon separated.[42] With Early still on the loose, the VI Corps received orders to move back toward Harper's Ferry. Detailed as the rear guard, the 77th stayed behind to deal with stragglers. Many suffering from overindulgence in bad whiskey, getting these men back to their commands was not an easy task. Early took advantage of the VI Corps' absence and routed General Crook's forces at Kernstown on July 24. On July 29, the 77th started at first light and marched 28 miles to catch up with their corps. On Monday, August 1, reports arrived that Early's cavalry had burned Chambersburg, Pennsylvania, to the ground on July 30.

Recovered from the wound that he received in the Wilderness, Brigadier General George W. Getty resumed command of the Second Division. He was one of the best, if not the best, division commander in the Union army. Born in Georgetown, the general was raised in Maryland. He graduated from West Point's Class of 1840. An artillery captain at the start of the Civil War, Getty was extremely cool under fire. The general employed innovation and resourcefulness as the means for dealing with any situations that he encountered.[43] Getty once remarked that he always obeyed an order, and if he was ordered to march his division across the Atlantic Ocean, he would do it. Observing grins on the faces of his audience, he then said, "At least, I would march them up to their necks in the sea, and then report that it was impracticable to carry out the order."[44]

Since the VI Corps left Washington, they had been subjected to constant marching day and night. They would just get settled into camp when orders arrived putting them on the march again. Other days they would march all day with only a short halt for breakfast. Grant directed Wright to follow Early until he was convinced that the raid was over and Early was on his way back to Richmond. On his own Major General Wright may have been capable of dealing with Old Jube, but his independent command lasted for only a week. The pursuit of General Early fell under the jurisdiction of four different military subdivisions. A telegram to General Grant from Assistant Secretary of War Charles A. Dana explained the situation: "General Hallack will not give orders except as he receives them; the president will give none, and until you direct positively and explicitly what is to be done, everything will go in the deplorable and fatal way in which it has gone on for the past week."[45] Other than running Early out of Washington, all their energy had been in vain.

Battle at Fort Stevens, D.C., on July 10, 1864

Courtesy of Stevens' *Three Years in the Sixth Corps*

**Captain Charles H. Davis,
77th New York State Volunteers, Company A**

Davis was wounded at the Wilderness.
Courtesy of Joseph Covais

– 18 –

Little Phil Takes Charge
Shenandoah Campaign, Winchester & Fisher's Hill
Early Fall 1864

One of those long-armed fellows with short legs that can scratch his shins without having to stoop over.
—President Abraham Lincoln describing Sheridan
Richard O'Connor, *Sheridan the Inevitable*

The first time Lincoln met Sheridan, the president was not impressed and commented to Grant that he seemed rather small to be handling cavalry. General Grant responded, "You will find him big enough for the purpose before we get through with him."[1] Based on Grant's recommendation, Lincoln authorized Sheridan's appointment as commander of the Army of the Shenandoah on August 7, 1864. His mission was to drive the rebels out of the Shenandoah and to strip the valley. Grant advised Sheridan to wait awhile and build up his strength before going after Early.[2]

Philip H. Sheridan was born in Albany, New York, and raised in Somerset, Ohio. "When Sheridan left Somerset to go to West Point he could whip any boy there."[3] In his third year at West Point Military Academy, he was suspended for breaking ranks with a fixed bayonet and pursuing a cadet officer who had treated him unjustly. From a poor Irish immigrant family, he was not polished at social skills, and this made it difficult for him in the peacetime army. He served as a lieutenant for eight years. In his element on the battlefield, Sheridan, nicknamed "Little Phil" by his soldiers, rose rapidly through the ranks.[4]

Little Phil Takes Charge

During early August the VI Corps' morale was at an all time low. Demoralized by the severe service and the recent battles, their guns were dirty and their camps were disorderly clusters of tents.[5] Surgeon Stevens felt that both the men and horses in the corps were played out. Their future performance would depend to a high degree on their new commander. When a general rose quickly through the ranks and gained a reputation as a fighter, these veterans knew who paid for that reputation. However, the men also understood that aimless maneuvering did not win wars either. Another battle, another campaign, and another general, this one's name is Sheridan. Big deal, so what? Would they fight for him?[6]

As time went on, the soldiers noticed the small things. If the army was on the move, Sheridan always went up near the front of the column and took charge. Whenever bottlenecks occurred, the officer who rode up to take care of things was usually Sheridan. Whether he was speaking in a very controlled soft voice or screaming obscenities, either way he got results. When the infantry gave way and marched in the fields, leaving the road for the wagons and guns, Sheridan went with the foot soldiers. Things started running smoother with fewer problems. Someone was in charge again.[7] He wasn't much on fuss and feathers. Little Phil's escort was usually one man bearing his flag, not an honor guard of cavalry. For headquarters, he made due with two tents and a couple of tent flies. The VI Corps veterans paid him their highest compliment when they said that having Sheridan in command was almost as good as having Uncle John back.[8]

On Wednesday, August 10, reveille was at 4:00 a.m. An hour later Sheridan's entire army was on the march from Harper's Ferry. Thursday they trekked to Winchester. The days were hot and the marching continued. Private John Mosher started out with the column, but the heat began to have an effect on him and he gradually fell behind. Toward evening, when he was too exhausted to walk any farther, a surgeon granted Mosher permission to ride in one of the ambulances. During the night, Private Mosher's condition deteriorated, and the doctors were unable to save him. The 77th retrieved his body, identified by a letter in his pocket, for burial. On the morning of August 13, his comrades buried Private Mosher along the bank of Cedar Creek. The chaplain offered a prayer, and they fired a parting salute, before slipping into the marching column.

On August 13, Sheridan's army fell back to Fisher's Hill. August 14 was a day of maneuvering with some scattered fighting along the skirmish lines. The next day was quiet, until Old Jube's infantry and artillery drove in the Union picket line. On August 16, they marched through Middletown. The next morning, with colors flying and bands playing, they marched through Winchester. On August 18 with their rations almost gone, they marched in the rain, halting that evening at Charlestown, West Virginia. From Friday, August 19, through Saturday, August 20, rain kept the VI Corps in camp at Charlestown. The men of the 77th spent the day resting or foraging. On Sunday during scattered fighting along the skirmish lines, in the 77th one man was killed and another wounded. The next day there was more skirmishing in the morning, but a heavy rain dominated the afternoon. On Tuesday, August 23, they marched through Charlestown, where John Brown had been hanged. To remind the citizens that Mr. Brown's soul was marching on, every Northern band played the tune and the troops all sang as they marched through the village.[9] Light skirmishing intensified to heavy skirmishing over the next two days. On September 4 the brigade dug rifle pits in the rain from sunset until dawn.

On September 13, at first light Getty's division, accompanied by both Wright and Sheridan, went on a reconnaissance of Opequon Creek. The Vermont Brigade was in the lead; by 10:00 a.m. they reached the creek. The Vermonters put out skirmishers who crossed the creek. The rest of the division, including the 77th, massed in a wooded area about a quarter of a mile back. Suffering light losses, the skirmishers quickly made contact with the rebel pickets and artillery. Finding the enemy in force, the division returned to camp.

On September 15, Grant visited the Shenandoah and gave Sheridan his orders to "Go in!"[10] Three days later word reached Sheridan that Early had divided his command and sent Gordon's division to Martinsburg, Virginia. Sheridan quickly took advantage of the situation. On September 19, Sheridan's army broke camp at 2:00 a.m., and with Bidwell's brigade in the lead they marched to Berryville. The day's march took them through the fields, over hills, and down into a deep valley where they forded a broad but shallow stream. From Berryville, they went along the Winchester pike. A woman kept a toll gate across the pike just outside of Winchester. As Sheridan and his staff rode up, she lowered the gate and demanded her usual fee to raise the gate. The general paid for himself and his staff, but said he couldn't afford to pay for the whole army. The toll keeper allowed the troops to pass, but she also counted each of the soldiers who marched by. After the war, she billed and collected the toll from the United States Government.[11]

The VI Corps crossed Opequon Creek and after sunrise they made their way through a wooded ravine. Filing out of the ravine, they passed General Sheridan's Headquarters. Sheridan personally supervised operations at the front, exposing himself to enemy fire. Bidwell's brigade led their division up the steep slope, and through a cornfield. They formed a line facing west. The Federal line extended from Abraham Creek on the left to the Berryville Pike on their right, with McKnight's and Cowan's batteries supporting them. Bidwell's troops were positioned along an open ridge and exposed to enemy fire. Woods shielded the other brigades. They relieved Wilson's cavalry and occupied a breastwork of rails. Once the regiment was in place, they had to wait for the brigade, division, their corps and the other corps to follow suit. The enemy opened on them with sharpshooters and a battery. Concentrating on the officers, the sharpshooters did considerable damage. Lieutenants George M. Ross, George H. Gillis, William W. Worden, and Lewis T. Van Derwerker in the 77th all went down wounded. Colonel French picked out a group of 20 of the regiment's best shots. He sent his shooters out in advance to make things unpleasant for the enemy.[12] With the entire brigade in position, a skirmish line was thrown out. The 77th deployed four companies under Major Babcock for its portion of the skirmish line. The VI Corps was in position and ready to charge, but the XIX Corps was nowhere in sight. They would need an additional two hours to get in position. Finally at noon the order was given to advance and attack. The Union battle line, three miles long, moved forward in splendid style with the various colors waving boldly in the bright sunlight. Bidwell ordered French to stay connected with the first brigade. Advancing, the 77th's main line closely followed the skirmishers. Early's troops, positioned along the top of a nearby hill, maintained a severe fire with both muskets and artillery. "Every step forward, men were dropping; some dead, some mortally hurt, and some with slight wounds. Now on this side, now on that they fell; still the line swept forward, leaving the ground behind it covered with victims."[13] With Sheridan's soldiers quickly closing in on them, the Confederates broke and ran. The blue line swiftly covered the balance of the field and continued through the wooded section. The 77th kept their connection with the first brigade but lost connection with the 122nd. They could hardly believe their eyes when they saw the Southerners formed up in the open. "Great God! If we could have got this kind of a lick at them last Spring! There wouldn't be no war now if we had!"[14]

Sheridan came dashing along the lines of the VI Corps. He drew up as he came upon his friend, Division Commander George Washington Getty. He shouted to him loudly, "General, I have put Tobert on the right and told him to give 'em hell and he is doing it. Crook is on the right, too, and is giving it to them! Now, press them, general, they'll run, I know they'll run!"[15] They did run over a long stretch of open plain, down into a deep hollow, and up again and over the rolling ground past the white farm house. Early's troops ran in wild disorder. The soldiers bearing the white crosses on their caps relentlessly pressed them, nipping at their heels. Runaway horses galloped about, and the ground was strewn with tents, kettles, officer's mess equipment, weapons, and baggage. Darkness halted the pursuit and allowed them to escape. It was ironic that when French advanced his line and the 77th was positioned near the ruins of an old church and graveyard, one of the graves covered with a plain marble tablet, broken across, read "Gen. Daniel Morgan." Morgan played a key role in the Battle of Bemis Heights during the Revolution. The regiment's colors, depicting the British surrender, were in sight of the general's grave.[16] Getty's division successfully wiped out everything that confronted them on September 19. Early had been driven from his position on the Opequon Creek, through Winchester, and beyond the city. The fighting had started at daylight with the last shots fired at about 7:00 p.m. The 77th suffered 29 wounded and one man was killed. Before dawn on September 20, Sheridan's army, including the VI Corps and the 77th, resumed their pursuit of the rebels. On the previous days' battlefield, the bodies of their fallen comrades lay, not in great concentrations but spread here and there, waiting for the burial details. At three in the afternoon, after marching eighteen miles, they halted at Strasburg. Old Jube's forces were entrenched at nearby Fisher's Hill. The two mountain chains that formed the valley approached one another, making the valley very narrow near Strasburg. Colonel French stated that Fisher's Hill was one of the most unattractive positions that he'd ever seen.

The heights were strongly fortified with batteries bearing on every approach.

The 49th and 77th New York Regiments were thrown ahead as pickets and skirmishers.[17] Later that morning, Sheridan and his staff rode the entire length of the picket line, carefully noting the nature of the ground. The next day was spent getting the army into position before Fisher's Hill. By mid-afternoon the divisions were almost in place. The XIX Corps was on the left, the VI was in the center, and Crook's corps was on the far right. Colonel French advanced his picket line and secured a good position to protect the movement. Once in position the Union divisions quickly began to entrench themselves.[18] Throughout the day, the sharp rifle cracks of the skirmishers could be heard.

Quietly using trails and mountain paths General George Crook's VIII Corps labored most of the day to get into position. With a high-pitched yell, Crook's troops rushed out of the woods and bore down on the surprised Confederates' flank. Both the 77th and 49th Regiments were deployed as skirmishers in front of the XIX Corps, commanded by Major General William H. Emory. With Crook's Yankees rolling up the Rebels' flank, confusion and panic ruled Early's rear and signaled advance to the rest of Sheridan's army. The advance described by Colonel French as "Dashing through the woods, over hills, into hollows, across gullies, over walls, fences, and every conceivable obstruction, and the enemy at the same time pouring us all his fiery vengeance, in the shape of shot and shell."[19] When the line was sufficiently swung around, a division of the XIX Corps charged. Sheridan, without escort, came riding down the line encouraging the troops and oblivious to the danger. He seemed to be everywhere he was needed that day. "The men rushed almost wildly forward, regardless of lines of battle, each striving to outdo the other in noble daring—Oh is there anything that will stir the deepest feelings of man's nature. Making ready and willing to die for our country, it is a battle.

The horrors and awful grandeur no one who has not seen one can imagine."[20]

The rebels fell back in complete disorder. Each of them ran for their lives as they scurried across the plain with the Union troops close behind. After chasing the Southerners off, the 49th and the 77th joined up with their brigade along the Winchester Pike. This ended the Battle of Fisher's Hill. The heights had been taken along with 16 pieces of artillery, battle flags, and many prisoners. Bidwell's brigade alone had captured six of the artillery pieces. All of Sheridan's army, including the 77th, were in the highest spirits and morale. After two days of staring at that impenetrable fortress and pondering their fates with a direct assault, to dislodge the Confederates in this manner was a pleasant surprise. Although other battles in the Shenandoah may have overshadowed the Battle at Fisher's Hill, the careful reconnoitering and skilled maneuvering, combined with a bit of military genius, resulted in an incredible victory. In the 77th, Private Isaac Kipp Jr. was killed and four men were wounded. Colonel French was slightly wounded in the chin and received a commendation by General Bidwell on the manner in which he handled the picket line.

The following day Sheridan's army marched up the valley to Woodstock located twelve miles south of Strasburg. On September 24 they resumed their advance in the early morning and passed through Mount Jackson. A few miles beyond, they were forced to form up in a line of battle when they came upon Early's Rear Guard. The VI Corps with Getty's division in the lead took the left of the road and the XIX Corps the right. Getty had his division in three parallel columns by brigade so that he could form into a divisional battle line in three minutes. The pursuit continued in this manner for 25 miles that day through New Market to Sparta. Thirteen of those miles were without a halt and with the rebels in sight. When the VI Corps abandoned the chase, the XIX Corps was over a mile or two behind them. Captain Martin Lennon commented that Union men in this vicinity are as scarce as blue sheep.[21]

Marching in the Shenandoah Valley was easier than marching in eastern Virginia or Maryland. There was less dust on the roads, and there were more trees alongside the roads to provide shade.[22] While in the valley, foragers from the 77th procured large amounts of both honey and apple butter. Other days they seized mutton, bacon, chickens, grapes, and potatoes. The boys of the Bemis Heights regiment nicknamed the Shenandoah Valley the land of "mutton and honey."[23]

Battle of Winchester on September 19, 1864 (Alfred Waud)

Courtesy of the Library of Congress

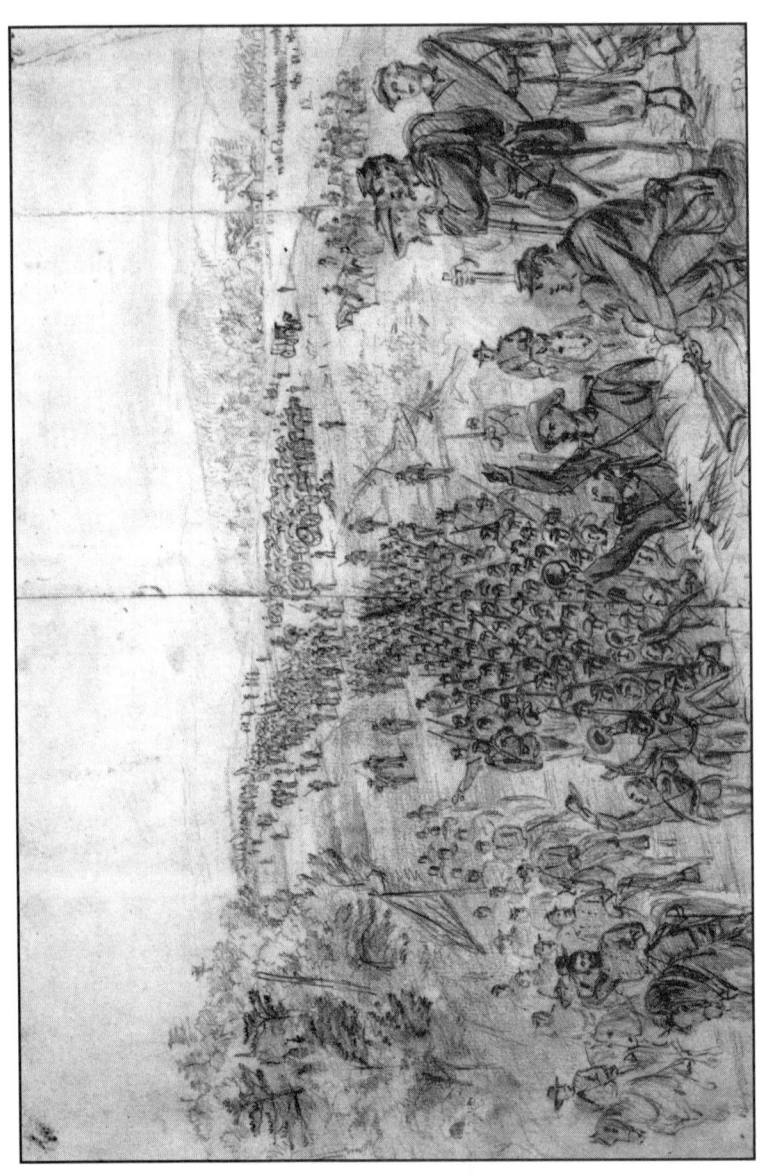

Sheridan's army chasing Early up the Valley (Alfred Waud)

Courtesy of the Library of Congress

– 19 –

Have to Drive Them from the Field
Shenandoah Campaign, Cedar Creek
Late Fall 1864

Don't run until the Vermonters do!

—Colonel Winsor B. French

Aldace Walker, *The Vermont Brigade in the Shenandoah*

After suffering his second defeat in four days, Early and the remnants of his army retreated to Rockfish Gap near Waynesboro to lick their wounds. This left the entire Shenandoah Valley open for implementation of Grant's order to strip the valley of all crops and provisions. Sheridan followed Early down the valley until he reached the end of his infantry's supply line at Harrisonburg. On October 6, 1864, Sheridan's army began the return trip through the valley. Called Red October, for three days they were shrouded in smoke as they burned barns, mills, haystacks, and grain. Sheridan's men put everything to the torch except houses, and they took all the cattle, horses, and mules that could be found. What they left was hardly enough to feed Mosby's guerillas. One of Sheridan's staff officers was killed while carrying orders to the picket line, and in retaliation Sheridan burned every house and barn within a five-mile radius.

On October 10, the VI Corps marched into Front Royal, a city of about four hundred residents. On arrival, the 77th was detailed as provost guard for the town and its bridges. The following afternoon, Captain Lennon and a detail went to gather the grapes in Mrs. Marcus Buck's large vineyard. He wrote, "Front Royal is the meanest secession town I have seen,"[1] while Sergeant Cyrille Fountain's diary entry for the same day read, "Went into the village in the evening with some of the boys and we had a grand concert with the secessh girls. They gave us an invitation to take dinner with them the next day."[2] One could conclude that in Front Royal it was better to bring music than take the grapes.

The following morning, the regiment broke camp at 3:00 a.m. and marched to Middletown. Sheridan set up his headquarters in Belle Grove plantation on the outskirts of Middletown. The Army of the Shenandoah was spread out around the plantation. The VIII and XIX Corps were camped closer to Cedar Creek while the VI Corps was camped on the army's right past Belle Grove. On October 17, Sheridan was called back to Washington for a meeting with President Lincoln. Believing that Old Jube was played out, Sheridan left for his meeting and placed General Wright in command.

Early had not been idle since his last defeat. He collected his scattered forces, regrouped, reorganized, and enlisted as many new recruits as he could find. One Sunday, General Early attended a Southern religious service. The minister closed his sermon by asking the congregation to consider the result if all those who are in their graves should arise from their resting places and come marching past them by the thousands in white shrouds. A hush ensued among the parishioners that was broken by a loud whisper from the general to his companion, "I'd conscript every damn one of them!"[3] Early followed Sheridan back through the valley and took possession of Fisher's Hill, waiting for an opportunity.

With Sheridan's departure, Early's break arrived. Just after dark on October 18, the Confederates began cautiously descending from Fisher's Hill. To avoid the noisy clatter of bayonet shanks against canteens, the rebel soldiers were not allowed to bring canteens. Early accompanied Kershaw's division. Confederate General Joseph B. Kershaw was the personification of a gentleman attorney turned soldier. By 3:30

a.m. they halted undetected and within sight of the fires burning in the Federal camps. The valley was blanketed with a thick morning fog. After a short rest, at 5:00 a.m. the rebels launched a well-coordinated surprise attack. After dealing with the pickets, Early's determined troops bore down on the VIII and XIX Corps.

In the early morning hours on October 19, Corporal Thomas King was looking forward to finishing up his three days of picket duty. The corporal was in charge of several posts on the right side of the main line and a few others stationed at the ford about thirty rods out in front. Distant firing broke the night's silence, followed by a period of stillness. More firing rang out in the darkness, but it was much louder and closer. Corporal King ordered his men to fall back toward the reserves. Just after they started back, another burst of firing erupted, so close that he felt the heat from the flashes of the rebels' guns. The corporal and his men quickly made tracks. In the darkness they became separated, and King headed for the nearest woods. Once there, he stopped and fired a few shots in the direction of the muzzle flashes. Looking about in the dim morning light, he found the woods around him were filled with rebels. Several gray-clad soldiers approached him from the darkness with their guns pointed at his belly, and Corporal King became a prisoner of war.

Concealed in the thick fog, Kershaw's division swept through the pickets, ignoring their scattered musketry and taking many prisoners. Unable to see precisely what was coming, the few soldiers in the trenches of the VIII Corps fired late or not at all. After a feeble struggle, the rebels controlled the breastworks and the seven guns positioned along them. The yelling rebels flooded into the VIII Corps' camp, where they shot and captured men who only moments before had been sleeping soundly. In darkness, Kershaw's division skillfully executed a successful surprise attack.[4] The same soldiers who fought with courage at both Winchester and Fisher's Hill, were now being driven in a mad rush. By seven-thirty that morning, two-thirds of the Union army had given way and was in full retreat.

The VI Corps was camped about two miles beyond the initial attack, with Getty's division on the extreme right. They heard the sounds of the impending battle and prepared themselves a quick breakfast in anticipation of a long day. Without orders, Getty had his men moving toward the sound of the guns in front of Middletown.[5] They marched through the dense fog over the plain, passing behind the camps of the artillery and other divisions. Swarms of officers and men were running wildly toward the rear. Most were shoeless, hatless, or coatless, but only a few were without their weapons. Beyond reasoning and consumed by fear, curses and blows would not rally them.[6] An XIX Corps captain, while trying to rally his troops, overheard one of the retreating soldiers comment to a friend, "The bloody Sixth is going in. They'll stop these blasted cusses. They say that, by Jesus, they'll hold 'em."[7]

Earlier that morning Corporal Albert Snyder was detailed with a few others to help load the officer's baggage. Finished with his assignment, Snyder returned to his tent. He found that the regiment had left with the rest of Getty's division. Corporal Snyder was deciding if he should make breakfast or wander off into the fog looking for the 77th. An officer rode up and ordered him to leave because the rebs were just minutes behind him. Corporal Snyder joined the crowd headed toward the rear. After a short distance, they halted and formed into a line of battle. When no rebels arrived, the process was repeated a few times. This battle line was composed of men and officers from different corps, who later were disbanded and ordered to rejoin their regiments.[8]

As Getty's column marched toward the sounds of the battle, they encountered numerous small bands of dispirited comrades. Some of these groups, in their rush to get away from the advancing rebels, chose a path through the column. The veteran soldiers, with the white cross on their caps, were not sympathetic to these intrusions. The front ranks fixed bayonets and used the points to encourage the fleeing soldiers to go around them.⁹ They arrived at Meadow Brook, a branch of Cedar Creek. The sounds of the impending battle were much louder and the air above their heads was filled with bullets whizzing and pinging past them. Getty realized the importance of the Pike Road, and positioned his division on the left by the road. The other two divisions of the VI Corps were farther off to the right. While his lines were forming, they began to receive fire from the rebel skirmishers in the woods across the brook, and a strong force of skirmishers was sent out to push them back. Thirty yards away on their right flank a well-dressed line of the first division extended into the fog. Getty advanced his brigades across the brook, swinging the left of his line forward toward the pike. They stopped to make adjustments before advancing into battle, and except for some annoying skirmish fire, they were not under attack. Confident that his right flank was secured by the first division, he issued orders to send his entire force moving forward while wheeling to the right. This maneuver would roll up Early's flank and put an end to their advance. Mounted on his horse, General Getty was in front of his line, waiting for the words from his brigade commanders that everything was ready for the advance.¹⁰ The general was stunned to observe First Division's troops breaking and falling back for no apparent reason. For as far as the dense fog allowed him to see, one after another, file after file, the troops were breaking and falling back. This was repeated until the last of the First Division's men sprang up from his place and ran back. The Second Division was now alone with both of their flanks exposed on the plain outside of Winchester. General Getty took stock of the situation: they were the only thing between Early's army and a complete victory.¹¹ He relocated his division to a better defensive position, three hundred yards back at a prominent semicircular, partially wooded crest. The crest was not a high one, but it was high enough that the top was not shrouded in the fog that covered the low lands. The brigades were positioned along the crest of the hill with Warner's First Brigade on the right in partly open terrain, Grant's Vermonters in the center in open terrain, and Bidwell on the left in mostly wooded terrain. The 77th was positioned between the 61st Pennsylvania and the 49th New York.

Viewing Getty's battle line from a distance, General Early, jubilant over the success of the morning, declared that it was only a rear guard and would leave by itself soon and their victory would be complete. However, General Gordon, seeing the distant banners that he had encountered in the Wilderness, felt otherwise. Gordon warned, "That is the Sixth Corps, General. It will not go unless we drive it from the field."[12] Under a cover of dense fog, Early's army drew down on the VI Corps Second Division.

Just behind the crest of their hill, Bidwell's veterans patiently waited, ready to fight. The 77th was not at full strength, 140 men plus four officers having been detailed for three days of picket duty. Colonel French deployed Captain Charles E. Stevens and his company as their skirmish line.[13] Stevens and his company disappeared into the fog in front of the regiment. The Georgians of Wofford's brigade from Kershaw's division made the first assault. A veteran of the Mexican War, Confederate General William Tatum Wofford was a plantation owner, newspaper publisher, and member of the North Carolina State Legislature.[14] The first assault was primarily directed at James M. Warner's brigade and Grant's brigades. Wofford's troops moved boldly up the slope approaching the crest and expecting to triumph. "It was like the clash of steel to steel. The astonished columns were checked. They had found an immovable obstacle to their march of victory."[15]

Shortly after the first assault, the second assault was made by the North Carolinians of Grime's brigade, part of Ramseur's division. Southern General Bryan Grimes, a graduate of Chapel Hill, had been a planter before the war. Grimes' attack was focused on the gap between Bidwell's and Grant's brigades and was more persistent than the first attack. Captain Stevens and his company of skirmishers came running out of the fog reporting that the enemy was close behind.[16] The thick fog concealed the rebels and allowed them to advance unseen to within 30 paces. Two lines of rebel infantry emerged out of the fog and stretched as far as one could see. When the first Southern faces became visible over the crest, simultaneously the men of the 77th and neighboring regiments jumped to their feet, dressed their line, sprang forward a couple of paces, aimed their weapons, and fired almost as one into the oncoming lines. The sudden appearance of the Yankees, out of nowhere, and the deadly accuracy of their volley staggered the rebel advance. Viewing the enemy's confusion, Colonel French immediately ordered a charge, which the adjoining regiments gallantly joined. With a loud, spontaneous cheer, the 77th, 61st, and 49th Regiments charged down the hill, driving the rebels like sheep back down the slope. The slower Southerners were taken as prisoners. Captain Martin Lennon took a ball in his right shoulder, his blood soaked into his diary and dried on the small remnant of a pencil that was in his pocket. Lennon died from his wounds on November 7. The gray-clad dead and wounded were left where they lay, scattered over the hillside. After the charge down the hill, the attackers were exposed and soon became prey for Early's cannons, captured earlier in the day. Recall was sounded and the soldiers made their way back up the slope. They resumed their positions behind the crest. Just out of rifle range, Kershaw's and Ramseur's divisions, who were chased past the base of the hill, quickly reformed their lines and began to press back up the hill.

With no reserves, every man and his musket were critically needed on the battle line. Assistant Surgeon William A. DeLong decided to help. During a battle, the drummers became stretcher-bearers. DeLong armed each of the eight drummers under his command with guns taken from the wounded. Drummers were non-combatants, and it was not their duty to fight, but the boys eagerly shouldered those rifles and fixed bayonets. The doctor formed them into a line that he used to stop the soldiers' stampeding to the rear. When they rounded up a group of six to eight, the doctor and his drummers herded their recruits up to the 77th where they were forced into service. One of the stampeding XIX Corps soldiers said, "I was making for the rear as fast as my legs would carry me, until a kid of an officer halted me, gave me a gun, and had me escorted to the firing line where with many others of mine and the VIII Corps we were sent by him. I didn't want to go but his damned drummers presented bayonets to our rears and we had to go."[17] Drummers John E. Evans and Charles E. Houghtaling were standing near DeLong when General Bidwell rode over and complimented him on his ingenuity.

Directing the brigade from his saddle, General Bidwell and staff were in front of the Union line. Detached from the 77th during the spring, Captain George Orr was assigned to the general's staff. In his reports, Bidwell noted both Orr's gallant conduct and his service as assistant inspector-general. A shell tore through the general's chest and exploded behind. Bidwell was knocked to the ground, his chest now a gaping hole, and the subsequent explosion tore off Captain Orr's arm. The general was placed in an ambulance and a surgeon was summoned. The 77th's Surgeon George Stevens responded quickly. Examining the general's wound, he saw that the man's entire right shoulder had been torn away by a shell. The general asked what his chances of recovery were, and Stevens responded that he feared that there was no hope. "Oh, my poor wife, Doctor, won't you see that my record is right at home; tell them I died at my post, and I did my duty."[18] Daniel Bidwell was beloved and respected by his men. His loss was mourned by the entire corps.

Colonel Winsor B. French, the senior regimental commander, assumed command of Bidwell's brigade. Every man was deployed on the line, fresh Confederate troops were pushing up the slope, plus his brigade and two neighboring regiments were in danger of being flanked. Immediately French challenged his troops, yelling out, "Don't run until the Vermonters do!"[19] Cheering loudly his men jumped up and advanced to the crest, where they delivered a devastating volley and charged down the slope into the face of the rebel attack. Stunned and unnerved by the sudden change in momentum, the gray line broke and reeled back, leaving the hillside covered with dead and wounded.[20] Shot in the bowel region, Lieutenant William J. Taber died about three minutes later. Corporal Augustus R. Walker and Lieutenant John Belding were wounded. Belding died days later from his wound.

All the rebel artillery was brought to bear on Getty's division for an intense bombardment lasting about thirty minutes. Fortunately, the shells were passing overhead and bursting far behind the soldiers crouched behind the ridgeline. Getty's entire force was in one thin line with not one single man in reserve. Early's whole army was up and about, ready to turn their flank. After holding his position for over an hour, Getty decided to pull back. At a lull in the artillery fire, each of the brigades faced by the rear flank and marched across the open fields to the crossroad north of Middletown known as Old Furnace Road. On arrival the brigades halted, about-faced, adjusted their lines, deployed skirmishers, and filled their cartridge boxes. Old Jube, unaware that Getty abandoned the crest, continued the bombardment.[21]

About 10:00 a.m. Sheridan, mounted on his big black horse Renzi, crested the final hill before the battlefield. Renzi was not an especially handsome animal and Little Phil was not graceful in the saddle. The two of them at top speed were not poetry in motion, but one felt that somehow they would get there. Unheralded and unanticipated, Sheridan came down the pike at full speed. Cresting the final hill, the general observed Getty's division formed up in the distance. Continuing on, Sheridan plowed through a group of routed soldiers. Swinging his arm in an arc toward the VI Corps Second Division, he shouted at them to "Turn about, you damn cowardly curs, or

I'll cut you down! I don't expect you to fight, but come and see some men who like to!"[22] He stopped briefly and made several inquiries to Colonel French, then he rode along the rear of the brigade making his presence felt.[23]

Getty and his fighting division checked the Southerners' advance and held them long enough to give the Union army time to regroup. Otherwise, Sheridan's dramatic ride might have been in vain. General Wright, his beard covered with dried blood from a wound, was well on the way to putting the army back together when General Sheridan resumed command. The army formed up on the Second Division's line. Little Phil established his command post on a crest behind Getty's line. Private Abram Cramer, standing in the battle line, overheard the general remark: "Boys, I find you in better position than I expected. We will lick them yet."[24] He gave orders for the rest of his army to form up on Getty's line. His plan was to have the army wheel to the left, using Getty's veterans as the pivot point. Just prior to the Union attack, Major General Sheridan rode the entire length of the line to fire up his troops.

The attack began at about 4:00 p.m.[25] Colonel French was in command of the third brigade, with the 77th positioned on the far left of the Union line. Ordered to advance slowly, French's brigade acted as the hinge, on which the gate or Union line would swing around. Advancing through an open meadow, the brigade came under intense fire. Across the meadow, Ramseur's troops were posted behind a stone wall, with his sharpshooters positioned in the houses, and a battery behind the mill. A fearless yet gentle young officer, Stephen D. Ramseur was a North Carolinian and an 1861 graduate from West Point.[26] The brigades on their right found cover behind a rock wall, but there was no such protection available for French's brigade. Men were being rapidly picked off as they tried to slowly advance. Approaching the brick mill, they came under a withering fire, especially the men carrying the 77th's colors. Within seconds, Color Sergeant Alonzo Briggs was shot down—seriously wounded. Next, Color Corporal Henry Clayton took up the colors and fell almost immediately.

Color Corporal Warren Earl was hit and went down trying to advance the colors. After Earl, Adjutant Lieutenant Gilbert Thomas grasped the flag and leaped over the fence in front of our line. With the flag in one hand and his sword in the other he cried out "Come on boys! . . . Forward, men, forward!"[27] As Lieutenant Thomas turned to advance, a rebel bullet struck his head and killed him instantly. Thomas fell forward onto his face, and the flag followed him down shrouding his body. Corporal Henry Reed took the colors and carried them from the field.[28] The brigade was forced to fall back. French informed General Getty of the situation, and received approval to advance quickly. Moments later they advanced at a double-quick over the same field, pushing the rebels in front of them. French's brigade quickly caught up with and passed the Vermonters on their right. The rebel lines broke, starting a wild race. The boys in blue took prisoners and arms without stopping to reload their weapons. Sheridan's army chased the fleeing rebels for more than three miles, driving them back across Cedar Creek. Early's army was eliminated as a fighting force. With darkness setting in, the tired and victorious soldiers made their way back to bivouac in their old camps. With darkness setting in, the tired and victorious soldiers made their way back to bivouac in their old camps.

During the advance, Private Abram Cramer was wounded in the leg. As Cramer made his way to the field hospital, twice mounted cavalrymen, with their swords drawn, stopped and questioned him as to where he was going. One of them offered Cramer a ride to the hospital. When he was some distance back, he encountered a wounded rebel lying on the ground. The man saw Cramer's bleeding leg and asked if he was on his way to the hospital. When Cramer nodded his head yes, the wounded rebel offered him greenbacks to take him along. The offer enraged the private, who had heard about rebels robbing the dead. He picked up a discarded rifle and started toward the man, intending to kill him. However, a rebel sharpshooter spotted him and "a bullet whizzed right under my nose. Why, it came so close that I could smell the grease on the bullet. I passed on and let the fellow live."²⁹

The men with the white crosses on their caps had saved the day. The victory did not come without a toll: the 77th had 3 missing, 21 wounded, and 12 men killed at Cedar Creek. The next day Sergeant Cyrill Fountain looked over the battlefield. Shockingly, Fountain found that the dead bodies of his comrades had been stripped of all their clothes and left naked on the ground. The VI Corps remained camped at Cedar Creek, and Colonel Thomas W. Hyde was placed in command of French's Third Brigade. On November 4, the entire army, including the VI Corps, withdrew to Camp Russell near Kernstown. On November 19, 1864, Colonel French and 119 men, with their three-year enlistments up, left camp and headed for home. This marked the end of the regiment's service and the start of the 77th Battalion.

General George W. Getty

Getty was division commander.
Courtesy of the
Massachusetts Commandery of
MOLLUS and
the USAMHI

General Sheridan on Renzi in the Shenandoah Valley, 1864 (L. Prang & Co.)
Courtesy of the Library of Congress

– 20 –

The 77th New York Battalion
Petersburg to Appomattox
Winter 1864–Spring 1865

They will make the fur fly!

—Major General Horatio G. Wright

Edwin Bearss, "The VI Corps Scores a Breakthrough"

In January of 1864, the future of the 77th was in question. The three-year terms of service for the men who enlisted during 1861 were drawing to a close. Colonel French spent several days in Washington, addressing these issues. Fortunately, enough of the 1861 volunteers re-enlisted to allow the 77th to remain in existence as a battalion.[1] During the late fall of 1864, French left with the men whose service was completed. The 420 men with remaining service were consolidated into a battalion of five companies. David J. Caw, the regiment's senior captain, was promoted to lieutenant colonel and placed in command. Caw, born in Scotia, New York, enlisted as a sergeant in 1861. "Knowing the mettle of that battalion as I do, I can confidently assure the ladies that the colors they gave to the Seventy-Seventh Regiment will never be disgraced in the hands of the battalion of the Seventy-Seventh."[2]

On November 24, Thanksgiving Day, drills and labor were suspended. The Sanitary Commission supplied the 77th Battalion with turkeys and chickens. Fearing Early might show up again, Sheridan kept Getty's division in the valley as long as he could. They were the last division released to return to the Army of the Potomac. On Thursday, December 8, 1864, Getty's division packed up and marched to Stevenson's Rail

Road Station.³ The next day they embarked on the Baltimore and Ohio Railroad. As the train was crowded, some of the men were forced to ride on the boxcars' roofs. The weather turned cold and snow began to fall. The train's engine was too small and could barely pull its load on dry tracks.⁴ The snow slowed up the train and frequently brought it to a complete halt. The men eagerly anticipated visiting Washington's Soldiers Retreat Barracks, where they could clean up, dry out, get warm, and have a hot meal. However, the train did not stop in Washington, instead it continued on past the city to the wharf. Later they learned that unappreciative small-minded politicians felt that the VI Corps was too rough and blocked the corps' admission into the city.⁵ Washington turned its back on the same men who only five months before had fought, bled, and died protecting them. At the wharf the disappointed soldiers were transferred onto waiting steamers. The 49th and the 77th New York shared a boat named the *City of Albany*.⁶ Captain David Caw was in command of both regiments. Sunday morning, December 11, after a warm breakfast, one of the officers suggested playing cards. Captain Caw forbade it, stating that there would be no card playing on Sundays while he was in command. Late that evening the steamers anchored off Hampton Roads.⁷ The following day the corps disembarked at City Point and boarded a train to rejoin the Army of the Potomac outside Petersburg.⁸

    Grant had not been idle during their absence. The Union line had been considerably advanced, extended, and fortified. Hyde's brigade took up a new position on the Squirrel Level Road behind Fort Fisher. The 77th was located on the Davis Farm, approximately eight miles from the position that they had occupied back in July.⁹ The ground they had been assigned was mostly swampy with muddy roads. The brigade dug a drainage ditch, called the Dutch Gap Canal, to drain the water off their new campsites.¹⁰ The 77th's boys wasted no time in erecting comfortable winter huts. The battalion was allowed to use the brigade's supply train to procure the required timber. The huts were constructed with walls made of chest-high, split pine logs using tents as roofs.[11] Their new camp consisted of five company streets with a sewer located at the foot of each street. Water was supplied by five good wells within the camp.[12]

The 77th's chain of command continued with Wright as corps commander and Getty at the division level. After Cedar Creek, Thomas W. Hyde became their brigade commander. Hyde was born in Italy while his parents were traveling. He graduated from Chicago University, where he met both Abraham Lincoln and Elmer Ellsworth. With the outbreak of the Civil War, he returned to Bath, Maine, and was elected major in the 7th Maine. For his actions at Antietam, Hyde received the Congressional Medal of Honor and promotion to lieutenant colonel.[13]

The Union line paralleled the strongly fortified rebel line. The rebel fortifications included several protective layers of dense abatis, a deep and broad ditch, and formidable breastworks made of logs and earth. Artillery earthworks were spaced along the line at the more accessible approaches. The area between the lines started out as a dense strip of timber. With the men in blue and gray trying to keep warm, as the winter progressed, the strip of trees became narrower and narrower until almost cleared.

As for Christmas in the 77th Battalion, indeed there was a Christmas. Private William C. Christmas enlisted on July 26, 1864, at Watertown, New York. Sergeant Fountain's diary listed December 25, 1864, as a pleasant but lonesome day.[14] The brigade held a dress parade every afternoon throughout the winter.[15] In late December a group of visitors from Saratoga Springs visited the camp.[16] During early January, the rebels attacked and drove in the picket line, capturing three of the 77th's pickets.[17]

Before dawn on Saturday, March 25, Hyde's brigade awoke to the sounds of heavy firing on the right. Covering his retreat to Danville, Lee ordered General John B. Gordon and his troops to capture the Union's Fort Steadman. Caught by surprise, the fort quickly fell to Gordon's men. The Union artillery from the neighboring forts and a strong counterattack kept the rebel flag's tenure over the fort short-lived.[18] Rationalizing that for the Southerners to have massed their forces for an attack, they would have to weaken their defenses someplace else. General Wright was ordered to feel out the enemy on his front. Wright gave the assignment to Getty's division. The first attempt to dislodge the rebel picket line with a beefed-up picket line was repulsed; next Getty called out his entire division. Forming up in a battle line in front of Fort Fisher, the division drew the attention of the enemy artillery. Soon shells were plowing up dirt among the troops. With a wave of the flag, the advance began with Hyde's brigade on the right. The rebel pickets and artillery kept up a hot fire on Getty's line advancing toward them. With the blue line bearing down on them, the Confederates quickly brought nine pieces of artillery into action.[19] The gray line began breaking up, and with a loud cheer Getty's troops swept over the rifle pits, capturing many of the defenders. Hyde, believing that their objective was the enemy forts, was almost to the main works when recall was sounded.[20] The division reformed and took up prone positions in and under the captured rifle pits to get some protection from the rebel artillery. General Hyde watched as a shell exploded in a rifle pit occupied by three officers, sending body parts flying. A boot with an ankle sticking out was blown over the general's head. Hyde looked into the pit and with remorse he recognized the mangled body of Lieutenant Stephen Pierce from the 77th New York. A few days earlier Hyde had been unable to grant Lieutenant Pierce's request for a leave of absence.[21] Later in the day the division held off several brigade-sized flanking attacks. After dark they refaced and strengthened the captured rifle pits. Posting a strengthened picket line, the division withdrew to their respective camps.[22] Driving in and capturing the rebels' picket line had netted 547 prisoners and casualties of 280 killed and wounded. Lieutenant Stephen Pierce, Captain Sumner Oakley, and Private Albert Chase were killed, plus four men were wounded in the 77th. The Union's picket line between Forts Fisher and Walsh was now only 800 yards from the main rebel line.[23]

On Saturday evening, April 1, the VI Corps used the captured picket line as the staging point for an assault. Confederate General James H. Lane's brigade of four North Carolina regiments manned the area targeted for the assault. Along Lane's battle line soldiers were spaced between six to ten paces apart.[24] Earlier in the day, General Hyde briefed his regimental commanders on the assault and instructed them to pass on the instructions to their regiments. At 10:00 p.m., the VI Corps' batteries opened up, sending shot and shell shrieking toward the rebel works. Later that night, Wright responded to a critical dispatch that he had confidence in his men's ability and promised: "The corps will go in solid, and I am sure will make the fur fly!"[25] General Wright also stated that if his troops did half as well as he expected, they would crack the rebel line within 15 minutes after he said, "go."

Falling in at midnight, the 77th left their knapsacks and canteens in camp. Their muskets were loaded but not capped. In the darkness, they formed up by brigade and then by division in column. The column passed the breastworks and abatis near Fort Welch. Halting behind the recently captured rifle pits, the VI Corps formed up in the darkness into a wedge-shaped assault formation. Getty's division was the advanced center, with the other two divisions of the corps placed in echelon. At the very tip of the wedge, the 49th New York was on the left and the 77th was on the right, with the balance of Hyde's brigade formed up behind them. Both of the tip regiments had been issued 40 axes, and it was their job to advance with rifles slung and clear a path through the abatis.

Knowing the formidable nature of the enemy positions, many of the soldiers had penciled their name, company, and regiment onto a piece of paper, which they pinned to their blouses. Lying quietly in that open field, the soldiers of the 77th waited anxiously, peering out into the darkness. The night was damp and chilly and as morning approached, a dense fog settled over the field. The pickets on both sides opened fire, and a number of brave men were killed and wounded in the staging area as a result of this unnecessary skirmish. Hyde's brigade suffered the greatest losses. After awhile the picket line's firing died down and stopped. Only disciplined soldiers could remain quietly in formation and take casualties without returning fire or breaking ranks.[26] Numbed and shivering, the assault force waited for the start signal.[27]

Early Sunday morning on April 2, General Wright delayed the start for 40 minutes due to darkness. The noise of the bombardment masked the sound of the signal gun. Realizing the problem, staff officers carried the start command to the waiting columns of prone soldiers. The Vermonters were the first to start, followed by Hyde's brigade, with the 77th and 49th New York Regiments in the lead. The distance between them and the enemy works was primarily covered with stumps. Using a rebel campfire as their guide, Colonel Caw and the 77th moved swiftly across the field. Initially the only sounds were the footsteps and heavy breathing of their comrades. The first lines almost made it to the rifle pits of the rebel picket line before being detected. The rebel pickets got off a few scattered shots at the dark blue cloud rolling toward them across the dark field. The advancing troops, shouting loudly, overran the rifle pits, capturing many of the rebel pickets. From this point on, officers and men were in an outright footrace for the enemy works that were emitting lines of flashing fire, sparkling in the darkness. The field was vividly illuminated off and on by the heavier artillery flashes. Shells with fiery tails blazed overhead, traveling through the gloom. The fastest men quickly advanced and soon came upon the barriers of abatis. Senior Captain Isaac D. Clapp and his men tore into the barrier of roots and branches. Using axes and even bare hands, they cleared a pathway. A rebel bullet wounded Captain Clapp as he battled with the tangled piles. At the far edge of the swamp Lieutenant Colonel Caw's deep loud voice was the beacon as he reformed his command on the 77th's colors. Regrouped, they continued to advance right to the base of the enemy works, up to eight feet high in places.[28] Quickly they scaled the main works. Sergeant William H. Wright claimed to be the first man over the rebel works and was rewarded with a Lieutenant's commission.[29] The 77th also claimed to have been the first to plant their colors on the rebels' works. Face to face with the enemy, the first group of about 50 men fought a fierce hand-to-hand battle with the rebel defenders. During the fight, Colonel Caw was bayoneted through the shoulder. Using their rifle butts and bayonets, stabbing and clubbing, the 77th triumphed over the defenders and drove them out of the works.[30] Colonel Caw's little brother William, six foot three, almost six foot four inches tall and 170 pounds, was also among the first group. With both Caw and Clapp wounded, command of the battalion shifted to Captain Charles Stevens. Private John H. Kipp was killed during the assault, and 11 men were wounded.[31] Captain Clapp was promoted to major and Lieutenant Colonel Caw to colonel for the gallantry and leadership they displayed.

By 5:00 a.m. on April 2, 1865, the VI Corps had torn a gap in Lee's impregnable line. They captured 3,000 prisoners and 40 pieces of artillery. The sounds of exulted cheering could be heard all over the battlefield. Five or more regiments, including the 77th, claimed to be the first to mount the enemy parapet. They are probably all correct, each storming the works on his front at almost the same instant.

The following day on Monday, April 3, Getty's Second Division was in the lead as the VI Corps advanced 14 miles westward and bivouacked on Whipponock Creek.[32] On Tuesday, April 4, the corps crossed Whipponock Creek and advanced another 12 miles.³³ The next day, late in the afternoon, the VI Corps vigorously in pursuit of Lee's Army, had advanced another 16 miles and stopped near Jetersville Station. They were posted on the right of the V Corps. The muddy roads impeded their deployment and Meade was forced to postpone his advance on the enemy positions until the next morning.³⁴ Dawn on April 6, the V Corps was positioned across the railroad, with the VI Corps on the right, and the II Corps on the left. The three corps advanced toward the Court House but Lee had pulled out. Later that morning, the rebels decided to make a stand near Sailor's Creek. This would be the last battle that the VI Corps was required to fight. Getty's Second Division was in the rear and not directly engaged. The other two divisions captured General Ewell and 9,000 men. General Custer rode past their camp followed by his escorts triumphantly bearing 37 captured battle flags. An old soldier commented: "Oh, yes, my boy, you have picked up the apples, but the VI Corps shook the tree for you."³⁵

The next day the corps marched 14 miles to Farmville. They arrived in the evening and made their way down the main street, which was well lighted by the glow of the bonfires. Sharp eyes recognized Grant sitting on the veranda of a country hotel. After four long, hard years of war, they knew that victory was near, and Grant was the man who had shown them the way. To show their appreciation, those closest to him broke ranks and made torches. Waving the torches and cheering hysterically, they paraded past him. Men without torches waved their caps. Brigade bands materialized and soon the air was filled with music. When the VI Corps had marched into the darkness past the last of the bonfires, Grant went inside the hotel and wrote a formal note asking General Lee to surrender. The corps continued on to the north side of the river where they bivouacked for the night.³⁶ On April 8, part of the 77th was detached for a few days to guard a supply train. Lee surrendered on April 9, 1865, at Appomattox. Grant's sense of honor would not allow his troops to witness the Southern surrender. Many of the men were disappointed, not because they wanted to exult but they were curious about the men they had been fighting. The VI Corps camped and rested for a few days at Clover Hill, just north of Appomattox. The corps then retraced their steps, marching back through Farmville, and on Wednesday April 13 they went into camp near Burkeville Junction. Late that night, profound grief swept through the Army of the Potomac as they learned of Lincoln's assassination.[37]

Senior Captain David J. Caw, 77th New York State Volunteers

Caw was promoted to lieutenant colonel. He was wounded in action at Petersburg.

Courtesy of the International Museum of Photography and Film; George Eastman House

Petersburg assault on April 2, 1865

Courtesy of Massachusetts MOLLUS and of the USAMHI

**Captain Sumner Oakley,
77th New York State Volunteers**

Oakley was killed in action at Petersburg.
Courtesy of the USAMHI and the New York State Division of Military
& Naval Affairs Adjutant General's Office, Albany, New York

– 21 –
The 77th Marched Home

Comrades, who would not be proud to be the bearer of the flag of such a regiment as ours.

—Corporal Charles E. Jennings
Report of the Thirty-Ninth Annual Reunion

With the close of the Shenandoah Campaign, Colonel French and 119 men with their three-year enlistments up, returned home on December 13, 1864. The veterans arrived in Albany, at 8:00 a.m., on the steamboat *Hendrick Hudson*. Discovering that the daily train for Saratoga Springs had already departed, the deputy superintendent ordered a special train for the regiment. The first stop was at Mechanicville where the Stillwater Band boarded the train, and at the next stop in Ballston Spa, Reverend Tully joined the group. The train arrived in Saratoga Springs at 2:00 p.m. and was greeted by a large crowd. Disembarking from the train, a procession was formed with Colonel French in front, followed by the 77th veterans, the band, and the welcoming citizens. Parading through the streets of Saratoga, the procession ended at Nicholas Hall. Colonel McKean gave the welcoming speech. Before he left the podium, McKean brought the regiment to attention, then saluted them for the last time. Colonel French took the stand and gave an account of the regiment's history. Frequently, he was forced to stop his speech and wait for the applause to die down. The regiment and the citizens adjourned to the American Hotel where Mr. McMichael, the regiment's unofficial quartermaster, served up a tasty banquet. After dinner, Mr. Charles S. Lester gave a speech paying tribute to the brave men of the

77th. He told of a young lieutenant who left as the regiment's adjutant—a man who put aside both his legal career and family when he exchanged his pen for a sword. The man returned four years later as the noble regiment's commander. More toasts and speeches were given, and the Johnnies of the 77th Regiment were home.

On April 22, 1865, after Lee's surrender, General Joseph E. Johnston and his rebel army of 30,000 men were still in the field near Danville, North Carolina. To deal with Johnston, the VI Corps, including the 77th Battalion, was placed under General Sheridan's command. The next day the corps broke camp and began a rapid march from Burnsville to Danville, a distance of one hundred miles. They arrived in four days and four hours—before the Union cavalry! Lieutenant William Caw remarked, "Oh how we did hop it down, but all things must have an end and when we got to this city we was about as tired a lot of men as you could find. I think that General Wright was just trying our mettle in the marching line."[1] The corps went into camp along the railroad line near Danville, and Hyde's brigade camped right in the city. Untouched by the war, the area in and around Danville was the prettiest country that they had seen in quite awhile. A few days after the VI Corps arrived, Johnston and his army surrendered. During the six weeks here, the men from the Third Brigade used the equipment of the *Danville Register* to publish a newspaper called *The Daily VI Corps*. The papers quickly sold out at twenty-five cents a copy. The men of Hyde's Third Brigade also performed provost guard duty, and issued rations to the population.[2] On May 1, Colonel Caw recovered from his wound and resumed command of the battalion.

On May 16, 1865, the VI Corps was ordered back to Washington. Traveling by train, each division disembarked at Manchester, Virginia. Their mundane march northward took them through many of the places where they had fought. May 23, 1865, was the first day since Lincoln's death that the flag was flown at full staff, the VI Corps was en route to Washington, and the Grand Armies of the Republic were honored with a grand review. Heavy rains slowed their progress, and it was early June before the VI Corps went into camp just south of Washington.[3]

To honor the VI Corps, Washington gave them a special review on June 8. Behind their war-torn banners adorned with Greek Crosses, twelve thousand proud soldiers marched up Pennsylvania Avenue to parade before President Andrew Johnson, cheering people lining both sides of the street. The day was very hot, and Private Herbert Schmidt was one among many overcome by the heat and sun. Schmidt had to be carried to the hospital.[4] The VI Corps had its day in the sun.

In the 77th a detachment of about 90 men were mustered out on June 16 in Washington. The men of the 43rd, 49th, and 77th New York regiments were loaded into a train of boxcars. Their train rolled out at sundown, but progress was slow due to the congestion caused by similar trains of soldiers. Private Charles H. Benedict was riding on top of a boxcar. Afraid of falling off if he fell asleep, Benedict lashed himself to the car with the straps of his backpack. Eventually Benedict did doze off and awoke intact and refreshed the next morning as the train pulled into Philadelphia. Leaving the boxcars, the veterans made their last visit to the Cooper Shop Refreshment Saloon.[5] After they cleaned up and enjoyed a fine breakfast, the men boarded a train. Arriving in New York City, the boys marched to the armory, which they used as headquarters for the day. Later that evening, the detail marched to the wharf and boarded the *Knickerbocker*. Steaming through the night, the old boat arrived the next morning in Albany.

A squad of the boys breakfasted at a hotel opposite the steamboat landing. The squad included Sergeants Obed M. Coleman, Augustus R. Walker, and Edward H. Thorn; Corporal Edward W. Smith; and Privates William B. Thorn, Nathan Tefft, and Charles H. Benedict. The boys were supposed to go into camp outside Albany in Clifton Park and wait to receive their discharges and pay. However, anxious to get home, they decided to forgo the formalities and go directly to Saratoga Springs. After convincing the ticket clerk that they were not deserters, they purchased train tickets using Sergeant Walker's silver watch. The squad boarded the passenger car on the Saratoga train, but their appearance and Private Bill Thorn's young bulldog puppy got them relocated to the baggage car. Once under way, the realization hit them that the war was over, they were alive, and they were on the final leg of their journey home. To the boys' surprise the conductor was an old friend. Had they known, Sergeant Walker might still have his watch. A cheering crowd surrounded them when they left the train at the depot in Saratoga Springs. In the depot they separated, with each man heading toward home. News of their return had spread quickly and the returning soldiers were met by cheering groups of family, friends, and neighbors.[6] By June 24, 1865, another 90 gallant soldiers from the 77th had returned home.[7]

During the end of June in 1865, the VI Corps was discontinued. After three years, seven months, and four days of service, on Tuesday, June 27, 1865, the remaining members of the 77th New York Volunteers were mustered out of service in Washington.[8] The following day, the Third Brigade of the VI Corps started for home by train. The 49th and 122nd New York regiments departed from the rest of the brigade at Baltimore. In Philadelphia the 61st Pennsylvania said their goodbyes. The 1st Maine went their separate way at New York City, while the 43th and 77th continued on together to Albany. The two regiments set up their camps a mile or two above the city.

On July 4, 1865, a ceremony for the reception of New York States Regimental Battle Flags was held in Albany at the Washington Parade Ground. Lieutenant General Grant and Major General Hooker attended the event. Major General

Daniel Butterfield presented 80 battle flags, including six from the 77th, to Governor Reuben E. Fenton. An excerpt from Butterfield's speech: "These standards are returned battle scarred, hallowed by the blood of your patriot sons—a precious treasure, a priceless legacy, for they shall tell your children's children of manhood and patriotism rising in their might to sustain the right. These are glorious insignia of the highest devotion and sacrifice of man for man, of man for country. I need not ask you to cherish them proudly."[9] Colonel Winsor B. French and Lieutenant Colonel David J. Caw represented the 77th New York Volunteers. Color Bearer Charles E. Jennings and others from the regiment carried the flags in the ceremonies. Jennings stated, "Comrades, who would not be proud to be the bearer of the flag of such a regiment as ours."[10] The Bemis Heights regiment turned in a regimental color, two national flags, and three guidons to the state for safekeeping.

On Thursday, July 20, 1865, a banquet and reception was held for the 77th Regiment in Congress Park of Saratoga Springs to show public appreciation for the soldiers' long and faithful service and to give the Saratoga boys a suitable reception. Colonel Winsor B. French was on the executive committee of arrangements. On July 7, 1865, the men of the 77th New York State Volunteers Battalion were paid off and dismissed. Of the original 50 men of Company A, who enlisted at Westport four years prior, only three returned at the end of the war. All of them had started out as privates, but they all returned home with commissions: Major Charles E. Stevens, Captain Charles A. Davis, and Lieutenant Cyrille Fountain.

In the year of 1865, the 77th Regiment had 410 men who were mustered out, 32 men were discharged for disability, and 6 men died from disease. During the year, 4 men were killed in action, 9 died from wounds received, and 1 man died in a Southern prison camp. There were 9 deserters, 15 men transferred, and 1 man was missing in action. The next year, 1866,

George T. Stevens completed his book entitled *Three Years in the Sixth Corps*. Stevens called his book a concise narrative of events in the Army of the Potomac, from 1861 to the close of the rebellion, April 1865.[11]

The VI Corps' Grand Review in Washington, D.C., on June 8, 1865

Courtesy of the Library of Congress

The 77th New York State Volunteers guidon (Red)
Author and the New York State Division of Military & Naval Affairs

The 77th New York State Volunteers national flag
Author and the New York State Division of Military & Naval Affairs

– 22 –

The Reunion Years from 1873

That so long as one Seventy-seventh be on earth a reunion will be held every year.

—Survivors of the Seventy-Seventh Regiment
"Report of the Forty-Fourth Annual Reunion"

Drinking from the same canteen, sharing tobacco, enduring hardships, experiencing victory and defeat tied these men together. Their experiences in the 77th from 1861 through 1865 created bonds that lasted a lifetime. The survivors of the regiment attended annual reunions dating from their first meeting in 1873 through the last, sometime in the 1920s. The majority of these meetings were held in Saratoga Springs; other assembly places included Ballston Spa, Galway, Gansevoort, Gloversville, Hagamans, Mechanicville, Schenectady, Schuylerville, Westport, Wilton, and Gettysburg.

On October 21, 1873, the First Annual Meeting of the 77th Survivors Association was held in Saratoga Springs, New York. The visiting veterans arrived on the morning trains. Stepping off the train, a blast of loud band music and a hardy handshake greeted the old soldiers. The regiment even had its own band, the Seventy-Seventh Regimental Band. After a few minutes of reminiscing, the group formed up, paraded through the streets, and marched to the meeting site. Their brigade's colors and a welcome banner were draped over the Church Street entrance to Town Hall. Inside headquarters decorations included arranging tables to form a Greek Cross. Coincidentally the special table held 77 plates. Four swords connected by an officer's sash were suspended by red, white, and blue ribbons from a chandelier. Three stacks of guns, a box of official government-issue hardtack, and the regiment's garrison flag were all prominently displayed in the headquarters room.

Many of the reunions began with Johnny Evans beating out assembly on his drum with just as much vim and vigor as he had when he was a lad of 14 years of age and the regiment charged up Marye's Heights.[1] General French called for three rousing cheers for the regiment's first commander, James B. McKean, which were deafeningly delivered and followed up with a regimental tiger "Grrrrrrrr." While Judge McKean, employed as the chief justice of Utah, was not there to enjoy the cheer, his mother was among the ladies present and appreciated the sentiment. General French, Colonel Caw, Private Keck, and Surgeon Stevens gave speeches. Just as Stevens began his speech, B. F. Judson thrust a bottle of Chickahominy into the doctor's hand. This flustered Stevens and drew loud applause from the veterans. A popular fever medication, Chickahominy was a mixture of quinine and whiskey. However, Surgeon Stevens did not approve of the mixture and would not prescribe it.[2]

A typical reunion included officer's reports. Secretary Fuller was continually discouraged with the response to the mailing of reunion invitations. The following year, Secretary Fuller, still angry over the poor response, said: "Had they not exhibited any more ardor twenty-eight to thirty-two years ago, they would still be carrying hardtack around for a square meal."[3] Treasurer Charles Thurber read his report and collected the voluntary annual dues of 50 cents per member.

One could not have a meeting of these old foragers without a banquet. At the appropriate time they would form up and march into the dining area. While they reminisced about the days when hardtack and salt pork were the main stays in their diet, none wanted to eat the ration of hardtack that was distributed with the meal—preferring to keep it as a souvenir. At a later reunion in Gansevoort's Dutch Reformed Church,

Edward Fuller commented: "More pie and cake was seen there that day than a Seventy-seventh boy saw in the field during the whole three years of his first enlistment."[4]

Time was always allowed to renew friendships and memories with old comrades. Edwin Ham, charmed by his service in the 77th, sought to make a career of military service, so he enlisted in the regular army for an additional 20 years. Ham relayed the following story to the boys:

> A Union soldier, who had lost both feet, both arms, and one eye during the war, was allowed to have a chair on the sidewalk of one of the business streets in a large western city. The average donation into the old soldier's cup was usually a nickel. One day a stranger put five dollars into the old soldier's cup. The old soldier was very appreciative and after he expressed his gratitude, he asked the donor for his name. The stranger refused to give his name but said: "My reasons for making the donation are that I am a Southerner and I too fought in the war, but for the South, and you are the first Yank that I have ever seen who has been trimmed up to suit my taste."[5]

Fulton County District Attorney Jeremiah Keck, unable to attend one of the reunions, sent five dollars to bc used toward the purchase of pipes and tobacco so the boys could have a smoke on him.[6] John Evans, the drummer and a ventriloquist, did his routine where he kicked his drum and projected the sound of a dog's yelping inside the drum, just like he had done to entertain the boys in blue—years before.[7] James Lawrence was the last of the one-legged Jims. James Allen was the first to die in 1889. The following year James Barnes, after visiting with James Lawrence of Nebraska at the reunion, died on his way home. Former Sergeant William H. Wright reminisced that in his four years of service seven of his tent mates were killed and he was wounded twice.[8]

Nothing pleased these old veterans more than to form up and march through friendly streets of upstate New York. The close of a reunion involved forming up with the band and marching back to the train station to see the departing old soldiers off. The association's presidents included David Caw, Winsor French, B. J. Judson, Charles Stevens, and J. Keck.

After the war the regiment was due $500 for company rations. The survivors voted to use this money as the nest egg for a monument fund to honor the regiment's dead. Under French's guidance over 10 years the amount grew to $1,000. The 77th's monument was the only monument in the entire country, other than the ones within the battlefields, that was dedicated to a single regiment.[9] On September 2, 1875, the 77th's survivors marched down Broadway in Saratoga Springs to the monument site at the entrance to Congress Park. Both the parade route and the monument site were crowded with spectators estimated at 7,000 to 10,000 people. Reverend Norman Fox gave the prayer and General Winsor French gave the dedication speech. At the close of French's speech, a signal gun was fired, music began to play, and the flag was dropped away, unveiling the monument in the center of the street. The Seventy-Seventh Regimental Band played during the unveiling ceremony.[10]

The 77th's final encounter with General Grant was 20 years after the war. The majority of the Captain Luther Wheeler Post was composed of men who had served in the 77th. On July 23, 1885, U. S. Grant died at Mount McGregor in Wilton, New York. While funeral arrangements were made, the Wheeler G.A.R. Post provided the honor guard to watch over the general. They kept away all except those who had business with Colonel Fred Grant. They continued to watch over the general until August 4 when a late-morning funeral service was held on the cottage's porch. After the service, Grant's body traveled by train through Saratoga Springs to Albany and eventually to New York.

The New York State Regimental Monument Dedications were held at Gettysburg Battlefield on October 16, 1889. The regiment's monument at Gettysburg was located on Powers

Hill near where Slocum's Headquarters had been.[11] The following segment is from French's dedication speech: "Saratoga's favorite Regiment, the Bemis Heights Battalion, has a record of noble deeds without a single blot. It never, by any act in the field, or the camp, or on the march, or in the fight, disgraced the county from which it was sent. It never flinched or wavered from the duty, however perilous, which was assigned to it. Nor, until it was ordered to do so, did it ever turn its back upon the foe."[12]

The regimental reunion pin, designed by Secretary Fuller, was worn for the first time at the 1906 meeting. The medallion was attached to a blue ribbon that had a white Greek Cross in its center and sold for 25 cents. Attendance ribbons were given to the reunion participants. The early reunions were documented by newspaper coverage. Sometime after Edward Fuller began his tenure as the 77th Survivors Association's secretary he printed the annual reports on newspaper broadsides. Later Fuller's annual reunion reports were printed up as booklets. The 50-year anniversary of the regiment's muster-in, celebrated in 1911, and the 50-year anniversary of the muster-out four years later in 1915 were recorded with 64-page booklets featuring a large quantity of photographs.

The main topic at the reunion in 1920 was the proposed relocation of their monument from the center of Broadway by the entrance to Congress Park in Saratoga Springs to the proposed location inside Congress Park. The increased number of automobiles made the relocation of the monument necessary to ensure the future safety of both the statue and the motorists. On December 1, 1921, the 77th Monument was moved inside the park.

Over the years several resolutions were made by the 77th Survivors Association. After the death of General French, Major Babcock commissioned Secretary Fuller to have a wreath of flowers shaped in a Greek Cross placed on his comrade's grave every Memorial Day. When Babcock passed away in 1917, Secretary Fuller continued the tradition for the duration of the 77th Survivors Association. "That so long as one Seventy-seventh be on earth a reunion will be held every year" was unanimously accepted.[13] Captain John R. Rockwell, Saratoga Springs, was the last known living member of the regiment.

77th Monument dedication at Saratoga Springs, New York, September 2, 1875

Courtesy of the George S. Bolster Collection of the Saratoga Springs Historical Society

77th Monument dedication at Gettysburg, October 19, 1889

Courtesy of the Saratoga Springs Historical Society

Veterans reunion in Ballston Spa, N.Y., during the late 1890s

Courtesy of the Author

77th Monument in Congress Park, Saratoga Springs, N.Y.

Courtesy of Robert F. Morrow Sr.

– 23 –

The Hard-Fighting Seventy-Seventh

The old 77th—They were all wool and a yard wide, none better!
—Major Andrew Cowan, 1st New York Battery
"Report of the Forty-Third Annual Reunion"

Praise the Lord and the Fighting VI Corps! Their history more than any other is filled with the glory, romance, and intensity of the Civil War.[1] Augustus Buell, the cannoneer, believed that the I and V Corps were tough outfits. "But a few days service in the 'Bloody Old VI' convinced me that the I and the V were Sunday schools by comparison."[2] In his writings, Buell praised the VI Corps, stating: "On the defense it was always a rock, in the attack a hurricane."[3] In the spring of 1865, General Sheridan requested the VI Corps once more so he could really smash things.[4] A noteworthy compliment to the corps came from an unlikely source. After the Chancellorsville Campaign, rebel pickets along the Rappahannock's southern bank bantering across the river with their Yankee counterparts, said that none of the Union army could ever cross the river again except for the fellows who captured Marye's Heights.[5]

Some historians wrote that the defenses at Fredericksburg on May 3, 1863, were undermanned. But the entire Army of the Potomac did not assault them, only one corps. One of Sedgwick's officers stated that if there had been an additional one hundred men on the heights that they would not have been able to take them.[6] For their part in the Chancellorsville Campaign, the VI Corps captured more prisoners, artillery pieces, and colors while sustaining greater losses than any other corps.[7]

Various historians stated that John Gordon ran out of daylight after he turned the Union flank in the Wilderness.[8] The facts were, Bidwell's brigade heard the approaching battle, formed a new line at a right angle to the rest of the brigade, and repulsed all of Gordon's attacks. Yes, Gordon may have run out of daylight, but he also ran into Bidwell, and the rout stopped here. This brigade's performance, before and after the Wilderness, supports that they were more than likely willing to fight to the last man than to skedaddle. For confirmation, refer to Gordon's comment to Early at Cedar Creek: "That is the VI Corps, general, it will not go unless we drive it from the field."[9]

Praise for the Second Division! Buell stated that "if anything yet written does full justice to Getty's Division at Cedar Creek it has escaped my notice . . . Nobody—General Sheridan or otherwise—ever 'rallied' these men, because they never required any rallying. Getty's division might have been buried at Cedar Creek, but not broken! The Second Division of the Sixth Corps had glory to spare before it ever saw the Shenandoah Valley . . . Such were the men of Warner's brigade . . . , of Lewis Grant's Vermont brigade, of Bidwell's brigade."[10] At Cedar Creek when Getty's Second Division made its stand, Jubal Early thought that he was fighting the entire VI Corps, not just one division. According to General Hazard Stevens, the First and Second Divisions were not surpassed by any troops in the army.[11]

Praise for the Third Brigade! General Stevens stated that Neill's brigade ranked second only to the Vermont Brigade, and that they were examples of the best in American soldiery.[12] Consolidated into one brigade, the Vermonters had their own identity. No matter who was in command, they were always referred to as the Vermont Brigade. The Third Brigade wasn't as recognizable, being from a mix of states and having served under many names, including Davidson's, Irwin's, Vinton's, Neill's, Bidwell's, French's, and

Hyde's brigades. If the Vermont Brigade was the best in the Union army, the Third Brigade was a close second. Colonel French challenged them at Cedar Creek, saying "Don't run until the Vermonters do!"[13] The brigade responded by charging into the face of a rebel assault and chasing them back.

Praise for the 77th New York State Volunteers! From the beginning this regiment was built on pride. From Bemis Heights to Appomattox, their sense of tradition was instilled in them and they were expected to perform at a level worthy of their name and number. To honor the charge and capture of Mechanicsville by the 77th New York Volunteers, musical composer J. W. Alfred Cluett from Troy, New York, wrote a spirited march. Called "Colonel McKean's Quickstep," the tune became popular and several editions of the sheet music were sold.[14] Considered a veteran regiment, the 77th was assigned as skirmishers at Antietam, Marye's Heights, the Wilderness, Fort Stevens, Fisher's Hill, and Cedar Creek. Comrade Major Andrew Cowan, commander of the 1st New York Battery, remarked, "The old 77th—They were all wool and a yard wide, none better: and Cowan's battery knows it."[15] After a long march the 77th did not limp into camp. Sometimes just for the fun of it, they would do the last one hundred yards into camp at the double-quick—yelling the entire distance.[16] Perhaps the greatest praise for the Bemis Heights Regiment was the fact that time after time, they were given, or picked for, the crucial assignments because their leaders knew that the boys from the 77th could always be counted upon to do all that men were capable of doing.

The Foxes were a patriotic family with two sons in both the 77th and the 107th New York Regiments. The chaplain's brother, William F. Fox, authored *Regimental Losses in the American Civil War*. The book included a list of three hundred fighting regiments; for whatever arbitrary reason he did not include the 77th New York. However, he did cite the 77th in a footnote as another fighting regiment, since their brigade had the distinction of having lost more officers than any other in the army. None of the three hundred regiments on Fox's list were in more engagements than the 77th.[17] Perhaps Fox was concerned about appearing biased since two of his brothers were in the 77th. Captain Charles H. Stevens wrote a letter to the *National Tribune* to address this discrepancy in 1908.[18] Stevens wrote that Fox's weekly articles in the *Tribune* designated some regiments as fighting regiments, implying that the others were not. Stevens defended the 77th by giving a sketch of the regiment's distinguished service. After each battle and mention of the comrades who fell there, he would sarcastically add that the 77th was not considered a fighting regiment. "Our regiment does not belong to Fox's noble 300, though it stood in its place from the organization to the disbandment."[19]

Funny, is it not, how history is preserved or presented? Take the men of a modest little regiment from upstate New York who just did their duty. Put them into critical roles in a number of different battles and the results were always the same. In over 50 engagements, the 77th New York State Volunteers were one of the best units in the Union army. Reflecting on the 1,549 men who were listed in the 77th, roughly one out of every three mustered out with the regiment or battalion. One out of every four men was discharged for disability. Also one out of every five died in the 77th's service; half of these were battle-related deaths and the rest mainly attributed to disease. Transfers, other reasons, and desertion accounted for the balance.

In conclusion, as Colonel Bidwell once stated, with the 77th he could drive the Johnnies all the way to Richmond. Perhaps Private Edward Fuller summed it up better when he wrote that "sojering was the 77th's business."

Winsor B. French, *front left*, and the 77th Survivors

Wilton Town Historian

Former Lieutenant Cyrille Fountain, 77th NYSV, with grandson

Courtesy of the Chipman Family

**Former Sergeant
David Wetherwax,
77th New York State Volunteers**

Courtesy of Suzanne
Weatherwax Bishop

**John Clements, son of a 77th veteran and
member of the 77th Regimental Band**

Courtesy of Ms. Minnie Clark Bolster

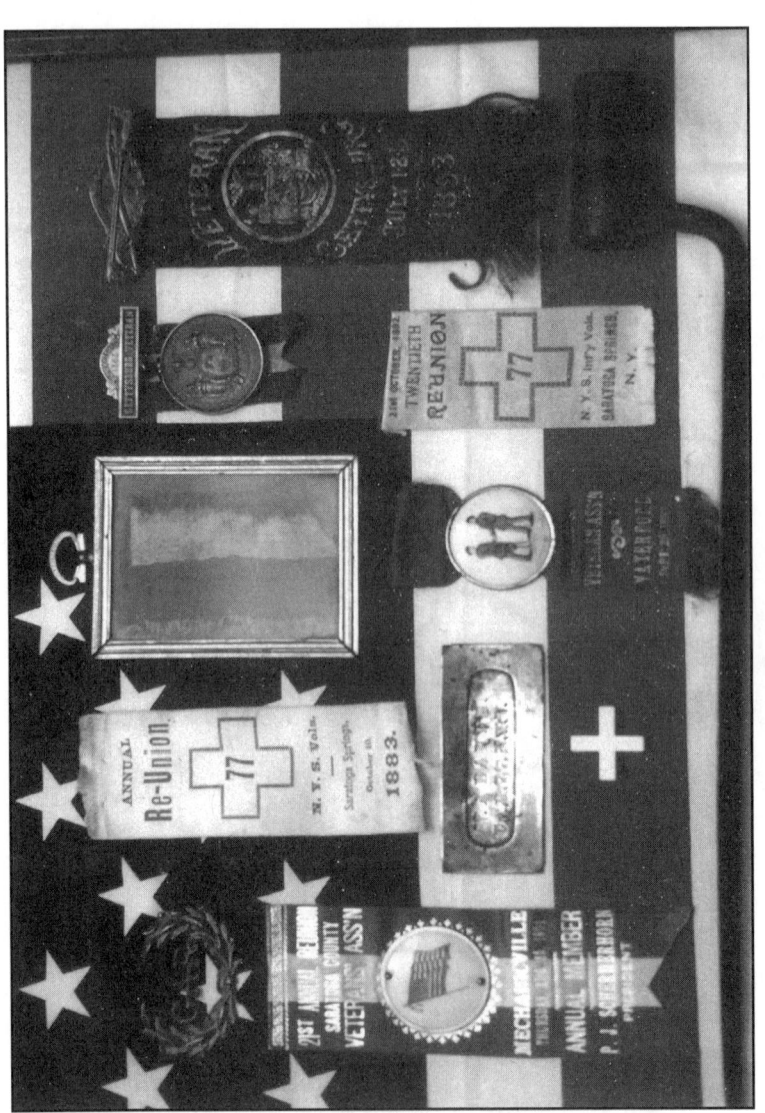

77th NYSV's artifacts inherited by the author

Appendix A

77th New York Battle Guide

Appendix A

Engagement	Date(s)	Army	Corps	Division	Brigade	Regiment	Casualties
Yorktown Seige	April 5, 1862–May 4, 1862	McClellan	Keyes	Smith	Davidson	McKean	–
Near Lee's Mills	April 5, 1862	McClellan	Keyes	Smith	Davidson	McKean	1
Lee's Mills	April 16, 1862	McClellan	Keyes	Smith	Davidson	McKean	0
Before Yorktown	April 26, 1862	McClellan	Keyes	Smith	Davidson	McKean	0
Lee's Mills	April 28, 1862	McClellan	Keyes	Smith	Davidson	McKean	2
Williamsburg	May 5, 1862	McClellan	Keyes	Smith	Davidson	McKean	1
Mechanicsville	May 24, 1862	McClellan	Franklin	Smith	Davidson	McKean	6
Golding's Farm	June 5, 1862	McClellan	Franklin	Smith	Davidson	Various–Temp.	1
Golding's Farm	June 24, 1862	McClellan	Franklin	Smith	Davidson	Various–Temp.	2
Seven Days' Battle	June 27, 1862–July 2, 1862	McClellan	Franklin	Smith	Davidson	Various–Temp.	14
Garnett's Farm	June 27, 1862	McClellan	Franklin	Smith	Davidson	Various–Temp.	included above
Garnett's & Golding's	June 28, 1862	McClellan	Franklin	Smith	Davidson	Various–Temp.	included above
Savage Station	June 29, 1862	McClellan	Franklin	Smith	Davidson	Various–Temp.	included above
White Oak Swamp	June 30, 1862	McClellan	Franklin	Smith	Davidson	Various–Temp.	included above
Malvern Hill	July 1, 1862	McClellan	Franklin	Smith	Davidson	Various–Temp.	included above
Harrison's Landing	July 3, 1862	McClellan	Franklin	Smith	Davidson	Various–Temp.	0
Crampton's Pass	September 14, 1862	McClellan	Franklin	Smith	Irwin	Babcock	0
Antietam	September 17, 1862	McClellan	Franklin	Smith	Irwin	Babcock	32
Fredericksburg	December 13, 1862	Burnside	Smith	Howe	Vinton	French	2
Marye's Heights	May 3, 1863	Hooker	Sedgwick	Howe	Neill	French	83

77th New York Battle Guide

Engagement	Date(s)	Army	Corps	Division	Brigade	Regiment	Casualties
Salem Church	May 3, 1863	Hooker	Sedgwick	Howe	Neill	French	included above
Banks' Ford	May 4, 1863	Hooker	Sedgwick	Howe	Neill	French	included above
Deep Run Crossing	June 5, 1863	Hooker	Sedgwick	Howe	Neill	French	5
Gettysburg	July 1, 1863	Meade	Sedgwick	Howe	Neill	French	0
Gettysburg	July 2–3, 1863	Meade	Slocum	-	-	French	1
Fairfield	July 5, 1863	Meade	Sedgwick	Howe	Neill	French	0
Marsh Run	July 7, 1863	Meade	Sedgwick	Howe	Neill	French	0
Funkstown	July 11, 1863	Meade	Sedgwick	Howe	Neill	French	0
Williamsport	July 14, 1863	Meade	Sedgwick	Howe	Neill	French	0
Chantilly	October 16, 1863	Meade	Sedgwick	Howe	Neill	French	0
Rappahannock Station	November 7, 1863	Meade	Sedgwick	Howe	Neill	French	0
Mine Run	November 26, 1863	Meade	Sedgwick	Howe	Neill	French	0
Germanna Ford	December 1, 1863	Meade	Sedgwick	Howe	Neill	French	0
Wilderness	May 5–7, 1864	Grant	Sedgwick	Getty	Neill	Babcock	66
Spotsylvania	May 8–21, 1864	Grant	Sedgwick	Neill	Bidwell	Babcock	107
North Anna	May 22–26, 1864	Grant	Wright	Neill	Bidwell	French	0
Totopotomoy	May 27–30, 1864	Grant	Wright	Neill	Bidwell	French	0
Cold Harbor	May 31, 1864–June 12, 1864	Grant	Wright	Neill	Bidwell	French	12
Petersburg	June 17, 1864–July 9, 1864	Grant	Wright	Neill	Bidwell	French	10
Weldon Railroad	June 21–23, 1864	Grant	Wright	Neill	Bidwell	French	7

Appendix A

Engagement	Date(s)	Army	Corps	Division	Brigade	Regiment	Casualties
Fort Stevens	July 12–13, 1864	Grant	Wright	Wheaton	Bidwell	French	20
Charlestown	August 21, 1864	Sheridan	Wright	Getty	Bidwell	French	2
Opequon Creek	September 13, 1864	Sheridan	Wright	Getty	Bidwell	French	0
Winchester	September 19, 1864	Sheridan	Wright	Getty	Bidwell	French	42
Fisher's Hill	September 22, 1864	Sheridan	Wright	Getty	Bidwell	French	5
Cedar Creek	October 18, 1864	Sheridan	Wright	Getty	Bidwell	French	36
Petersburg	March 25, 1865	Grant	Wright	Getty	Hyde	Caw	11
Petersburg	April 2, 1865	Grant	Wright	Getty	Hyde	Caw	15
Sailor's Creek	April 6, 1865	Grant	Wright	Getty	Hyde	Stevens	0
Appomattox	April 9, 1865	Grant	Wright	Getty	Hyde	Stevens	0

Appendix B

77th New York Officers Chart

Appendix B

REGIMENTAL STAFF

Colonels	**Through**
James B. McKean	June 1862

Lieutenant Colonels
Joseph C. Henderson | June 17, 1862
Winsor B. French | December 13, 1864
David J. Caw | June 27, 1865

Majors
Selden Hetzel | May 15, 1862
Winsor B. French | July 18, 1862
Nathan S. Babcock | December 13, 1864
David J. Caw | December 24, 1864

Adjutants
Winsor B. French | June 1, 1862
Isaac D. Clapp | May 4, 1863
William H. Fursman | February 12, 1864
Lawrence Van Demark | September 30, 1864
Gilbert F. Thomas | October 19, 1864
William W. Worden | December 13, 1865
Charles H. Davis | April 22, 1865
Thomas M. White | June 27, 1865

Quartermasters
Lucius E. Shurtliff | June 21, 1862
Jacob F. Hayward | December 13, 1864
Charles W. Thurber | June 27, 1865

Surgeons
John L. Perry | January 21, 1862
Augustus Campbell | February 9, 1863
George T. Stevens | December 13, 1864
Justin G. Thompson | June 27, 1865

Assistant Surgeons
George T. Stevens | November 11, 1862
John W. Fay | December 21, 1862
Justin G. Thompson | December 13, 1864
William DeLong | December 30, 1864

Chaplains
David Tully | July 8, 1862
Norman Fox Jr. | December 13, 1864

77th New York Officers Chart 211

COMPANY A
Essex County
Westport, New York

Captains	**Through**
Renel W. Arnold	April 3, 1862
George S. Orr	November 19, 1864
Isaac D. Clapp	June 27, 1865

First Lieutenants

William Douglas | August 21, 1862
Stephen S. Hastings | December 26, 1862
Charles E. Stevens | July 26, 1864
Robert E. Nelson | January 1, 1865
Stephen H. Pierce | March 25, 1865
Thomas S. Harris | June 27, 1865

Second Lieutenants

James S. Farnsworth | February 8, 1862
Charles E. Stevens | December 26, 1862
Lewis Van Derwerker | April 1863
William F. Lyon | May 10, 1864
William E. Merrill | May 5, 1865
Cyrille Fountain | June 27, 1864

COMPANY B
Saratoga County
Ballston Spa, New York

Captains	**Through**
Clement C. Hill	July 1, 1862
Stephen S. Horton	May 21, 1863
Frederick Smith	September 1, 1864
Joseph H. Loveland	December 13, 1864
George M. Ross	June 27, 1865

First Lieutenants

Noble H. Hammond | July 24, 1862
Frederick Smith | June 18, 1863
Sidney O. Cromack | March 31, 1865
Alonzo Holland | June 26, 1865
Adam Flansburgh | June 27, 1865

Second Lieutenants

Stephen S. Horton | May 11, 1862
George K. McGunigle | October 4, 1862
Sumner Oakley | January 9, 1865
William Caw | June 27, 1865

COMPANY C
Saratoga County
Saratoga Springs, New York

Captains

	Through
Benjamin F. Judson	April 1, 1862
Luther M. Wheeler	May 3, 1863
Isaac D. Clapp	November 19, 1864
Charles E. Stevens	June 27, 1865

First Lieutenants

Luther M. Wheeler	April 2, 1862
John Patterson	September 8, 1862
Edward W. Winne	May 17, 1863
Lawrence Van Demark	February 13, 1864
Charles H. Davis	February 18, 1865
William E. Merrill	June 27, 1865

Second Lieutenants

John Patterson	April 19, 1862
Edward W. Winne	September 9, 1862
Lawrence Van Demark	May 17, 1865
Charles H. Davis	January 2, 1865
Adam Flansburgh	June 19, 1865

COMPANY D
Saratoga County
Wilton, New York

Captains

	Through
John Carr	May 18, 1862
Seth W. Deyoe	July 26, 1864
Charles E. Stevens	November 19, 1864
George S. Orr	December 13, 1864
Sumner Oakley	March 25, 1864
Charles H. Davis	June 27, 1865

First Lieutenants

Winsor B. French	November 23, 1861
Seth W. Deyoe	May 19, 1862
Joseph H. Loveland	November 15, 1863
Lewis Van Derwerker	December 13, 1864
Robert E. Nelson	June 27, 1865

Second Lieutenants

Chester F. Fodow	May 1862
Robert H. Skinner	September 19, 1862
Lewis F. Van Derwerker	November 15, 1863
Jeremiah Stebbins	March 16, 1863
Thomas S. Harris	March 26, 1865
William H. Quackenbush	June 27, 1865

77th New York Officers Chart

COMPANY E
Saratoga County

Captains — **Through**
Lewis Wood — October 4, 1862
David J. Caw — December 28, 1862
William B. Carpenter — May 10, 1864
David A. Thompson — June 27, 1865

First Lieutenants
William B. Carpenter — December 25, 1862
Henry C. Rolland — December 13, 1864
James A. Monroe — June 27, 1865

Second Lieutenants
Halsey Bowe — August 14, 1862
David Lyon — December 13, 1864
Thomas M. White — June 15, 1865
Charles D. Thurber — June 27, 1865

COMPANY F
Saratoga County

Captains — **Through**
Judson B. Andrews — July 16, 1862
Jessie White — February 20, 1863
Edward W. Winne — August 15, 1864
David A. Thompson — November 19, 1864

First Lieutenants
Jessie White — July 17, 1862
Ansel Denison — February 27, 1863
David A. Thompson — September 19, 1864

Second Lieutenants
John J. Cameron — May 11, 1862
Emmett J. Peterson — December 18, 1862
David A. Thompson — February 28, 1862
Jeremiah Stebbins — December 9, 1863
Thomas W. Fowler — August 12, 1864
Robert E. Nelson — August 30, 1864

Appendix B

COMPANY G
Saratoga County

Captains	**Through**
Calvin A. Rice	January 8, 1863
Orrin P. Rugg	May 12, 1864
George M. Ross	September 28, 1864

First Lieutenants
George S. Orr | April 3, 1862
Edward S. Armstrong | January 5, 1863
George M. Ross | August 25, 1864

Second Lieutenants
Lucius E. Shurtliff | November 22, 1862
William K. Young | April 15, 1862
Orrin P. Rugg | October 5, 1862
George M. Ross | January 5, 1863
George H. Gillis | December 13, 1864

COMPANY H
Saratoga County
Charlton, New York

Captains	**Through**
Albert F. Beach	January 30, 1862
N. Hollister Brown	December 25, 1862
David J. Caw	November 19, 1864

First Lieutenants
N. Hollister Brown | January 30, 1862
George D. Story | May 30, 1862
David J. Caw | October 4, 1862
Frank Thomas | August 30, 1864
Alonzo Howland | December 6, 1864

Second Lieutenants
George D. Story | January 30, 1864
David J. Caw | June 1, 1864
Alonzo Howland | September 19, 1864

77th New York Officers Chart

COMPANY I
Essex County
Keeseville, New York

Captains — **Through**
Franklin Norton — August 18, 1862
Martin Lennon — October 19, 1864

First Lieutenants
Jacob F. Hayward — June 21, 1862
John W. Belding — October 19, 1864

Second Lieutenants
Martin Lennon — August 18, 1862
John W. Belding — February 25, 1863
Carlos Rowe — December 13, 1864

OLD COMPANY K (*)
Fulton County
Gloversville, New York

*Note—during Oct. 1862, old Company K was consolidated into Company F and the new company from Schuylerville became Company K.

Captains — **Through**
Nathan S. Babcock * — September 1, 1862
John R. Rockwell — October 2, 1863
Joseph H. Loveland — November 19, 1864

First Lieutenants
John W. McGregor * — February 6, 1862
Philander A. Cobb * — May 11, 1862
Ansel Dennison * — September 19, 1862
William H. Fursman — May 3, 1863
William J. Taber — October 19, 1864

Second Lieutenants
Philander A. Cobb * — February 6, 1862
Ansel Dennison * — May 12, 1862
Emmett J. Peterson — October 31, 1862
Cyrus F. Rich — November 30, 1862
Frank Thomas — February 28, 1863
Stephen Reesham — October 8, 1863
William W. Worden — October 20, 1864

NEW COMPANY K
Saratoga County
Schuylerville, New York

Appendix C

77th New York Roster

Appendix C

Abbot, John
Abbott, Harlin
Abbott, John
Abbs, Adna Jr.
Adams, John H.
Ageter, Solomon
Ahreets, William F.
Aley, Dennis
Aley, Jacob
Aley, Madison
Allen, Calvin B.
Allen, Charles H.
Allen, Eber N.
Allen, Francis J.
Allen, George
Allen, George G.
Allen, Henry
Allen, James G.
Allen, John
Allen, Merritt H.
Allen, Reuben
Ambler, Daniel R.
Anable, Alexander

Anable, Lucien
Ancock, Robert
Andress, Charles
Andrews, Daniel V.
Andrews, John A.
Andrews, Judson B.
Armar, Thomas
Armstrong, Edward S.
Armstrong, John R.
Armstrong, William
Arnold, John W.
Arnold, Renel W.
Arnold, William
Atkins, Frasur
Atkinson, Charles D.
Austin, Amos E.
Austin, Elam
Austin, Gideon A.
Austin, Ira
Austin, James F.
Austin, Orville W.
Austin, Philip J.
Austin, William H.

Avery, Dennis
Avery, Dudley
Avery, Russell
Babcock, Nathan S.
Bacon, James W.
Bailett, Timothy
Bailey, Edward M.
Baker, Cladius
Baker, Henry
Baker, Henry H.
Baker, Jeremiah
Baker, William
Baker, William A.
Baldwin, William H.
Ballou, Case
Ballou, Chauncey A.
Bame, John
Barber, James C.
Barber, Stephen
Barhydt, William G.
Barker, David
Barker, David S.
Barker, John

Barnes, Hiram
Barnes, James E.
Barnes, Merritt L.
Barrass, Harry
Barringer, Dennis S.
Bartlett, Charles H.
Bartman, William
Barton, Samuel
Barton, Wilson
Bath, James
Batte, James
Beach, Alfred F.
Beagle, William
Belding, John W.
Bell, Peter
Bemis, Isaac
Benedick, Charles H.
Benham, Samuel
Bennett, Benjamin Jr.
Bennett, Benjamin Sr.
Bennett, Julius P.
Bennett, Oliver
Benoist, Francis

Benson, James
Benson, Thomas
Bentley, Hector
Bentley, Oslin G.
Berg, Maximillian
Berry, George C.
Bethman, Henry
Betts, John
Bevens, George
Bigelow, George W.
Bignall, James R.
Birdsill, Peter
Bissell, Edwin
Bissell, Mills H.
Bisson, Luis
Blair, Alexandria
Blanchard, Charles
Bliss, Marcellus W.
Blount, George
Bobenreath, Edwin
Boice, George W.
Bois, Isaac
Bois, William H.

Bolin, Patrick
Bolton, George E.
Bootier, Nelson
Bordon, Victor
Bordwell, Charles
Borst, David
Bortel, James
Bortle, George W.
Bortle, Lysander
Boughton, Henry
Boulton, Samuel D.
Bourst, David
Bowe, Halsey
Bowen, James
Bowen, Marian
Bowers, George
Bowers, Hermanus A.
Boyle, Patrick
Bradshaw, William G.
Brady, Edward
Brainard, John
Braman, William W.
Branch, Erskine B.

Brant, John
Brasier, George W.
Bratt, Thomas G.
Brazier, George W.
Breut, Henry
Brewer, Abraham
Brewer, Cornelius
Brewer, William
Briggs, Benjamin A.
Briggs, Charles A.
Briggs, John H.
Briggs, Michael S.
Brine, Edward
Brisbane, James C.
Bristol, John D.
Britton, John R.
Britton, William R.
Brodt, Henry
Brooks, Levi A.
Brooks, Silas R.
Broughton, Hiram
Broughton, Louis
Broughton, Thomas

Brower, Andrew
Brown, George H.
Brown, Loren
Brown, N. Hollister
Brown, Nathan
Brown, Paul A.
Brown, William
Brown, William H.
Brunson, Noah
Bruse, Clarence
Bruse, Mansfield
Bruyn, George A.
Bryant, John
Buchanan, James W.
Bull, Francis M.
Bullard, George
Bump, Alonzo D.
Bumyea, George
Burch, Seymour
Burdick, Frederick
Burgess, George
Burk, Lewis
Burlingham, Jesse

Burnes, James
Burnes, John P.
Burnham, Charles
Burns, Harvey
Burns, John
Burns, Oscar
Burpee, Samuel
Burroughs, Albert M.
Burrows, William H.
Burt, Edgar O.
Burt, Hiram
Bushnell, Darius G.
Butler, John R.
Cabana, Raymond
Cadman, Seth
Cady, Frank
Cady, John
Cady, Oscar
Cahoo, Joseph
Cain, Edward
Calborn, Louis
Calkins, Byron
Calkins, Lewis

Callahan, Daniel
Callahan, Thomas
Cameron, John J.
Cammel, James
Campbell, Augustus
Campbell, George W.
Campbell, Sanford E.
Canfield, Josephus
Carey, Seymour A.
Carlow, William
Carnes, Lyman B.
Carney, James
Carp, Albert
Carpenter, Alonzo
Carpenter, Peter
Carpenter, William B.
Carr, Benjamin H.
Carr, James
Carr, Joel
Carr, John
Carragan, Anthoney W.
Carrigan, Owen
Carter, James D.

Appendix C

Cartwright, Joseph
Cary, Simon
Casey, Charles
Casey, Michael
Casey, Thomas
Casey, William
Cath, William H.
Caughland, William
Caw, David J.
Caw, William
Chapman, Charles
Chapman, John
Chase, Alford
Chase, John A.
Cheedell, Charles E.
Cherry, James W.
Christman, Lawrence
Christmas, William C.
Church, James
Clancey, James
Claper, Levi
Clapp, Isaac D.
Clark, Alonzo B.

Clark, Frank
Clark, Jacob
Clark, John
Clark, Louis
Clark, Samuel
Clark, Slocum
Clayton, Henry
Cleland, Alexander
Clement, Albert H.
Clements, John J.
Close, Albert
Close, George W.
Clothier, James S.
Clunis, Henry
Clute, John L.
Cobb, Philander A.
Coffenger, William
Cole, Charles S.
Cole, Daniel H.
Cole, James
Cole, Lorin
Cole, Lorrin
Cole, Lyman

Cole, William
Cole, William A.
Coleman, Walter
Coleman, Oped M.
Collins, Clark
Collins, Henry
Compton, Charles W.
Comstock, J. D.
Comstock, William S.
Conde, Isaac H.
Conklin, John
Conklin, Otis
Conlen, James
Conley, Michael
Conners, Edward
Conners, John
Cook, Augustus
Cook, Charles
Cook, John H.
Coon, Elias
Coon, John C.
Cooney, Francis
Cooney, James

Cooney, John
Cooney, John
Cooney, Thomas
Cooney, William
Coonradt, Abraham
Coonradt, Philip S.
Cooper, Minor
Corey, John
Cornell, Chester P.
Cornell, George W.
Cornelle, Charles
Corrigan, George W.
Coster, Norman
Cotrill, Franklin
Cotrill, George
Couse, James E.
Cowhey, James
Coy, Zera
Cozzens, John H.
Craig, Henry G.
Craig, Samuel S.
Craig, William
Cramer, Abram

Crandell, Henry
Crane, Volney
Cristman, Lawrence
Cromack, Joseph
Cromack, Sidney O.
Cronk, Albert
Crosby, Simeon W.
Cross, John
Crouch, Charles H.
Crowningshield, Enos
Cutler, Charles
Daivenson, James
Daley, Stillman
Danby, Michael
Dance, John
Darrow, Henry C.
Darrow, John B.
Dater, David H.
Davenport, David
Davenport, George
Davenport, Harrison
Davenport, John
Davidson, Gilbert C.

Davis, Charles	Delavergue, Seneca	Diamond, William	Dowen, William	Dwyer, Edward
Davis, Charles H.	DeLong, George	Dickenson, Roswell B.	Dowling, Michael	Dwyer, Edward H.
Davis, Darius S.	DeLong, Robert N.	Dingman, George W.	Downs, Alexander	Dwyer, Rawson O.
Davis, Egbert W.	DeLong, William A.	Divine, William	Dows, James L.	Dwyer, Walter
Davis, Harvey J.	Demore, Levi	Dixon, Robert	Doyle, Henry H.	Dye, Able B.
Davis, Henry J.	Deneffe, James	Dodge, Dennison	Doyle, John	Dyer, John
Davis, John	Denmark, Alexander	Dodge, Samuel	Drake, Albert A.	Eames, James
Davis, Martin	Dennison, Ansel	Doevee, William	Drummond, James Jr.	Earls, Warren
Davis, Samuel E.	Denton, Weston	Dolan, Michael	Drummond, James Sr.	Eastham, William
Davis, Thomas	Derby, Charles	Dolan, Patrick	Duboise, Andrew J.	Eastman, Joseph
Day, Benjamin H.	Derby, John W.	Doolittle, Emery	Dudley, Chancy	Edmonds, James
Day, Benjamin H.	Deuel, Charles E.	Dorley, James	Dudley, Charles	Edmonds, Willard
Day, Joseph R.	Deuel, James G.	Dorvee, Joseph	Duel, Andrew P.	Edwards, George L.
De Witt, Burton	Deuel, John E. L.	Dorvee, William	Duel, Truman	Eldridge, Nathan
Deal, George	Deuel, Seth B.	Doty, George W.	Dugan, Henry	Elliot, Henry
Dean, Jonathan J.	Dewel, Edwin B.	Doud, Chester	Dunham, Augustus	Ellison, George H.
Dean, Josiah	Deyoe, George R.	Douglass, Jacob	Dunham, Charles S.	Ellison, James
Dean, Thomas	Deyoe, Minot C.	Douglass, William	Dunn, Plany F.	Elms, Thomas
DeGraff, Charles L.	Deyoe, Peter A.	Dowen, Andrew J.	Dunson, Edgar W.	Emperor, James
DeGraff, Joseph	Deyoe, Renliff K.	Dowen, Barnet	Dupre, Joseph	Ennis, Ezera
Delano, Macy	Deyoe, Seth W.	Dowen, John	Dutcher, Thomas	Ensign, William C.
Delany, Thomas	Deyoe, William	Dowen, John H.	Duval, Andrew	Evans, Edward
Delavergue, George	Deyoe, William H.	Dowen, Josiah	Duval, Henry	Evans, John E.

Appendix C

Eagle, William	Flansburgh, Nicholas	Freeman, Walter
Fairchilds, James O.	Flansburgh, Simon	Freeman, William
Falen, Michael	Fletcher, Leonard	Freeman, William H.
Fancher, Michael	Flood, William	French, Winsor B.
Farley, John	Flury, Richard	Frey, Jacob
Farmer, George	Fodow, Chester H.	Frirabend, Frederick
Farnsworth, James H.	Fogg, James V.	Frost, Stephen R.
Farrell, Andrew	Forrister, John H.	Fry, George
Farthing, James A.	Foster, Horace	Fuller, Edward H.
Fay, Clinton B.	Foster, John	Fuller, George
Fay, Cyrus M.	Fountain, Cyrille	Fuller, Thomas S.
Fay, John W.	Fowler, Herman H.	Funk, Lawrence
Fell, Charles E. H.	Fowler, Oren	Fursman, William H.
Ferguson, Jeffery	Fowler, Thomas W.	Gaff, Charles
Ferris, George D.	Fowler, William	Gains, Abram W.
Ferry, John	Fox, George H.	Gallup, Herbert
Fetters, Bernard	Fox, Norman Jr.	Galvin, Patrick
Finch, Isaac R.	Franc, Henry	Gardiner, George
Finch, William W.	Francisco, William	Gardner, Perry
Fisher, Charles R.	Frank, George	Gates, Edward H.
Fitzgerald, Michael	Freeman, Elisha R.	Gates, Stephen C.
Flanders, John	Freeman, George S.	Gazley, John
Flansburgh, Adam	Freeman, Schuyler	Geltzschiter, Nicholas

Geoghan, John	Goodspeed, Rodolphus
George, Orwin	Goodwin, Michael
Gick, George	Gorden, Andrew I.
Gifford, Hiram B.	Goss, Charles H.
Gifford, Walter	Goucher, William
Gifford, William H.	Goudie, Robert B.
Gilbert, Freeman	Gould, Jacob V.
Gilbert, Henry N.	Gower, Jesse
Gildersleeve, Elcauh	Graff, Leonard
Gillis, George H.	Graham, George T.
Gilroy, Patrick	Gray, Terrance
Gilson, Justus M.	Green, Albert S.
Gingall, Robert	Green, Davis
Glass, George	Green, Earl
Gleesattel, Frederick	Green, Isaac
Gleesattel, Gotfried	Green, James O.
Glen, Allen S.	Green, John H.
Glok, George	Green, John H.
Glusha, George	Green, Joseph A.
Glusha, James	Green, Wells
Glusha, James K.	Green, William
Goffe, David E.	Greene, William
Goodspeed, Charles	Greenfield, William

77th New York Roster

Gregory, Lorenzo	Hall, Warren C.	Harris, Mark C.
Gregory, William F.	Hall, William	Harris, Thomas S.
Griffin, Orville	Halligan, Thomas	Harrison, James W.
Grooms, James	Halsapple, Gilbert	Hart, Charles M.
Groosbeck, Jonah D.	Ham, Edwin	Hart, William H.
Grovensteen, Garret	Ham, John W.	Haseltine, Joseph
Grovensteen, Harvey	Hammond, Alonzo	Hass, Henry
Grovensteen, John	Hammond, Delos	Hassett, Andrew
Gruber, Albert	Hammond, George	Hastings, Stephen S.
Guest, John J.	Hammond, Noble P.	Hatch, Alanson E.
Guest, Stephen H.	Hammond, William J.	Havens, Rex A.
Gurney, Henry G.	Harder, Philip	Hawkins, Lemuel
Hackett, Thomas	Hare, William H.	Hawley, William
Haggart, Gilbert W.	Harrington, Benjamin A.	Hayden, Henry
Haight, Charles	Harrington, James	Hayes, Clark
Haight, Sylvester S.	Harrington, Manfried M.	Hayes, George S.
Haight, Warren M.	Harrington, William H.	Hayes, Hiram
Hains, Francois	Harrington, William H.	Hayes, Joseph H.
Hall, Ayron B.	Harris, Ezera	Haynes, Francis
Hall, Charles	Harris, Frank	Hays, John W.
Hall, Edward	Harris, John	Hays, Nelson
Hall, Frank	Harris, John T.	Hayward, Ashton M.
Hall, John R.	Harris, Lyman W.	Hayward, Jacob F.

Haze, Aaron	Hilton, John
Hazzard, James H.	Hilton, John W.
Heartt, John	Hinckley, Henry
Henderson, Joseph C.	Hinds, Hiram
Hendrick, James	Hines, James B.
Hendricks, William	Hines, James R.
Hermance, Theodore	Hines, John W.
Herrick, Smith	Hodges, Charles H.
Hert, Heinrich	Hodges, Isaac S.
Hess, George	Hoey, Thomas
Hetzel, Selden	Hoffman, William
Hewitt, Jerome	Hoisington, Frank
Hewitt, William H.	Holbrook, Amasa A.
Heydon, George L.	Holbrook, Otis
Hichcock, Franklin	Holden, Charles
Hickok, Alfred	Holesaple, James
Hickok, Edward	Hollen, Edward
Hicks, John H.	Holmes, Alexander C.
Hill, Christopher C.	Holmes, George R.
Hill, Clement C.	Holmes, Morgan L.
Hill, John W.	Hopkins, Eugene
Hill, Peter	Hopkins, Freeman E.
Hill, William	Hopkins, Jonathan

Appendix C

Hopkins, Nelson
Hopkins, Silas
Horrigan, John
Horton, Frank W.
Horton, Stephen S.
Hotkins, Charles
Houghtaling, Charles
Houghtaling, George
Houseman, George
Hovey, Henry
Howard, George A.
Howe, Benjamin
Howe, David H.
Howe, William C.
Howland, Alonzo
Hoyt, Alexander
Hoyt, Dallas
Hoyt, George
Hoyt, Le Roy
Hubbard, Frank
Hubbell, Alonzo C.
Hudson, Benjamin
Hudson, James H.

Hudson, Jerome
Hudson, John
Hudson, John J.
Hudson, Miles
Hudson, Nathan B.
Huested, David R.
Hulburt, John H.
Hull, Charles A.
Huntington, George
Hurd, Henry J.
Hurlburt, Erebus
Hurley, George W.
Husted, James H.
Huyck, Cornelius S.
Huyck, Isaac B.
Hyer, Christopher
Ingersoll, George W.
Ingerson, Charles E.
Ingham, William
Inman, Leonard
Ireland, William
Irish, Aaron
Irish, Luther

Irish, Reuben W.
Jackson, John
Jacobs, Norman
Jacques, James H.
James, Henry
Jaques, Henry
Jaquis, Timothy S.
Jaquith, Ebenezer W.
Jeffords, Francis J.
Jeffords, James
Jeffords, James H.
Jeffords, Orville
Jeffords, Samuel D.
Jennings, Edward
Jerome, Joseph
Jerome, Jules
Jervis, Courteen
Jewel, Altus H.
Johnson, Charles
Johnson, James B.
Johnson, James B.
Johnson, Philip
Johnson, William E.

Johnson, William H.
Johnson, William H.
Jones, Benjamin J.
Jones, Elihu
Jones, Henry
Jones, Israel
Jones, James H.
Jones, John
Jones, John
Jones, Joseph F.
Jones, Lyman
Jones, Oliver
Jones, Thomas
Jones, William H.
Jordan, William
Juber, Charles
Jucket, Franklin H.
Judson, Benjamin F.
Jump, John
Jump, Joseph
Kearnes, John
Keck, Jeremiah
Kee, Samuel

Keeholts, Frederick
Kehne, Peter
Kelley, William
Kelley, William
Kenedy, James
Kent, George
Kested, Joseph
Ketchum, Charles
Kidd, Samuel E.
Kildea, Michael
Kimpton, William
King, Jacob
King, Sidney B.
King, Thomas
Kingsley, Alfred H.
Kingsley, Joseph F.
Kipp, John H.
Kipp, Isaac Jr.
Kipp, Tennis
Kirchen, Henry
Kirkland, Franklin
Kitchner, John G.
Klein, George E.

Knapp, Benjamin P.
Knapp, George
Knickerbocker, Peter
Knight, James
Krank, Joseph
Krintly, John L.
La Clair, John
La Morey, Edward
La Pierre, Francis
Lackely, Lewis
Ladd, Noah B.
Laidy, Patrick
Lama, Michael
Lamson, Benjamin
Landers, Octavius
Lane, George T.
Lansing, Oliver R.
Lansing, Wendell
Lapean, Isaac
Lapham, Abram
Larmouth, John G.
Latimore, William J.
Latta, George W.

Lavaer, Charles
Lawrence, Edward
Lawrence, Edwin
Lawrence, James A.
Lawson, George
Layon, John
Leak, Charles
Lee, John
Leek, Francis
Lefferts, George W.
Lenhien, John
Lennon, Martin
Lent, Abram
Leonard, Andrew V.
Lewis, Aaron
Lewis, Ezra
Lewthwaite, John
Like, Addison
Lobdell, Isaac D. M.
Lockwood, Edwin A.
Lockwood, Edwin L.
Lockwood, Oscar F.
Lohnes, Elisha

Love, Francis
Love, Matthew
Loveland, Joseph H.
Loveless, Arial
Lowery, Martin
Luther, John
Lynch, James
Lyon, David
Lyon, William F.
Mab, Stephen
Mack, Andrew
Mackay, Lewis
Madden, Thomas
Madigan, Timothy
Mahan, Thomas
Mainhood, Thomas
Malby, Alexander
Mann, William H.
Manning, Andrew
Marfitt, John
Marsh, William H.
Marshall, Edward P.
Marshall, Ewin

Marshman, Edwin
Martin, Albert
Martin, Lewis
Martin, Oscar
Martin, Patrick
Mathews, Albert P.
Matott, Ambrose
Matteews, Alfus H.
Mattison, Edward
Mattison, Samuel
Mattison, Zina H.
McAdoo, William
McCall, William
McCann, John
McConhie, George
McConkie, George
McConkie, Joel A.
McCormick, George
McCullough, Edward
McCumber, Alonzo
McDade, Michael
McDaniel, Patrick
McDonald, James

McDonald, John
McElwain, Andrew
McGannegle, George
McGoffin, George
McGoffin, William
McGovern, Terrence
McGovern, Thomas
McGown, Samuel
McGregor, John W.
McGuire, John
McGuire, Michael
McIntosh, Alexander
McIntosh, Charles P.
McIntosh, James
McKean, James B.
McKee, George A.
McKenzie, Stanford
Mclain, Allen
McLain, William H.
McLannon, John
McLean, James H.
McLean, John
McLure, John

Appendix C

McMahon, Hugh
McNaughton, Charles
McNeal, Ira
McNeal, David Jr.
McNeil, William
McNulty, William
McOdach, Ambrose
McOmber, Amos
McOmber, Ezra W.
McPherson, Edwin
McPherson, Herman
McPherson, Robert
McWilliams, Michael
Mead, Alexander
Mead, Ralph E.
Mead, Walter
Mead, Walton
Mehan, Michael
Mercellus, Charles E.
Mero, George
Merrhiew, Stephen F.
Merrill, Henry H.
Merrill, Jeffry

Merrill, William E.
Meurer, Joseph
Michaels, John J.
Miller, Andrew
Miller, James
Miller, Lyman E.
Miller, Manfield
Miller, Riley
Miller, Samuel C.
Miller, Warren E.
Miller, William
Miller, William H.
Miller, William R.
Millerd, Richard
Milliman, Ambrose B.
Milliman, William W.
Miln, Robert
Miner, Ezra
Mitchell, John
Monroe, James A.
Monroe, John L.
Monroe, William H.
Moodey, Henry A.

Mooney, Peter M.
Moore, James H.
Moore, John
Moran, Edward
Morehouse, F. D.
Morgan, Amsa N.
Morgan, Henry
Morgan, Jonathan
Morris, John
Morris, Peter
Morrison, Wallace
Morrison, Alexander
Morrison, Prosper
Morrison, Thomas
Morse, Daniel
Morse, Daniel E.
Morse, Silvanus
Mosher, David
Mosher, John
Mosher, John T.
Mosier, Charles W.
Moss, Hubbard M.
Mott, Wesley

Mowrey, Alvarah
Muffleman, Herman
Muliken, Leander
Mulkin, Henry
Mulligan, Christopher
Mulligan, Matthew
Mulliken, Alfred
Munn, Charles
Munn, Henry
Munroe, Allen
Munroe, Nathan
Munster, Michael
Murphy, Peter
Murphy, Thomas
Murphy, William
Murry, Charles H.
Murry, Edward
Mushgrove, Thomas
Myers, Henry M.
Myers, James H.
Myers, John A.
Myert, Lawrence
Myres, James A.

Myres, Lafayette
Myres, Orin
Myres, Thomas
Nash, Martin
Neilson, Samuel
Nelson, Joseph
Nelson, Robert E.
Newell, Taylor J.
Newman, Jacob
Nichels, Franklin J.
Nisbeth, Stephen
Nisbeth, Tunis
Nolan, James
Nolan, James
Nolan, Michael
Northrup, Benjamin
Northrup, John
Norton, Franklin
Norton, Martin V.
Noys, Frederick W.
Noys, Newton S.
Oakley, Sumner
Obrie, Frank

77th New York Roster

O'Brien, Edward	Owens, Frederick S.	Peltvill, George F.	Place, Charles E.	Putney, Alpha Jr.
O'Bryan, James	Packer, George	Perkins, Frederick W.	Place, Monroe	Quackenbus, William
Odell, Lewis	Padelford, James A.	Perry, Charles A.	Plant, Henry	Quackenbush, Tunis
Ogden, Albert	Page, Benjamin H.	Perry, Gardner	Pool, Yale A.	Quackenbush, William
Ogilvey, Henry	Palmatier, Anson J.	Perry, Harmon E.	Porter, Isaac	Quant, Frederick
Olmsted, Ellia	Palmatier, Charles	Perry, John	Porter, Robert	Quigley, Patrick
O'Neil, Henry	Palmer, Charles	Perry, John L.	Porter, Samuel	Quinn, Cornelius
Ormsby, John	Palmer, James	Persons, Hiram B.	Post, Horace A.	Quivey, Aaron B.
Orr, George S.	Palmer, James S.	Peterson, William D.	Post, Peter M.	Quivey, William H.
Orsborne, Charles M.	Palmer, John W.	Peton, James M.	Potter, Seth W.	Quivey, William H.
Orsburn, Samuel	Pangburne, David	Pettit, George W.	Poucher, James E.	Radley, John H.
Orton, Benjamin	Patterson, Emmett J.	Phelan, John	Poucher, Seneca	Radshaw, Stephen
Orton, William	Patterson, James	Phelps, Charles S.	Powers, Thomas	Read, Harry A.
Ost, Adam	Patterson, John	Phillips, Alonzo	Pratt, Lester	Rector, John
Ostrender, Charles	Peacock, George N.	Phillips, Archey	Premean, Joseph	Reed, Albert J.
Ott, Albert H.	Peacock, Thomas	Phillips, Charles E.	Price, Robert	Reese, Albert
Outing, Thomas F.	Pearsall, Edward S.	Phillips, Edmond	Provost, Louis	Regan, Patrick
Overocker, Elias T.	Pearson, Thomas	Phillips, Samuel	Pulling, George E.	Reid, Frank
Owen, Frederick	Peck, Cornelius	Pickette, Alfred	Pung, Jacob	Reidy, Patrick
Owen, Gilbert	Peck, Dyer	Pierce, Charles	Purdy, George	Reinhardt, Godfried
Owen, Henry	Peck, Gibbs	Pierce, Stephen H.	Purdy, Jerome	Rellinger, John
Owen, John W.	Peck, Horatio G.	Pike, William	Putnam, Joseph	Relyea, Mathew
Owen, William H.	Peck, Taylor A.	Pinley, James	Putnam, Thomas	Relyea, William

Appendix C

Reno, George R.
Reuchler, John A.
Rey, Joseph R.
Rhoades, Jonathan J.
Rice, Calvin A.
Rice, George
Rice, Nathan N.
Rich, Cyrus F.
Rich, Zopher C.
Richards, George
Richards, Henry H.
Richards, William
Richardson, Charles
Richmond, Orlando
Riley, Henry C.
Riley, John D.
Riley, Patrick
Ringer, Obed
Robear, Moses
Robertson, Henry
Robinson, John
Robinson, Ruben E.
Rockwell, John R.

Rodgers, William R.
Rooney, Patrick D.
Root, George W.
Root, John C.
Root, Seth B.
Rose, Cornelius
Rose, Gilbert
Rose, John
Rose, John S.
Rose, Nelson A.
Rose, William A.
Ross, George M.
Rowe, Carlos
Rowland, Henry C.
Rowley, Charles W.
Rowley, John J.
Rowley, Simon
Rowly, Gideon M.
Royce, Henry
Rugg, Orrin P.
Ruggles, Charles H.
Russell, George B.
Russell, Jervis W.

Russell, Simon D.
Ryan, Thomas
Safford, Job S.
Safford, Nathaniel
Sanbourn, John
Saunders, George
Savage, Patrick
Savage, Peter
Sawyer, John H.
Sawyer, John T.
Schermerhorn, L.
Schmidt, Adolph C. F.
Schmitz, Herbert
Schoonmaker, William
Scidmore, George H.
Scott, Arthur
Scott, George
Scott, George A.
Scott, James G.
See, Alfred M.
See, Dudley E.
Seeley, Frank
Seeley, John T.

Serviack, Edmond
Settle, Paul Jr.
Severance, Charles R.
Sexton, Charles E.
Sexton, Thomas H.
Sexton, William H.
Seymour, Russel
Shaffer, Richard N.
Shannon, Oscar
Sharp, Erastus
Shaw, John
Shaw, Oliver
Shay, Patrick
Shean, John
Shears, Eugene
Sheehan, Patrick
Sheldon, Daniel
Sheppard, Samuel D.
Sheran, Dennis
Sherman, Charles H.
Sherman, Daniel C.
Sherman, Philo D.
Sherman, Rowland

Sherman, Washington
Shill, Henry H.
Shippee, Amasa D.
Shires, John H.
Short, Frank
Shouts, Lewis
Showdy, Seward
Shreeves, Henry B.
Shumway, Tophfield
Shurtliff, Lucas E.
Shuster, James W.
Sicord, Louis
Sil, Simon
Sill, Charles
Simmons, John
Simmons, Peter B.
Simon, Benjamin F.
Simonds, Daniel C.
Simpson, Henry
Skene, William
Skinner, Robert H.
Slater, Jacob
Slingerland, James N.

77th New York Roster

- Slocum, William W.
- Smidt, Earnest
- Smith, Alvin
- Smith, Andrew J.
- Smith, Andrew J.
- Smith, Daniel
- Smith, Dennis B.
- Smith, Edward L.
- Smith, Edward W.
- Smith, Eli
- Smith, Elias W.
- Smith, Frederick
- Smith, George
- Smith, George B.
- Smith, George W.
- Smith, Henry
- Smith, Henry A.
- Smith, James
- Smith, James H.
- Smith, John
- Smith, John
- Smith, Louis
- Smith, Richard
- Smith, Richard
- Smith, Samuel
- Smith, Seneca
- Smith, Thomas
- Smith, Warren L.
- Smith, William
- Smith, William H.
- Smith, William H.
- Snow, Jerome
- Snow, Harvey
- Snow, Lafayette
- Snyder, Albert
- Snyder, George I.
- Snyder, William J.
- Spencer, Varner
- Spicer, Arnold
- Spring, Andrew J.
- Springer, George E.
- Squares, Samuel
- Starrett, Andrew
- Staunton, David
- Stay, Franklin
- Stearns, Melvin W.
- Stebbins, Jeremiah
- Sterling, William
- Steuder, William
- Stevens, Charles E.
- Stevens, George T.
- Stevens, James
- Stevens, James A.
- Stevenson, Jacob
- Stewart, Charles A.
- Stewart, John
- Stewart, Thomas
- Stickney, Pierpont
- Stiles, Horace L.
- Stilwell, Benjamin F.
- Stone, George
- Stone, John
- Stores, Hiram
- Storms, George M.
- Story, George R.
- Straing, John G.
- Strancher, Frederick
- Stratton, Josiah
- Stringham, Dana M.
- Strong, Legare
- Sulivan, Murtz
- Sullivan, Michael
- Sutherland, James
- Sutliff, Edward
- Sutliff, Oliver
- Swartz, Joseph
- Sweet, Milton P.
- Sweet, William
- Taber, William J.
- Tabour, Henry H.
- Tack, Gustavus
- Tafft, Kenyon
- Tanner, George
- Tanner, Henry
- Tanner, Israel
- Tatro, Moses
- Taylor, James
- Taylor, James
- Taylor, William Jr.
- Taylor, Peter
- Taylor, William
- Tefft, Nathan
- Tefft, Oscar
- Tenney, Royal M.
- Thackery, Thomas
- Thomas, Dennis
- Thomas, Frank
- Thomas, Gilbert F.
- Thomas, Harlon A.
- Thompson, Moses
- Thompson, Reuben K.
- Thompson, David A.
- Thompson, Jacob W.
- Thompson, James
- Thompson, Justin G.
- Thompson, Orris P.
- Thorn, Edward H.
- Thorn, Jesse B.
- Thorn, William B.
- Thornton, John
- Thurber, Charles D.
- Tighe, James
- Titus, Flavius A.
- Tobee, Henry
- Todd, James

Tombs, Frederick
Tombs, Lorin M.
Tracy, John
Trepp, Ephraim
Tripp, Gideon A.
Tripp, Ira
Tripp, Martin B.
Tripp, Perry
Troax, Jonathan B.
Truman, James
Truman, Joshua
Trumball, Stephen
Tubbs, Henry C.
Tucker, George C.
Tully, David
Tunison, John M.
Twomey, Patrick
Tyrrell, Hiram
Van Anden, Barnard
Van Antwerp, George
Van Antwerp, Richard
Van Antwerp, Winant
Van Arnum, Jacob H.

Van Arnum, William
Van Denmark, Lauran
Van Derwerker, Lewis
Van Dusen, William
Van Dyke, Asa
Van Dyke, George
Van Horn, Michael
Van Kleer, Charles
Van Natta, Peter E.
Van Ness, Seneca
Van Ornam, James
Van Salsbury, William
Van Schaick, Levi
Van Steenburg, Ben
Van Steenburgh, Jacob
Van Steenburgh, John
Van Steenburgh, Sandy
Van Steinburgh, Barker
Van Wie, Andrew G.
Van Wie, Henry J.
Van Wie, Newman
Vandenberg, Lewis W.
Vandenburg, Cornelius

Vandenburgh, Alonzo
Vandenburgh, Bradley
Vandenburgh, Lyman
Vandenburgh, Sidney
Vanderworker, Taylor
Vanderworker, Taylor
Vandinburgh, James
Vanslike, Cornelius
Vanslyke, Robert
Veile, Benjamin R.
Velie, Isaac N.
Velie, Stephen O.
Velie, William W.
Vining, Charles
Vroman, Nelson
Wade, Erastus
Waite, Charles H.
Walch, Joseph
Waldron, Alexander
Walker, Andrew J.
Walker, Augustus R.
Walroth, John A.
Walton, William

Ward, Lewis C.
Warner, Henry
Warren, James M.
Warren, Manley
Washburn, John W.
Watson, Elbert J.
Watson, John E.
Watson, William J.
Watters, John
Wayne, Joseph S.
Weatherwax, Andrew
Weatherwax, Hiram
Weatherwax, Jerome
Weatherwax, Joseph
Weaver, Alfred
Weaver, Hiram
Weaver, Horace
Webb, George
Webb, Thomas H.
Webster, James E.
Wedall, George L.
Weeks, Samuel
Welch, George W.

Welch, James
Welch, Stephen
Welch, William
Welden, Samuel H.
Wells, Joseph
Welsh, George H.
Welsh, John B.
Welsh, Richard
Werner, Eugene
Wescott, Francis G.
West, George N.
West, Henry A.
West, Shallum
Westcott, William H.
Weston, Clifford
Weston, James
Wetherbee, Charles E.
Wetherwax, David N.
Whaley, James H.
Wheeler, Amos
Wheeler, Charles
Wheeler, Luther M.
Whipple, Harvey L.

Whitcomb, Smith C.
White, George
White, Hamilton
White, Jesse
White, Silas S.
White, Thomas M.
Whitman, Henry
Whitman, Leroy
Whitman, Thomas
Whitmarsh, John W.
Whitmarsh, Riley C.
Whitney, Frank
Whittaker, John W.

Wickam, Wallace W.
Wicks, Alexander H.
Wilbur, Datus E.
Wilbur, Henry
Wilcox, Charles E.
Wilcox, Hiram P.
Wilcox, Kinner
Wilcox, Wallace
Wilder, William E.
Wildey, William
Will, George F.
Willard, Denison J.
Williams, Alonzo

Williams, Edmund
Williams, Henry E.
Williams, John
Williams, William
Williamson, Andrew
Willis, James
Wills, Joseph
Willsey, Charles
Wilson, Isaac H.
Wilson, James K.
Winchop, Frank
Wing, Patrick
Winkler, James

Winne, Edward W.
Winnie, George W.
Wood, Antoine
Wood, Benjamin
Wood, George M.
Wood, Henry
Wood, James M.
Wood, Lewis
Wood, Washington H.
Woodard, Frederic G.
Woodworth, John
Woolsey, William H.
Worden, William W.

Wright, John
Wright, William H.
Wyatt, William
Yale, William H.
Yattan, Sidney
Yatton, Frederick
Young, Harvey
Young, Henry
Young, William K.
Zears, Walter W.
Zinsture, William

Notes

INTRODUCTION

1. New York Monuments Commission, *New York at Gettysburg*, vol. 2 (Albany, N.Y.: Lyon Company, State Printers, 1902), 623.

CHAPTER 1

1. Nathaniel Bartlett Sylvester, *History of Saratoga County, New York* (Interlaken, N.Y.: Heart of the Lakes Publishing, 1979), 117.
2. Edward H. Fuller, *Battles of the Seventy-Seventh New York State Foot Volunteers*, United States Army Military History Institute Collection, Carlisle Barracks, Pa.
3. Nathaniel Bartlett Sylvester, *History of Saratoga County, New York* (Interlaken, N.Y.: Heart of the Lakes Publishing, 1979), 195.
4. Ibid., 106–107.
5. Ibid., 116.
6. Edward F. Gross, *Centennial History of the Village of Ballston Spa* (Ballston Spa, N.Y.: Ballston Journal, 1847), 147.
7. 29th Reunion of the 77th New York State Volunteers Survivors Association, "The Survivors' Association of the Seventy-Seventh Regiment New York Volunteers, 1901," United States Army Military History Institute Collection, Carlisle Barracks, Pa.
8. "Special Notices Volunteers," *Saratogian*, Saratoga Springs, N.Y., September 26, 1861.
9. *Saratogian, Our County and Its People, A Descriptive and Bibliographic Record of Saratoga County* (The Boston History Company Publishers, 1899), 493–494.
10. Caroline Halstead Royce, *Bessboro: A History of Westport* (Essex County, N.Y.: Privately Published, 1885), 513.
11. "Ballston Spa Company," *Saratogian*, Saratoga Springs, N.Y., September 24, 1861; "Special Order No. 360," *Saratogian*, Saratoga Springs, N.Y., September 6, 1861.

CHAPTER 2

1. 43rd Reunion of the 77th New York State Volunteers Survivors Association, "Report of the Forty-Third Annual Reunion of the Survivors Association of the Seventy-Seventh Regiment, 1915," Saratoga Springs Public Library, Saratoga Room, Saratoga Springs, N.Y.
2. "Special Order No. 360," *Saratogian*, Saratoga Springs, N.Y., September 6, 1861.
3. Nathaniel Bartlett Sylvester, *History of Saratoga County, New York* (Interlaken, N.Y.: Heart of the Lakes Publishing, 1979), 107.
4. "The Bemis Heights Regiment," *Saratogian*, Saratoga Springs, N.Y., October 17, 1861.
5. "Fatal Casualty—Death of a Volunteer," *Saratogian*, Saratoga Springs, N.Y., November 3, 1861; "Mustering in Saratoga for Civil War Service," *Sunday Gazette*, Schenectady, N.Y., November 3, 1996.

6. Nathaniel Bartlett Sylvester, *History of Saratoga County, New York* (Interlaken, N.Y.: Heart of the Lakes Publishing, 1979), 107.
7. "The Bemis Heights Regiment," *Saratogian*, Saratoga Springs, N.Y., October 17, 1861.
8. "Union Meeting on Bemis Heights," *Saratogian*, Saratoga Springs, N.Y., October 10, 1861.
9. Nathaniel Bartlett Sylvester, *History of Saratoga County, New York* (Interlaken, N.Y.: Heart of the Lakes Publishing, 1979), 107.
10. 39th Reunion of the 77th New York State Volunteers Survivors Association, "Report of the Thirty-Ninth Annual Reunion of the Survivors Association of the Seventy-Seventh Regiment, 1911," Saratoga Springs Public Library, Saratoga Room, Saratoga Springs, N.Y.
11. Ibid.
12. Ibid.
13. Ibid.
14. "When Caw and Cramer Were Defending the Union," *Schenectady Union Star*, N.Y., April 30, 1912.
15. *Saratogian*, "Our County and its People, New York, A Descriptive and Bibliographic Record of Saratoga County" (The Boston History Company, Publishers, 1899), 495.

CHAPTER 3

1. 43rd Reunion of the 77th New York State Volunteers Survivors Association, "Report of the Forty-Third Annual Reunion of the Survivors Association of the Seventy-Seventh Regiment, 1915," Saratoga Springs Public Library, Saratoga Room, Saratoga Springs, N.Y.; "Bemis Heights Regiment in Washington," *Saratogian*, Saratoga Springs, N.Y., January 5, 1861.
2. Jack Coggins, *Arms and Equipment of the Civil War* (Garden City, N.Y.: Doubleday and Company, Inc., 1962), 38–39.
3. "The Regimental Flag," *Saratogian*, Saratoga Springs, N.Y., December 19, 1861, Nathaniel Bartlett Sylvester, *History of Saratoga County, New York* (Interlaken, N.Y.: Heart of the Lakes Publishing, 1979), 117–118.
4. 43rd Reunion of the 77th New York State Volunteers Survivors Association, "Report of the Forty-Third Annual Reunion of the Survivors Association of the Seventy-Seventh Regiment, 1915," Saratoga Springs Public Library, Saratoga Room, Saratoga Springs, N.Y.
5. James Moore, M.D., *History of the Cooper Shop Volunteer Refreshment Saloon* (Philadelphia: Jas. B. Rodgers Publishers, 1866), 49.
6. Nathaniel Bartlett Sylvester, *History of Saratoga County, New York* (Interlaken, N.Y.: Heart of the Lakes Publishing, 1979), 118.
7. George T. Stevens, *Three Years in the Sixth Corps* (Albany, N.Y.: S. R. Gray Publisher, 1866), 4–5.
8. Ibid., 7.
9. 39th; "Letters from the Army," *Saratogian,* Saratoga Springs, N.Y., August 16, 1862. Reunion of the 77th New York State Volunteers Survivors Association, "Report of the Thirty-Ninth Annual Reunion of the Survivors Association of the Seventy-Seventh Regiment, 1911," Saratoga Springs Public Library, Saratoga Room, Saratoga Springs, N.Y.
10. Robert H. Skinner, Letter to Adam Clark Works, January 16, 1862, Adam Clark Works Papers, Univ. of Rochester, Rush Rhees Library Department of Rare Books, Manuscripts, and Archives, Rochester, N.Y.

11. Ibid.
12. Nathaniel Bartlett Sylvester, *History of Saratoga County, New York* (Interlaken, N.Y.: Heart of the Lakes Publishing, 1979), 108.
13. "Army Reminiscences," *Saratogian*, February 28, Saratoga Springs Public Library, Saratoga Room, Saratoga Springs, N.Y.
14. George T. Stevens, *Three Years in the Sixth Corps* (Albany, N.Y.: S. R. Gray Publisher, 1866), 221.
15. Charles Stevens, Letter to Friend Cone, December 17, 1863; Letter, Ed Italo Collection, Ojai, Calif.
16. George T. Stevens, *Three Years in the Sixth Corps* (Albany, N.Y.: S. R. Gray Publisher, 1866), 11.
17. Ibid.
18. Nathaniel Bartlett Sylvester, *History of Saratoga County, New York* (Interlaken, N.Y.: Heart of the Lakes Publishing, 1979), 118.
19. "The Holidays with the 77th," *Saratogian*, Saratoga Springs, N.Y., January 6, 1862.
20. Robert H. Skinner, Letter to Adam Clark Works, December 23, 1861, Adam Clark Works Papers, Univ. of Rochester, Rush Rhees Library Department of Rare Books, Manuscripts, and Archives, Rochester, N.Y.
21. George T. Stevens, *Three Years in the Sixth Corps* (Albany, N.Y.: S. R. Gray Publisher, 1866), 12.
22. "The Camp of the 77th—How the Boys are Getting Along," *Saratogian*, Saratoga Springs, N.Y., January 16, 1862.
23. 39th Reunion of the 77th New York State Volunteers Survivors Association, "Report of the Thirty-Ninth Annual Reunion of the Survivors Association of the Seventy-Seventh Regiment, 1911," Saratoga Springs Public Library, Saratoga Room, Saratoga Springs, N.Y.
24. 34th Reunion of the 77th New York State Volunteers Survivors Association, "Stories, Sketches, History of Saratoga Soldier Boys, interesting account of Annual Reunion Seventy-Seventh Regiment Survivors Association, 1906," Saratoga Springs Historical Society, Saratoga Springs, N.Y.
25. Robert H. Skinner, Letter to Adam Clark Works, December 3, 1861, Adam Clark Works Papers, Univ. of Rochester, Rush Rhees Library Department of Rare Books, Manuscripts, and Archives, Rochester, N.Y.
26. George T. Stevens, *Three Years in the Sixth Corps* (Albany, N.Y.: S. R. Gray Publisher, 1866), 8–15.
27. Ibid.
28. Robert H. Skinner, Letter to Adam Clark Works, January 16, 1861, Adam Clark Works Papers, Univ. of Rochester, Rush Rhees Library Department of Rare Books, Manuscripts, and Archives, Rochester, N.Y.

CHAPTER 4

1. George T. Stevens, *Three Years in the Sixth Corps* (Albany, N.Y.: S. R. Gray Publisher, 1866), 8–15.
2. Homer K. Davidson, *Black Jack Davidson: A Cavalry Commander on the Western Frontier, The Life of John W. Davidson* (Glendale, Calif.: Arthur H. Clarke Company, 1974), 47.
3. *Diary of William G. Watson for the Years of 1862 & 1863*, Eastern Washington Universities Libraries, Archives and Special Collections, Robert E. Lingow Family Papers, Cheny, Wash.

4. George T. Stevens, *Three Years in the Sixth Corps* (Albany, N.Y.: S. R. Gray Publisher, 1866), 14.
5. "Our War Correspondence," *Saratogian,* Saratoga Springs, N.Y., March 13, 1862.
6. Robert H. Skinner, Letter to Adam Clark Works, January 16, 1862, Adam Clark Works Papers, Univ. of Rochester, Rush Rhees Library Department of Rare Books, Manuscripts, and Archives, Rochester, N.Y.
7. "Reconnaissance of the 77th," *Saratogian,* Saratoga Springs, N.Y., March 6, 1862.
8. Martin Lennon, Letters and Diary. *Fifth Annual Report of the New York State Bureau of Military Statistics.* New York State Library, Albany, N.Y.
9. 39th Reunion of the 77th New York State Volunteers Survivors Association, "Report of the Thirty-Ninth Annual Reunion of the Survivors Association of the Seventy-Seventh Regiment, 1911," Saratoga Springs Public Library, Saratoga Room, Saratoga Springs, N.Y.
10. Herbert M. Schiller, *Autobiography of Major General William F. Smith 1861–1864* (Dayton, Ohio: Morningside, 1990), 47.
11. George T. Stevens, *Three Years in the Sixth Corps* (Albany, N.Y.: S. R. Gray Publisher, 1866), 22–23.
12. 23rd Reunion of the 77th New York State Volunteers Survivors Association, "The Bemis Heights Battalion, Annual Reunion of the Seventy-Seventh Survivors, 1895," City Historian, Saratoga Springs, N.Y.
13. Robert H. Skinner, Letter to Adam Clark Works, March 28, 1862, Adam Clark Works Papers, Univ. of Rochester, Rush Rhees Library Department of Rare Books, Manuscripts, and Archives, Rochester, N.Y.
14. "Army Reminiscences," *Saratogian*, February 28, Saratoga Springs Public Library, Saratoga Room, Saratoga Springs, N.Y.

CHAPTER 5

1. Robert H. Skinner, Letter to Adam Clark Works, March 28, 1862, Adam Clark Works Papers, Univ. of Rochester, Rush Rhees Library Department of Rare Books, Manuscripts, and Archives, Rochester, N.Y.
2. George T. Stevens, *Three Years in the Sixth Corps* (Albany, N.Y.: S. R. Gray Publisher, 1866), 27–28.
3. Steven W. Sears, *George B. McClellan—The Young Napoleon* (New York: Ticknor & Fields, 1988), 63, 132–135, 163.
4. 43rd Reunion of the 77th New York State Volunteers Survivors Association, "Report of the Forty-Third Annual Reunion of the Survivors Association of the Seventy-Seventh Regiment, 1915," Saratoga Springs Public Library, Saratoga Room, Saratoga Springs, N.Y.; George T. Stevens, *Three Years in the Sixth Corps* (Albany, N.Y.: S. R. Gray Publisher, 1866), 30–31; Edward H. Fuller, "Battles of the Seventy-Seventh New York State Foot Volunteers," United States Army Military History Institute Collection, Carlisle Barracks, Pa.
5. Caroline Halstead Royce, *Bessboro: A History of Westport* (Essex County, N.Y.: Privately Published, 1885), 526.
6. Frederick David Bidwell, *History of the 49th New York Volunteers* (Albany, N.Y.: J. B. Lyon Company, 1916), 8; 33rd Reunion of the 77th New York State Volunteers Survivors Association, "Veterans of Civil Conflict in Annual Reunion at Gansevoort, 1905," New York City Public Library, New York; Stephen W. Sears, *To the Gates of Richmond, The Peninsular Campaign* (New York: Ticknor & Fields, 1992), 342; Steven W. Sears, *George B. McClellan—The Young Napoleon* (New York: Ticknor & Fields, 1988).
7. 43rd Reunion of the 77th New York State Volunteers Survivors Association, "Report of the Forty-Third Annual Reunion of the Survivors Association of the

Seventy-Seventh Regiment, 1915," Saratoga Springs Public Library, Saratoga Room, Saratoga Springs, N.Y.
8. Ibid.
9. George T. Stevens, *Three Years in the Sixth Corps* (Albany, N.Y.: S. R. Gray Publisher, 1866), 30–31.
10. Orrin Rugg, Letter to his parents and friends, April 9, 1862, David Handy Collection, Cobleskill, N.Y.
11. George T. Stevens, *Three Years in the Sixth Corps* (Albany, N.Y.: S. R. Gray Publisher, 1866), 30–35.
12. Luther M. Wheeler, Letter to his mother, April 12, 1862, Newspaper Clipping, "Interesting from the 77th Before Yorktown," Chris Morley Collection, Ballston Spa, N.Y.
13. 37th Reunion of the 77th New York State Volunteers Survivors Association, "Report of the Thirty-Seventh Annual Reunion, 1909," United States Army Military History Institute Collection, Carlisle Barracks, Pa.
14. Ibid.
15. Luther M. Wheeler, Letter to his mother, April 12, 1862, Newspaper Clipping, "Interesting from the 77th Before Yorktown," Chris Morley Collection, Ballston Spa, N.Y.
16. Ibid.
17. Martin Lennon, Letters and Diary. *Fifth Annual Report of the New York State Bureau of Military Statistics.* New York State Library, Albany, N.Y.
18. 43rd Reunion of the 77th New York State Volunteers Survivors Association, "Report of the Forty-Third Annual Reunion of the Survivors Association of the Seventy-Seventh Regiment, 1915," Saratoga Springs Public Library, Saratoga Room, Saratoga Springs, N.Y.
19. "Army Reminiscences," *Saratogian*, Saratoga Springs, N.Y., February 28, Saratoga Springs Public Library, Saratoga Room, Saratoga Springs, N.Y.
20. 23rd Reunion of the 77th New York State Volunteers Survivors Association, "The Bemis Heights Battalion, Annual Reunion of the Seventy-Seventh Survivors, 1895," City Historian, Saratoga Springs, N.Y.
21. "Army Reminiscences," *Saratogian*, Saratoga Springs, N.Y., February 28, Saratoga Springs Public Library, Saratoga Room, Saratoga Springs, N.Y.
22. Walter H. Hebert, *Fighting Joe Hooker* (New York: The Bobbs Merrill Company, 1944), 78.
23. 43rd Reunion of the 77th New York State Volunteers Survivors Association, "Report of the Forty-Third Annual Reunion of the Survivors Association of the Seventy-Seventh Regiment, 1915," Saratoga Springs Public Library, Saratoga Room, Saratoga Springs, N.Y.
24. George T. Stevens, *Three Years in the Sixth Corps* (Albany, N.Y.: S. R. Gray Publisher, 1866), 45.
25. "From the 77th," *Saratogian*, Saratoga Springs N.Y., July 3, 1862.
26. Nathaniel Bartlett Sylvester, *History of Saratoga County, New York* (Interlaken, N.Y.: Heart of the Lakes Publishing, 1979), 118.
27. Executive Committee, *Maine at Gettysburg—Report of Maine Commissioners* (Portland, Maine: Lakeside Press, 1898), 442.
28. "From the 77th," *Saratogian,* Saratoga Springs, N.Y., July 3, 1862.

CHAPTER 6

1. New York Monuments Commission, *New York at Gettysburg, vol. 2* (Albany, N.Y.: J. B. Lyon Company, State Printers, 1902), 443.

2. Jack Coggins, *Arms and Equipment of the Civil War* (Garden City, N.Y.: Doubleday and Company, Inc., 1962), 23.
3. "From the 77th," *Saratogian*, Saratoga Springs, N.Y., May 29, 1862.
4. Stephen W. Sears, *To the Gates of Richmond, The Peninsular Campaign* (New York: Ticknor & Fields, 1992), 70–71.
5. "From the 77th," *Saratogian*, Saratoga Springs, N.Y., August 29, 1862.
6. 25th Reunion of the 77th New York State Volunteers Survivors Association. "The Boys of the Seventy-Seventh, Full Account of their Annual Reunion,1897." City Historian, Saratoga Springs, N.Y.
7. Ibid.
8. George T. Stevens, *Three Years in the Sixth Corps* (Albany, N.Y.: S. R. Gray Publisher, 1866), 58–62.
9. Ibid., 63.
10. War Rebellion, A Compilation of the Official Records of the Union and Confederate Armies (Washington, D.C.: Government Printing Office, 1891), Official Reports–Series I, Volume 12/1, Report no.10.
11. "From the 77th," *Saratogian*, Saratoga Springs, N.Y., May 14, 1862.
12. "From the 77th," *Saratogian*, Saratoga Springs, N.Y., June 3, 1862.
13. "Skirmish of the 77th," *Saratogian*, Saratoga Springs, N.Y., June 3, 1862.
14. 39th Reunion of the 77th New York State Volunteers Survivors Association, "Report of the Thirty-Ninth Annual Reunion of the Survivors Association of the Seventy-Seventh Regiment, 1911," Saratoga Springs Public Library, Saratoga Room, Saratoga Springs, N.Y.
15. "From the 77th," *Saratogian*, Saratoga Springs, N.Y., May 14, 1862.
16. 24th Reunion of the 77th New York State Volunteers Survivors Association, "Veterans Reunion, The Gathering of the Survivors of the Seventy-Seventh, 1896," City Historian, Saratoga Springs, N.Y.
17. Robert H. Skinner, Letter to Adam Clark Works, July 11,1862, Adam Clark Works Papers, Univ. of Rochester, Rush Rhees Library Department of Rare Books, Manuscripts, and Archives, Rochester, N.Y.
18. 39th Reunion of the 77th New York State Volunteers Survivors Association, "Report of the Thirty-Ninth Annual Reunion of the Survivors Association of the Seventy-Seventh Regiment, 1911," Saratoga Springs Public Library, Saratoga Room, Saratoga Springs, N.Y.
19. Nathaniel Bartlett Sylvester, *History of Saratoga County, New York* (Interlaken, N.Y.: Heart of the Lakes Publishing, 1979), 108, 118.

CHAPTER 7

1. Nathaniel Bartlett Sylvester, *History of Saratoga County, New York* (Interlaken, N.Y.: Heart of the Lakes Publishing, 1979), 118.
2. Executive Committee, *Maine at Gettysburg—Report of Maine Commissioners* (Portland, Maine: Lakeside Press, 1898), 445; Alexander S. Webb, *The Peninsula: McClellan's Campaign of 1862* (New York: Charles Scribner's Sons, 1881), 115.
3. John Michael Priest, *Turn Them Out to Die Like a Mule* (Leesburg, Va.: Gauley Mount Press, 1995), 104.
4. George T. Stevens, *Three Years in the Sixth Corps* (Albany, N.Y.: S. R. Gray Publisher, 1866), 74–75.
5. "Home Matters," *Saratogian*, Saratoga Springs, N.Y., July 10, 1872.
6. Ibid.
7. Ezra J. Warner, *Generals in Blue* (Baton Rouge: Louisiana University, 1964), 179–183; Mark Mayo Boatner, *Civil War Dictionary* (New York: David McKay Co., 1921), 476–479.

8. "From the 77th," *Saratogian,* Saratoga Springs, N.Y., July 24, 1862.
9. Ibid.
10. Ibid.
11. Ibid.
12. Martin Lennon, Letters and Diary. *Fifth Annual Report of the New York State Bureau of Military Statistics.* New York State Library, Albany, N.Y.
13. George T. Stevens, *Three Years in the Sixth Corps* (Albany, N.Y.: S. R. Gray Publisher, 1866), 91.
14. Executive Committee, *Maine at Gettysburg—Report of Maine Commissioners* (Portland, Maine: Lakeside Press, 1898), 447.
15. "The 77th and the Late Battles," *Saratogian,* Saratoga Springs, N.Y., July 10, 1862; George T. Stevens, *Three Years in the Sixth Corps* (Albany, N.Y.: S. R. Gray Publisher, 1866), 100–102.
16. "Interesting from the 77th," *Saratogian,* Saratoga Springs, N.Y., July 17, 1862.
17. Washington Frothingham, *History of Fulton County* (Syracuse, N.Y.: D. Mason & Co. Printers and Publishers, 1892), 128; "From the 77th Interesting Letter from Adjutant French," *Saratogian,* Saratoga Springs, N.Y., July 24, 1862.
18. Ibid.

CHAPTER 8

1. Homer K. Davidson, *Black Jack Davidson, A Cavalry Commander on the Western Frontier: The Life of General John W. Davidson* (Glendale, Calif.: Arthur H. Clarke Company, 1974), 105–107.
2. "Col. Caw Called Out," *Saratogian,* Saratoga Springs, N.Y., October 22, 1873.
3. George T. Stevens, *Three Years in the Sixth Corps* (Albany, N.Y.: S. R. Gray Publisher, 1866), 115–117.
4. "Home Matters," *Saratogian,* Saratoga Springs, N.Y., July 10, 1862; "A Cool Reception," *Saratogian,* Saratoga Springs, N.Y., July 31, 1862.
5. George T. Stevens, *Three Years in the Sixth Corps* (Albany, N.Y.: S. R. Gray Publisher, 1866), 118–119.
6. Frank L. Welcher, *The Union Army 1861–1865, Organization and Operations, Vol. 1: The Eastern Theater* (Indianapolis, Ind.: Indiana University Press, 1989), 394.
7. Orrin Rugg, Letter to his parents, May 11, 1863, David Handy Collection, Cobleskill, N.Y.
8. "Col. Caw Called Out," *Saratogian,* Saratoga Springs, N.Y., October 22, 1873.
9. "Recruiting for the 77th," *Saratogian,* Saratoga Springs, N.Y., October 2, 1862.
10. Cornelius E. Durkee, "Reminiscences of Saratoga," Reprinted from *Saratogian,* Saratoga Springs, N.Y.
11. "Appointments in the 77th," *Saratogian,* Saratoga Springs, N.Y., August 7, 1861.
12. Nathaniel Bartlett Sylvester, *History of Saratoga County, New York* (Interlaken, N.Y.: Heart of the Lakes Publishing, 1979), 110.
13. George T. Stevens, *Three Years in the Sixth Corps* (Albany, N.Y.: S. R. Gray Publisher, 1866), 130.
14. Ibid.
15. Ibid.
16. Nathaniel Bartlett Sylvester, *History of Saratoga County, New York* (Interlaken, N.Y.: Heart of the Lakes Publishing, 1979), 118.

CHAPTER 9

1. 40th Reunion of the 77th New York State Volunteers Survivors Association, "Report of the Fortieth Annual Reunion,1912," United States Army Military History Institute Collection, Carlisle Barracks, Pa.
2. Ezra J. Warner, *Generals in Blue* (Baton Rouge: Louisiana University, 1964), 159–160.
3. Thomas W. Hyde, *Following the Greek Cross or Memories of the Sixth Corps* (Boston: Houghton Mifflin and Co., 1894), 97.
4. "Obituary, Nathan S. Babcock," Nebraska Signal, Geneva, Nebr., March 1, 1917.
5. 39th Reunion of the 77th New York State Volunteers Survivors Association, "Report of the Thirty-Ninth Annual Reunion of the Survivors Association of the Seventy-Seventh Regiment,1911," Saratoga Springs Public Library, Saratoga Room, Saratoga Springs, N.Y.
6. 24th Reunion of the 77th New York State Volunteers Survivors Association, "Veterans Reunion, The Gathering of the Survivors of the Seventy-Seventh, 1896," City Historian, Saratoga Springs, N.Y.
7. Robert H. Skinner, Letter to Adam Clark Works, October 1, 1862, Adam Clark Works Papers, Univ. of Rochester, Rush Rhees Library Department of Rare Books, Manuscripts, and Archives, Rochester, N.Y.
8. Thomas W. Hyde, *Following the Greek Cross or Memories of the Sixth Corps* (Boston: Houghton Mifflin and Co., 1894), 94–95.
9. 24th Reunion of the 77th New York State Volunteers Survivors Association, "Veterans Reunion, The Gathering of the Survivors of the Seventy-Seventh, 1896," City Historian, Saratoga Springs, N.Y.
10. Nathaniel Bartlett Sylvester, *History of Saratoga County, New York* (Interlaken, N.Y.: Heart of the Lakes Publishing, 1979), 110.
11. Stephen W. Sears, *Landscape Turned Red, The Battle of Antietam* (New York: Ticknor & Fields, 1992), 251.
12. Ibid.
13. Ibid.
14. Frederick David Bidwell, *History of the 49th Regiment New York Volunteers* (Albany, N.Y.: J. B. Lyon Co., 1916), 20.
15. Nathaniel Bartlett Sylvester, *History of Saratoga County, New York* (Interlaken, N.Y.: Heart of the Lakes Publishing, 1979), 110.
16. Thomas Hyde, *Following the Greek Cross or Memories of the Sixth Corps* (Boston: Houghton Mifflin and Co., 1894), 94–95.
17. George Contant, *Path of Blood* (Savannah, N.Y.: Seeco Printing Services, 1997), 238–239.
18. Robert H. Skinner, Letter to Adam Clark Works, October 11, 1862, Adam Clark Works Papers, Univ. of Rochester, Rush Rhees Library Department of Rare Books, Manuscripts, and Archives, Rochester, N.Y.
19. Ibid.
20. George Contant, *Path of Blood* (Savannah, N.Y.: Seeco Printing Services, 1997), 238–239.
21. War Rebellion, A Compilation of the Official Records of the Union and Confederate Armies (Washington, D.C.: Government Printing Office, 1891) Official Reports–Series I, Volumn 19/1, Report No. 136.
22. Edward H. Fuller, "Battles of the Seventy-Seventh New York State Foot Volunteers," United States Army Military History Institute Collection, Carlisle Barracks, Pa.

23. Frederick David Bidwell, *History of the 49th Regiment New York Volunteers* (Albany, N.Y.: J. B. Lyon Co., 1918), 20–21.
24. War Rebellion, A Compilation of the Official Records of the Union and Confederate Armies (Washington, D.C.: Government Printing Office, 1891 Official Reports–Series I, Volume 19/1, Report No. 136.
25. John Michael Priest, *Antietam: The Soldiers' Battle* (Shippensburg, Pa.: White Mane Publishing, 1989), 200.
26. Robert H. Skinner, Letter to Adam Clark Works, October 11, 1862, Adam Clark Works Papers, Univ. of Rochester, Rush Rhees Library Department of Rare Books, Manuscripts, and Archives, Rochester, N.Y.
27. 40th Reunion of the 77th New York State Volunteers Survivors Association, "Report of the Fortieth Annual Reunion,1912," United States Army Military History Institute Collection, Carlisle Barracks, Pa..
28. Thomas Hyde, *Following the Greek Cross or Memories of the Sixth Corps* (Boston: Houghton Mifflin and Co., 1894), 96–97.
29. "Killed and Wounded in the 77th," *Saratogian,* Saratoga Springs. N.Y., October 2, 1862.
30. Herbert M. Schiller, *Autobiography of Major General William F. Smith 1861–1864* (Dayton, Ohio: Morningside, 1990), 54–55.
31. Stephen W. Sears, *Landscape Turned Red, The Battle of Antietam* (New York: Ticknor & Fields, 1992), 293–294.
32. 40th Reunion of the 77th New York State Volunteers Survivors Association, "Report of the Fortieth Annual Reunion, 1912," United States Army Military History Institute Collection, Carlisle Barracks, Pa.
33. Ibid.
34. 34th Reunion of the 77th New York State Volunteers Survivors Association, "Stories, Sketches, History of Saratoga Soldier Boys, interesting account of Annual Reunion Seventy-Seventh Regiment Survivors Association, 1906," Saratoga Springs Historical Society, Saratoga Springs, N.Y.
35. 30th Reunion of the 77th New York State Volunteers Survivors Association. "Reunion of Bemis Heights Battalion 77th foot regiment N.Y. S. vols. at Schuylerville, September 17, 1902." United States Army Military History Institute Collection, Carlisle Barracks, Pa.

CHAPTER 10

1. "Thanksgiving in the 77th," *Saratogian*, Saratoga Springs, N.Y. December 11, 1862.
2. Ibid.
3. T. Scott Fuller, Letter to his mother, December 21, 1863, Saratoga Historical Society Collection, Saratoga Springs, N.Y.
4. George T. Stevens, *Three Years in the Sixth Corps* (Albany, N.Y.: S. R. Gray Publisher, 1866), 165.
5. William Marvel, *Burnside* (Chapel Hill, N.C.: University of North Carolina Press, 1991), 4.
6. Mark Mayo Boatner, *Civil War Dictionary* (New York: David McKay Co., 1921), 107–108; Ezra J. Warner, *Generals in Blue* (Baton Rouge: Louisiana University, 1964), 57–58; William Marvel, *Burnside* (Chapel Hill, N.C.: University of North Carolina Press, 1991), 39, 97, 157.
7. Ezra J. Warner, *Generals in Blue* (Baton Rouge: Louisiana University, 1964), 239–240; Larry Tagg, *The Generals of Gettysburg* (Campbell, Calif.: Savas Printing Co., 1998), 111–112.
8. Ezra J. Warner, *Generals in Blue* (Baton Rouge: Louisiana University, 1964), 528–529.

9. Isaac O. Best, *History of the 121st New York State Infantry* (Chicago, Ill.: Published by Lieutenant Jas. H. Smith, 1921), 40–41.
10. Martin Lennon, Letters and Diary. *Fifth Annual Report of the New York State Bureau of Military Statistics.* New York State Library, Albany, N.Y.
11. War Rebellion, A Compilation of the Official Records of the Union and Confederate Armies (Washington, D.C.: Government Printing Office, 1891), series I, vol 31/1, reports no. 252 & 259.
12. Mason W. Tyler, *Recollections of the Civil War* (New York: G. Putnam's Sons, 1912), 232.
13. Ezra J. Warner, *Generals in Blue* (Baton Rouge: Louisiana University, 1964), 342–343.
14. Martin Lennon, Letters and Diary, *Fifth Annual Report of the New York State Bureau of Military Statistics.* New York State Library, Albany, N.Y.
15. Ibid.
16. Isaac O. Best, *History of the 121st New York State Infantry* (Chicago, Ill.: Published by Lieutenant Jas. H. Smith, 1921), 42–48.
17. Martin Lennon, Letters and Diary, *Fifth Annual Report of the New York State Bureau of Military Statistics,* New York State Library, Albany, N.Y.
18. Bruce Catton, *Mr. Lincoln's Army* (New York: Anchor Books, Doubleday, 1951), 110.
19. T. Scott Fuller, Letter to his mother, December 21, 1863, Saratoga Historical Society Collection, Saratoga Springs, N.Y.
20. Ibid.
21. George T. Stevens, *Three Years in the Sixth Corps* (Albany, N.Y.: S. R. Gray Publisher, 1866), 174.
22. 21st Reunion of the 77th New York State Volunteers Survivors Association, "The Brave Seventy-Seventh, A Jolly Reunion Held by the Boys at Schenectady, 1893," City Historian, Saratoga Springs, N.Y.
23. Martin Lennon, Letters and Diary, *Fifth Annual Report of the New York State Bureau of Military Statistics,* New York State Library, Albany, N.Y.
24. George T. Stevens, *Three Years in the Sixth Corps* (Albany, N.Y.: S. R. Gray Publisher, 1866), 177.
25. John Sedgwick, *Correspondence of John Sedgwick, Major General, vol. 2* (Privately Printed: 1903), 189; Ezra Warner, *Generals in Blue* (Baton Rouge: Louisiana University, 1964), 430–431.

CHAPTER 11

1. Thomas P. Lowry,*The Story the Soldiers Wouldn't Tell* (Harrisburg, Pa.: Stackpole Books, 1994), 145–149; Walter H. Hebert, *Fighting Joe Hooker* (New York: Bobbs Merrill Company, 1944), 180; Ezra J. Warner, *Generals in Blue* (Baton Rouge: Louisiana University, 1964), 333–335; Gabor S. Boritt, *Lincoln's Generals* (New York: Oxford University Press, 1994), 54; Stephen W. Sears, *Chancellorsville* (New York: Houghton Mifflin Company, 1996); Alan A. Siegel, *For the Glory of the Union: Myth, Reality, and the Media in Civil War New Jersey* (Rutherford, N.J.: Fairleigh Dickinson University Press, 1984).
2. Mason W. Tyler, *Recollections of the Civil War* (New York: G. Putnam's Sons, 1912), 75.
3. George T. Stevens, *Three Years in the Sixth Corps* (Albany, N.Y.: S. R. Gray Publisher, 1866), 215.
4. Orrin Rugg, Letter to his parents, May 11, 1863, David Handy Collection, Cobleskill, N.Y.

5. Norman Fox Jr., Letter to his brother about May 3, 1863, Louise Barker's Fox Family Collection, Winchester, Ma.
6. Jay Luvaas & Harold W. Nelson, *The U.S. Army War College Guide to the Battles of Chancellorsville and Fredericksburg* (New York: Harper & Row Publishers, 1988), 341.
7. Ezra J. Warner, *Generals in Gray* (Baton Rouge: Louisiana University, 1964), 16–17.
8. Edward H. Fuller, "Battles of the Seventy-Seventh New York State Foot Volunteers," United States Army Military History Institute Collection, Carlisle Barracks, Pa.
9. Nathan S. Babcock, Letter to Mort Brockway, May 20, 1863, Jerry Babcock Collection, Omaha, Nebr.
10. 38th Reunion of the 77th New York State Volunteers Survivors Association, "Report of the Thirty-Eighth Annual Reunion, 1910," United States Army Military History Institute Collection, Carlisle Barracks, Pa.
11. Edward F. Gross, *Centennial History of the Village of Ballston Spa* (Ballston Spa, N.Y.: Ballston Journal, 1847), 149.
12. Orrin Rugg, Letter to his parents, May 11, 1863, David Handy Collection, Cobleskill, N.Y.
13. Ibid.
14. William M. Owen, *In Camp and Battle with the Washington Artillery of New Orleans* (Baton Rouge, La.: LSU Press, 1999).
15. Martin Lennon, Letters and Diary. *Fifth Annual Report of the New York State Bureau of Military Statistics.* New York State Library, Albany, N.Y.
16. Ibid., 734.
17. Orrin Rugg, Letter to his parents, May 11, 1863, David Handy Collection, Cobleskill, N.Y.
18. William M. Owen, *In Camp and Battle with the Washington Artillery of New Orleans* (Baton Rouge, La.: LSU Press, 1999).
19. 39th Reunion of the 77th New York State Volunteers Survivors Association, "Report of the Thirty-Ninth Annual Reunion of the Survivors Association of the Seventy-Seventh Regiment, 1911," Saratoga Springs Public Library, Saratoga Room, Saratoga Springs, N.Y.
20. Ibid.
21. "Further from the 77th," *Saratogian,* Saratoga Springs, N.Y., May 11, 1863.
22. Saratogian, "Our County and Its People, A Descriptive and Bibliographic Record of Saratoga County" (The Boston History Company, Publishers, 1899), 495.
23. *Ballston Journal*, Ballston Spa, N.Y., February 26, 1896.
24. *Ballston Journal*, February 22, 1896.
25. Erskine Branch, Pamphlet on his Service in the 77th, United States Army Military History Institute Collection, Carlisle Barracks, Pa.
26. "From the 77th," *Saratogian,* Saratoga Springs, N.Y., July 7, 1913.
27. 39th Reunion of the 77th New York State Volunteers Survivors Association, "Report of the Thirty-Ninth Annual Reunion of the Survivors Association of the Seventy-Seventh Regiment, 1911," Saratoga Springs Public Library, Saratoga Room, Saratoga Springs, N.Y.
28. Christopher Ford, *Over the Wall—The VI Corps, Fredericksburg, 1863* (Fredericksburg, Va.: Fredericksburg Press, 1996), 57.
29. Executive Committee, *Maine at Gettysburg—Report of Maine Commissioners* (Portland, Maine: Lakeside Press, 1898), 453–456.

30. Martin Lennon, Letters and Diary, *Fifth Annual Report of the New York State Bureau of Military Statistics,* New York State Library, Albany, N.Y.
31. Orrin Rugg, Letter to his parents, May 11, 1863, David Handy Collection, Cobleskill, N.Y.
32. War Rebellion, A Compilation of the Official Records of the Union and Confederate Armies (Washington, D.C.: Government Printing Office, 1891), Official Reports–series I, vol 39/1, report no. 231.
33. Nathan S. Babcock, Letter to Mort Brockway, May 20, 1863, Jerry Babcock Collection, Omaha, Nebr.
34. Eveyln Barrett Britten, *Chronicles of Saratoga* (Privately Published, 1957), 257.

CHAPTER 12

1. Edward H. Fuller, "Battles of the Seventy-Seventh New York State Foot Volunteers," United States Army Military History Institute Collection, Carlisle Barracks, Pa.
2. T. Scott Fuller, Letter to his mother, June 6, 1863, Saratoga Historical Society, Saratoga Springs, N.Y.
3. George T. Stevens, *Three Years in the Sixth Corps* (Albany, N.Y.: S. R. Gray Publisher, 1866), 223.
4. New York Monuments Commission, *New York at Gettysburg, vol. 2* (Albany, N.Y.: J. B. Lyon Co., State Printers, 1902), 622.
5. 33rd Reunion of the 77th New York State Volunteers Survivors Association, "Veterans of Civil Conflict in Annual Reunion at Gansevoort, 1905," New York City Public Library; George T. Stevens, *Three Years in the Sixth Corps* (Albany, N.Y.: S. R. Gray Publisher, 1866), 223.
6. Altus Jewel, Letter to his sister, dated June 16, 1863, United States Army Military History Institute, Warren K. Tice Collection, Carlisle Barracks, Pa.
7. George T. Stevens, *Three Years in the Sixth Corps* (Albany, N.Y.: S. R. Gray Publisher, 1866), 236–237.
8. Ezra J. Warner, *Generals in Blue* (Baton Rouge: Louisiana University, 1964), 315–317; Gabor S. Boritt, *Lincoln's Generals* (New York: Oxford University Press, 1994), 87.
9. 26th Reunion of the 77th New York State Volunteers Survivors Association, "The Fighters of 61, The Seventy-Seventh Boys Recall Their Battles, 1898," Saratoga Springs Historical Society, Saratoga Springs, N.Y.
10. 46th Reunion of the 77th New York State Volunteers Survivors Association, "The Forty-Sixth Annual Reunion of the Saratoga Regiment, the 77th Infantry Volunteers at 1861–65, 1918," City Historian, Saratoga Springs, N.Y.; New York Monuments Commission, *New York at Gettysburg, vol. 2* (Albany, N.Y.: J. B. Lyon Co., State Printers, 1902), 626.
11. John Sedgwick, *Correspondence of John Sedgwick, Major General, vol. 2* (Privately Printed, 1903), 203.
12. Richard E. Winslow, *General John Sedgwick, Union Corps Commander* (Novato, Calif.: Presidio Press, 1982), 101.
13. Ibid., 94.
14. New York Monuments Commission, *New York at Gettysburg, vol. 2* (Albany, N.Y.: J. B. Lyon Co., State Printers, 1902), 623.
15. Ezra J. Warner, *Generals in Gray* (Baton Rouge: Louisiana University, 1964), 451–452.
16. Ibid., 34.

17. 46th Reunion of the 77th New York State Volunteers Survivors Association, "The Forty-Sixth Annual Reunion of the Saratoga Regiment, the 77th Infantry Volunteers at 1861–65, 1918," City Historian, Saratoga Springs, N.Y.
18. 33rd Reunion of the 77th New York State Volunteers Survivors Association, "Veterans of Civil Conflict in Annual Reunion at Gansevoort, 1905," New York City Public Library.
19. Ibid.
20. George T. Stevens, *Three Years in the Sixth Corps* (Albany, N.Y.: S. R. Gray Publisher, 1866), 258.
21. Ibid., 258–259.
22. Ibid., 301.
23. Nathaniel Bartlett Sylvester, *History of Saratoga County, New York* (Interlaken, N.Y.: Heart of the Lakes Publishing, 1979), 111.
24. Edward H. Fuller, "Battles of the Seventy-Seventh New York State Foot Volunteers," United States Army Military History Institute Collection, Carlisle Barracks, Pa.
25. Martin Lennon, Letters and Diary, *Fifth Annual Report of the New York State Bureau of Military Statistics,* New York State Library, Albany, N.Y.
26. *Saratogian*, Saratoga Springs, N.Y., November 12, 1863.
27. 39th Reunion of the 77th New York State Volunteers Survivors Association, "Report of the Thirty-Ninth Annual Reunion of the Survivors Association of the Seventy-Seventh Regiment, 1911," Saratoga Springs Public Library, Saratoga Room, Saratoga Springs, N.Y.
28. Ibid.
29. Ibid.
30. George T. Stevens, *Three Years in the Sixth Corps* (Albany, N.Y.: S. R. Gray Publisher, 1866), 297.
31. Ibid.
32. Ibid.

CHAPTER 13

1. Timothy B. Mudgett, *Make the Fur Fly: A History of a Union Volunteer Division* (Shippensburg, Pa.: Burd Street Press, 1997), 63.
2. Norman Fox Jr., Letter to his father dated Wednesday, January 27, 1863, Louise Barker's Fox Family Collection, Winchester, Mass.
3. Orrin Rugg, Letter to his parents and friends, May 11, 1863, David Handy Collection, Cobleskill, N.Y.
4. Donald Chipman, "An Essex County Soldier in the Civil War: The Diary of Cyrille Fountain," New York History: Quarterly Journal of the New York Historical Society (Cooperstown, N.Y.: New York Historical Society, 1985), 289.
5. John D. Billings, *Hardtack and Coffee: The Unwritten Story of Army Life* (Williamstown, Mass.: Corner House Publishers, 1973), 231–249.
6. Martin Lennon, Letters and Diary. *Fifth Annual Report of the New York State Bureau of Military Statistics.* New York State Library, Albany, N.Y.
7. Ibid.
8. 25th Reunion of the 77th New York State Volunteers Survivors Association, "The Boys of the Seventy-Seventh, full account of their Annual Reunion, 1897," City Historian, Saratoga Springs, N.Y.

9. Donald Chipman, "An Essex County Soldier in the Civil War: The Diary of Cyrille Fountain," New York History: Quarterly Journal of the New York Historical Society (Cooperstown, N.Y.: New York Historical Society, 1985), 285.
10. T. Scott Fuller, Letter to his mother, March, Saratoga Springs Historical Society Collection, Saratoga Springs, N.Y.
11. Charles E. Stevens, Letter to friend Cone, December 17, 1863, Ed Italo Collection, Ojai, Calif.
12. Norman Fox Jr., Letter to his father, Wednesday, January 27, 1863, Louise Barker's Fox Family Collection, Winchester, Mass.
13. Ibid.
14. George T. Stevens, *Three Years in the Sixth Corps* (Albany, N.Y.: S. R. Gray Publisher, 1866), 300–301.
15. Charles E. Stevens, Letter to friend Cone, December 17, 1863, Ed Italo Collection, Ojai, Calif.
16. Donald Chipman, "An Essex County Soldier in the Civil War: The Diary of Cyrille Fountain," New York History: Quarterly Journal of the New York Historical Society (Cooperstown, N.Y.: New York Historical Society, 1985), 288.
17. Ibid., 290.
18. "From the 77th," *Saratogian*, Saratoga Springs, N.Y., May 26, 1864.
19. *Waterville Times*, N.Y., October 11, 1861.
20. Alan A. Siegel, *For the Glory of the Union: Myth, Reality, and the Media in Civil War New Jersey* (Rutherford, N.J.: Fairleigh Dickinson University Press, 1984), 133–134.
21. Donald Chipman, "An Essex County Soldier in the Civil War: The Diary of Cyrille Fountain," New York History: Quarterly Journal of the New York Historical Society (Cooperstown, N.Y.: New York Historical Society, 1985), 288.
22. Ibid., 287.
23. William A. Frassanito, *Grant and Lee: The Virginia Campaigns, 1864–1865* (New York: Scribner, 1983), 36.
24. "The Fighters of 61, The Seventy-Seventh Boys Recall Their Battles" (Report Twenty-Sixth Annual Reunion, 1898), Saratoga Springs Historical Society, N.Y.
25. "From the 77th," *Saratogian*, Saratoga Springs, N.Y., March 8, 1864.
26. Donald Chipman, "An Essex County Soldier in the Civil War: The Diary of Cyrille Fountain," New York History: Quarterly Journal of the New York Historical Society (Cooperstown, N.Y., 1985), 288.
27. "From the 77th," *Saratogian*, Saratoga Springs, N.Y., October 3, 1865.
28. Donald Chipman, "An Essex County Soldier in the Civil War: The Diary of Cyrille Fountain," New York History: Quarterly Journal of the New York Historical Society (Cooperstown, N.Y.: New York Historical Society, 1985), 289.

CHAPTER 14

1. Ezra Warner, *Generals in Blue* (Baton Rouge: Louisiana University, 1964), 183–186.
2. Mark Mayo Boatner, *Civil War Dictionary* (New York: David McKay and Co., 1921), 153.
3. George T. Stevens, *Three Years in the Sixth Corps* (Albany, N.Y.: S. R. Gray Publisher, 1866), 300–302.
4. Papers of the Military Historical Society of Massachusetts, "*The Wilderness Campaign May–June 1864*" (Boston, Mass.: Cadet Armory, 1905), 15–19.

5. Robert Garth Scott, *Into the Wilderness with the Army of the Potomac* (Bloomington, ind.: University Press, 1985), 17.
6. Papers of the Military Historical Society of Massachusetts, *The Wilderness Campaign May-June 1864* (Boston, Mass.: Cadet Armory, 1905), 15–19.
7. George T. Stevens, *Three Years in the Sixth Corps* (Albany, N.Y.: S. R. Gray Publisher, 1866), 303–306.
8. Ibid.
9. 39th Reunion of the 77th New York State Volunteers Survivors Association, "Report of the Thirty-Ninth Annual Reunion of the Survivors Association of the Seventy-Seventh Regiment, 1911," Saratoga Springs Public Library, Saratoga Room, Saratoga Springs, N.Y.
10. "From the 77th," *Saratogian*, Saratoga Springs, N.Y., June 23, 1864.
11. 43rd Reunion of the 77th New York State Volunteers Survivors Association, "Report of the Forty-Third Annual Reunion of the Survivors Association of the Seventy-Seventh Regiment, 1915," Saratoga Springs Public Library, Saratoga Room, Saratoga Springs, N.Y.
12. John Michael Priest, *Nowhere to Run: The Wilderness May 4th and 5th, 1864* (Shippensburg, Pa.: White Mane Publishing, 1995), 47.
13. Ibid., 98–99.
14. George T. Stevens, *Three Years in the Sixth Corps* (Albany, N.Y.: S. R. Gray Publisher, 1866), 304–307.
15. 33th Reunion of the 77th New York State Volunteers Survivors Association, "Veterans of Civil Conflict in Annual Reunion at Gansevoort, 1905," Saratoga Springs Historical Society, Saratoga Springs, N.Y.
16. John Michael Priest, *Nowhere to Run, The Wilderness May 4th and 5th, 1864* (Shippensburg, Pa.: White Mane Publishing, 1995), 213.
17. Papers of the Military Historical Society of Massachusetts, *The Wilderness Campaign May-June 1864* (Boston, Mass.: Cadet Armory, 1905), 136.
18. Ibid., 189.
19. Gordon C. Rhea, *The Battle of the Wilderness, May 5–6, 1864* (Baton Rouge: Louisiana State University Press, 1994), 318–319.
20. George T. Stevens, *Three Years in the Sixth Corps* (Albany, N.Y.: S. R. Gray Publisher, 1866), 309.
21. Gordon C. Rhea, *The Battle of the Wilderness, May 5–6, 1864* (Baton Rouge: Louisiana State University Press, 1994), 319.
22. Ibid.
23. New York Monuments Commission, *New York at Gettysburg, vol. 2* (Albany, N.Y., J.B. Lyon Co., State Printers), 622.
24. Ibid.
25. Robert Garth Scott, *Into the Wilderness with the Army of the Potomac* (Bloomington, Ind.: Indiana University Press, 1985), 110.
26. 39th Reunion of the 77th New York State Volunteers Survivors Association, "Report of the Thirty-Ninth Annual Reunion of the Survivors Association of the Seventy-Seventh Regiment, 1911," Saratoga Springs Public Library, Saratoga Room, Saratoga Springs, N.Y.
27. John Michael Priest, "*Victory Without Triumph: The Wilderness May 6th & 7th, 1864, vol. 2* (Shippensburg, Pa.: White Mane Publishing, 1996), 6, 177.
28. William A. Frassanito, *Grant and Lee: The Virginia Campaigns, 1864–1865* (New York: Scribner, 1983), xxxiv.

29. Robert Garth Scott, *Into the Wilderness with the Army of the Potomac* (Bloomington, Indiana University Press, 1985), 172–174.
30. John Michael Priest, *Victory Without Triumph: The Wilderness May 6th & 7th, 1864*, vol. 2 (Shippensburg, Pa.: White Mane Publishing, 1996), 184.
31. Robert Garth Scott, *Into the Wilderness with the Army of the Potomac* (Bloomington, Ind.: Indiana Univ. Press, 1985), 172, 174.
32. 31st Reunion of the 77th New York State Volunteers Survivors Association, "Reunion of Survivors Association, 77th Foot Regiment, N. Y. S. Vols. at Schenectady, Sept. 22, 1903," New York City Public Library.
33. 39th Reunion of the 77th New York State Volunteers Survivors Association, "Report of the Thirty-Ninth Annual Reunion of the Survivors Association of the Seventy-Seventh Regiment, 1911," Saratoga Springs Public Library, Saratoga Room, Saratoga Springs, N.Y.
34. Nathaniel Bartlett Sylvester, *History of Saratoga County, New York* (Interlaken, N.Y.: Heart of the Lakes Publishing, 1979 reprint of 1878 edition), 502.
35. Isaac Lobdell, Letter to his wife, May 12, 1864, Jerry Babcock Collection, Omaha, Nebr.
36. 43rd Reunion of the 77th New York State Volunteers Survivors Association, "Report of the Forty-Third Annual Reunion of the Survivors Association of the Seventy-Seventh Regiment, 1915," Saratoga Springs Public Library, Saratoga Room, Saratoga Springs, N.Y.
37. Gordon C. Rhea, *The Battle of the Wilderness May 5–6, 1864* (Baton Rouge, Louisiana State Univ. Press, 1994), 424–425.
38. Ibid.
39. Ibid.
40. Gordon C. Rhea, *The Battle of the Wilderness May 5–6, 1864* (Baton Rouge: Louisiana State Univ. Press, 1994), 414–424.
41. John Michael Priest, *Nowhere to Run: The Wilderness, May 4th & 5th, 1864* (White Mane Publishing, 1995), 123.
42. Frederick David Bidwell, *History of the 49th New York Volunteers* (Albany, N.Y.: J. B. Lyon Company, 1916), 43–45.
43. Ibid.
44. Issac Lobdell, Letter to his wife, May 12, 1864, Jerry Babcock Collection, Omaha, Nebr.
45. "Report of the Thirty-Ninth Annual Reunion of the Survivors Association of the Seventy-Seventh Regiment" (Report of the Thirty-Ninth Annual Reunion, 1911), Saratoga Room, Saratoga Springs Public Library, N.Y.
46. Bruce Catton, *A Stillness at Appomattox* (New York, Anchor Books, Doubleday, 1951), 92–93; Hazard Stevens, *The Sixth Corps in the Wilderness*, Papers of the Military Historical Society of Mass. Vol. 4, 1905, 175–203; Edward Steere, *The Wilderness Campaign* (Harrisburg, Pa.: Stackpole Company, 1960).

CHAPTER 15

1. 43rd Reunion of the 77th New York State Volunteers Survivors Association, "Report of the Forty-Third Annual Reunion of the Survivors Association of the Seventy-Seventh Regiment, 1915," Saratoga Springs Public Library, Saratoga Room, Saratoga Springs, N.Y.; James M. Greiner, Janet L. Coryell, & James R. Smither, *A Surgeon's Civil War, The Letters and Diary of Daniel M. Holt* (Kent, Ohio: The Kent State University Press, 1994), 184; Bruce Catton, *A Stillness at Appomattox* (New York: Anchor Books, Doubleday, 1951), 92–94.
2. "Report of the Thirty-Ninth Annual Reunion of the Survivors Association of the Seventy-Seventh Regiment" (report of the Thirty-Ninth Annual Reunion, 1911), Saratoga Room, Saratoga Springs Public Library, N.Y.

3. George T. Stevens, *Three Years in the Sixth Corps* (Albany, N.Y.: S. R. Gray Publisher, 1866), 334.
4. Edward H. Fuller, "Battles of the Seventy-Seventh New York State Foot Volunteers," United States Army Military History Institute Collection, Carlisle Barracks, Pa., 17.
5. Augustus Buell, *The Cannoneer Recollections of Service in the Army of the Potomac* (Washington, D.C.: National Tribune,1890), 194.
6. Ibid., 184–185.
7. Bruce Catton, *A Stillness at Appomattox* (New York: Anchor Books, Doubleday, 1953), 109.
8. Ezra J. Warner, *Generals in Blue* (Baton Rouge: Louisiana University, 1964), 575–576.
9. Bruce Catton, *A Stillness at Appomattox* (New York: Anchor Books, Doubleday, 1953), 116.
10. Stephen E. Ambrose, *Upton and the Army* (Baton Rouge: Louisiana State University, 1964), 30–31.
11. Ibid., 6.
12. New York Monuments Commission, *New York at Gettysburg, vol. 3* (Albany, N.Y.: J. B. Lyon Co., State Printers, 1902), 834–835.
13. Donald Chipman, "An Essex County Soldier in the Civil War: The Diary of Cyrille Fountain," New York History: Quarterly Journal of the New York Historical Society (Cooperstown, N.Y.: New York Historical Society,1985), 291.
14. Gordon C. Rhea, *The Battles for Spotsylvania Court House and the Road to the Yellow Tavern* (Baton Rouge: Louisiana State University Press, 1997), appendix.
15. 43rd Reunion of the 77th New York State Volunteers Survivors Association, "Report of the Forty-Third Annual Reunion of the Survivors Association of the Seventy-Seventh Regiment, 1915," Saratoga Springs Public Library, Saratoga Room, Saratoga Springs, N.Y.
16. Bell Irvin Wiley, *Embattled Confederates* (New York: Bonanza Books, 1964), 97.
17. Donald Chipman, "An Essex County Soldier in the Civil War: The Diary of Cyrille Fountain," New York History: Quarterly Journal of the New York Historical Society (Cooperstown, N.Y., 1985), 291.
18. 23rd Reunion of the 77th New York State Volunteers Survivors Association, "The Bemis Heights Battalion, Annual Reunion of the Seventy-Seventh Survivors, 1895," City Historian, Saratoga Springs, N.Y.
19. 24th Reunion of the 77th New York State Volunteers Survivors Association, "Veterans Reunion, The Gathering of the Survivors of the Seventy-Seventh, 1896," City Historian, Saratoga Springs, N.Y.
20. 43rd Reunion of the 77th New York State Volunteers Survivors Association, "Report of the Forty-Third Annual Reunion of the Survivors Association of the Seventy-Seventh Regiment, 1915," Saratoga Springs Public Library, Saratoga Room, Saratoga Springs, N.Y.
21. 23rd Reunion of the 77th New York State Volunteers Survivors Association, "The Bemis Heights Battalion, Annual Reunion of the Seventy-Seventh Survivors, 1895," City Historian, Saratoga Springs, N.Y.
22. *Confederate Veteran*, Vol. 6, No. 9, Nashville, Tenn., September 1898.
23. William D. Matter, *If It Takes All Summer* (Chapel Hill, N.C.: University of North Carolina Press, 1988), 208–209.
24. Gordon C. Rhea, *The Battles for Spotsylvania Court House and the Road to the Yellow Tavern* (Baton Rouge: Louisiana State University Press, 1997), 262.

25. Frederick David Bidwell, *History of the 49th New York Volunteers* (Albany, N.Y., J. B. Lyon Co., 1916), 56–57.
26. "From the 77th," *Saratogian,* Saratoga Springs, N.Y., May 17, 1864.
27. Donald Chipman, "An Essex County Soldier in the Civil War: The Diary of Cyrille Fountain," New York History: Quarterly Journal of the New York Historical Society (Cooperstown, N.Y., 1985), 291.
28. Mason W. Tyler, *Recollections of the Civil War* (New York: G. Putnam's Sons, 1912), 195–196.
29. "From the 77th," *Saratogian,* Saratoga Springs, N.Y., June 23, 1864.
30. Norman Fox Jr., Letter to his brother, Louise Barker's Fox Family Collection, Winchester, Mass.
31. George T. Stevens, *Three Years in the Sixth Corps* (Albany, N.Y.: S. R. Gray Publisher, 1866), 345–346.
32. Ibid., 337.

CHAPTER 16

1. "From the 77th," *Saratogian,* Saratoga Springs, N.Y., July 1864.
2. George T. Stevens, *Three Years in the Sixth Corps* (Albany, N.Y.: S. R. Gray Publisher, 1866), 348.
3. Ibid., 349.
4. Ibid., 162.
5. George Bolton's Widows Pension Request, Rita O'Brien's Private Collection, Woodstock, Ill.
6. Martin Lennon, Letters and Diary, Fifth Annual Report of the New York State Bureau of Military Statistics, 1866, New York State Library, Albany, N.Y., 741–742.
7. George T. Stevens, *Three Years in the Sixth Corps* (Albany, N.Y.: S. R. Gray Publisher, 1866), 354.
8. 37th Reunion of the 77th New York State Volunteers Survivors Association, "Report of the Thirty-Seventh Annual Reunion, 1909," United States Army Military History Institute Collection, Carlisle Barracks, Pa.
9. George T. Stevens, *Three Years in the Sixth Corps* (Albany, N.Y.: S. R. Gray Publisher, 1866), 96–97.
10. James M. Greiner, Janet L. Coryell, & James R. Smither, *A Surgeon's Civil War, The Letters and Diary of Daniel M. Holt* (Kent, Ohio: The Kent State University Press, 1994), 203.
11. "From the 77th," *Saratogian*, Saratoga Springs, N.Y., July 1864.
12. Nathan S. Babcock, Letter to Mort Brockway, June 21, 1864, Jerry Babcock Collection, Omaha, Nebr.
13. Martin Lennon, Letters and Diary, Fifth Annual Report of the New York State Bureau of Military Statistics, 1866, New York State Library, Albany, N.Y., 742–743.
14. Lewis A. Grant, "The Old Vermont Brigade at Petersburg," A paper read before the Minnesota Commandery of the Military Order of the Loyal Legions (M.O.L.L.U.S.) (Minneapolis, Minn.: Minnesota State Library, 1887), 10.
15. Nathan S. Babcock, Letter to Mort Brockway, June 21, 1864, Jerry Babcock Collection, Omaha, Nebr.; 21st Reunion of the 77th New York State Volunteers Survivors Association, "The Brave Seventy-Seventh, A Jolly Reunion Held by the Boys at Schenectady 1893," City Historian, Saratoga Springs, N.Y.
16. Caroline Halstead Royce, *Bessboro: A History of Westport* (Essex County, N.Y.: Privately Published, 1885), 521.

17. George T. Stevens, *Three Years in the Sixth Corps* (Albany, N.Y.: S. R. Gray Publisher, 1866), 364; 21st Reunion of the 77th New York State Volunteers Survivors Association, "The Brave Seventy-Seventh, a Jolly Reunion Held by the Boys at Schenectady 1893," City Historian, Saratoga Springs, N.Y.; Caroline Halstead Royce, *Bessboro: A History of Westport* (Essex County, N.Y.: Privately Published, 1885), 521.
18. Lewis A. Grant, "The Old Vermont Brigade at Petersburg," A paper read before the Minnesota Commandery of the Military Order of the Loyal Legions (M.O.L.L.U.S.), (Minneapolis, Minn.: Minnesota State Library, 1887), 10; Ernest B. Furguson, *Not War But Murder, Cold Harbor 1864* (New York: Alfred A. Knopf, 2000).
19. Nathan S. Babcock, Letter to Mort Brockway, June 21, 1864, Jerry Babcock Collection, Omaha, Nebr.
20. Martin Lennon, Letters and Diary, Fifth Annual Report of the New York State Bureau of Military Statistics, 1866, New York State Library, Albany, N.Y., 745.
21. Ibid., 744.
22. Nathan S. Babcock, Letter to Mort Brockway, June 21, 1864, Jerry Babcock Collection, Omaha, Nebr.
23. James E. Reid, Curtis Scrap Book of Clippings from the Ballston Journal (Saratoga Springs Public Library, Saratoga Room, Saratoga Springs, N.Y.)
24. Martin Lennon, Letters and Diary, Fifth Annual Report of the New York State Bureau of Military Statistics, 1866, New York State Library, Albany, N.Y., 745.

CHAPTER 17

1. Bruce Catton, *A Stillness at Appomattox* (New York: Anchor Books, Doubleday, 1953), 262.
2. George T. Stevens, *Three Years in the Sixth Corps* (Albany, N.Y.: S. R. Gray Publisher, 1866), 371.
3. 29th Reunion of the 77th New York State Volunteers Survivors Association, "The Survivors' Association of the Seventy-Seventh Regiment New York Volunteers, 1901," United States Army Military History Institute Collection, Carlisle Barracks, Pa.
4. Larry Tagg, *The Generals of Gettysburg* (Campbell, Calif.: Savas Printing Company, 1998), 256.
5. Ibid., 257.
6. Ibid., 258–259; Ezra J. Warner, *Generals in Gray* (Baton Rouge: Louisiana University, 1959), 79–80; Millard Kessler Bushong, *Old Jube, A Biography of General Jubal A. Early* (Boyce, Va.: Carr Publishing Co., 1955), 235.
7. 43rd Reunion of the 77th New York State Volunteers Survivors Association, "Report of the Forty-Third Annual Reunion of the Survivors Association of the Seventy-Seventh Regiment, 1915," Saratoga Springs Public Library; Saratoga Room, Saratoga Springs, N.Y.
8. Joseph Judge, *Season of Fire, The Confederate Strike on Washington* (Berryville, Va.: Rockbridge Publishing Company, 1994), 235–236.
9. 29th Reunion of the 77th New York State Volunteers Survivors Association, "The Survivors' Association of the Seventy-Seventh Regiment New York Volunteers,1901," United States Army Military History Institute Collection, Carlisle Barracks, Pa.
10. Edward H. Fuller, "Battles of the Seventy-Seventh New York State Foot Volunteers," United States Army Military History Institute Collection, Carlisle Barracks, Pa.

11. Isaac O. Best, *History of the 121st New York State Infantry* (Chicago, Ill.: Published by Lieutenant Jas. H. Smith, 1921), 170.
12. 29th Reunion of the 77th New York State Volunteers Survivors Association, "The Survivors' Association of the Seventy-Seventh Regiment New York Volunteers,1901," United States Army Military History Institute Collection, Carlisle Barracks, Pa.; Augustus Buell, *The Cannoneer Recollections of Service in the Army of the Potomac* (Washington, D.C.: The National Tribune, 1890), 268; Isaac O. Best, *History of the 121st New York State Infantry* (Chicago, Ill.: Published by Lieut. Jas. H. Smith, Chicago, Ill, 1921), 170.
13. Ibid.
14. Augustus Buell, *The Cannoneer Recollections of Service in the Army of the Potomac* (Washington, D.C., *The National Tribune*, 1890), 269–270.
15. George T. Stevens, *Three Years in The Sixth Corps* (Albany, N.Y.: S. R. Gray Publisher, 1866), 373.
16. Donald Chipman, "An Essex County Soldier in the Civil War: The Diary of Cyrille Fountain," New York History: Quarterly Journal of the New York Historical Society (Cooperstown, N.Y., 1985), 300.
17. 43rd Reunion of the 77th New York State Volunteers Survivors Association, "Report of the Forty-Third Annual Reunion of the Survivors Association of the Seventy-Seventh Regiment, 1915," Saratoga Springs Public Library, Saratoga Room, Saratoga Springs, N.Y.
18. Frederick David Bidwell, *History of the 49th New York Volunteers* (Albany, N.Y.: J. B. Lyon Company, 1916), 102.
19. Ezra J. Warner, *Generals in Blue* (Baton Rouge: Louisiana University, 1964), 32–33.
20. Frederick David Bidwell, *History of the 49th New York Volunteers* (Albany, N.Y.: J. B. Lyon Company, 1916), 102.
21. Joseph Judge, *Season of Fire: The Confederate Strike on Washington* (Berryville, Va.: Rockbridge Publishing Company, 1994), 249.
22. Benjamin Franklin Cooling, *Symbol, Sword, and Shield: Defending Washington during the Civil War* (North Haven, Conn.: Archon Books, 1975), 204–208.
23. Ibid., 249.
24. George T. Stevens, Letter to his wife, July 12, 1864, George T. Stevens Papers, William L. Clements Library, University of Michigan, Schoff Civil War Collection.
25. James M. Greiner, Janet L. Coryell, and James R. Smither, *A Surgeon's Civil War, The Letters and Diary of Daniel M. Holt* (Kent, Ohio: The Kent State University Press, 1994), 220.
26. Ibid.
27. George T. Stevens, Letter to his wife, July 12, 1864, George T. Stevens Papers, William L. Clements Library, University of Michigan, Schoff Civil War Collection.
28. Frederick David Bidwell, *History of the 49th New York Volunteers* (Albany, N.Y.: J. B. Lyon Company, 1916), 64.
29. Aldace Walker, *The Vermont Brigade in the Shenandoah* (Burlington, Vt.: Free Press, 1869).
30. 42nd Reunion of the 77th New York State Volunteers Survivors Association, "Report of the Forty-Second Annual Reunion, 1914," United States Army Military History Institute Collection, Carlisle Barracks, Pa.
31. Nathaniel Bartlett Sylvester, *History of Saratoga, New York* (Interlaken, N.Y.: Heart of the Lakes Publishing, 1979), 112.
32. Elisha Hunt Rhodes, *All for the Union: The Civil War Diary and Letters of Elisha Hunt Rhodes* (New York: Orion Books, 1985), 169–170.

33. James M. Greiner, Janet L. Coryell, and James R. Smither, *A Surgeon's Civil War, The Letters and Diary of Daniel M. Holt* (Kent, Ohio: The Kent State University Press, 1994), 218.
34. Ibid.
35. 43rd Reunion of the 77th New York State Volunteers Survivors Association, "Report of the Forty-Third Annual Reunion of the Survivors Association of the Seventy-Seventh Regiment, 1915," Saratoga Springs Public Library; Saratoga Room, Saratoga Springs, N.Y.
36. 33rd Reunion of the 77th New York State Volunteers Survivors Association, "Veterans of Civil Conflict in Annual Reunion at Gansevoort, 1905," New York City Public Library.
37. Aldace Walker, *The Vermont Brigade in the Shenandoah* (Burlington, Vt.: Free Press, 1869).
38. Ibid.
39. George T. Stevens, *Three Years in the Sixth Corps* (Albany, N.Y.: S. R. Gray Publisher, 1866), 378.
40. Benjamin Franklin Cooling, *Symbol, Sword, and Shield, Defending Washington during the Civil War* (North Haven, Conn.: Archon Books, 1975), 210.
41. 29th Reunion of the 77th New York State Volunteers Survivors Association, "The Survivors' Association of the Seventy-Seventh Regiment New York Volunteers,1901," United States Army Military History Institute Collection, Carlisle Barracks, Pa.
42. Thomas P. Lowry, *The Story the Soldiers Wouldn't Tell, Sex in the Civil War* (Harrisburg, Pa.: Stackpole Books, 1994), 68; Shelby Foote, *The Civil War: A Narrative, vol. 2, Fredericksburg to Meridian* (New York: Random House, 1958–74), 152.
43. Mark Mayo Boatner, *Civil War Dictionary* (New York: David McKay and Co., 1959), 329–330.
44. Papers of the Military Historical Society of Massachusetts, *The Wilderness Campaign May–June 1864* (Ferdinand Street, Boston: Cadet Armory, 1905), 180.
45. Richard O'Connor, *Sheridan the Inevitable* (Indianapolis, Ind.: Bobbs-Merrill Company, 1953), 188.

CHAPTER 18

1. Richard O'Connor, *Sheridan the Inevitable* (Indianapolis, Ind.: Bobbs-Merrill Company, 1953), 150–151.
2. Millard Kessler Bushong, *Old Jube, A Biography of General Jubal A. Early* (Boyce, Va.: Carr Publishing Company, 1955), 231.
3. Richard O'Connor, *Sheridan the Inevitable* (Indianapolis, Ind.: Bobbs-Merrill Company, 1953), 21–53.
4. Ibid.
5. John William DeForest, *A Volunteer's Adventures: A Union Captain's Record of the Civil War* (New Haven, Conn.: Yale University Press, 1904), 165.
6. Bruce Catton, *A Stillness at Appomattox* (New York: Anchor Books, Doubleday, 1951), 280.
7. George T. Stevens, *Three Years in the Sixth Corps* (Albany, N.Y.: S. R. Gray Publisher, 1866), 391.
8. Ibid.
9. Aldace Walker, *The Vermont Brigade in the Shenandoah* (Burlington, Vt.: Free Press, 1869), 70–88.
10. Edward H. Fuller, "Battles of the Seventy-Seventh New York State Foot Volunteers," United States Army Military History Institute Collection, Carlisle Barracks, Pa.

11. Millard Kessler Bushong, *Old Jube, A Biography of General Jubal A. Early* (Boyce, Va.: Carr Publishing Company, 1955), 237.
12. War Rebellion, A Compilation of the Official Records of the Union and Confederate Armies (Washington, D.C.: Government Printing Office, 1891 Official Reports–series I, vol. 90/1, report no. 46.
13. George T. Stevens, *Three Years in the Sixth Corps* (Albany, N.Y.: S. R. Gray Publisher, 1866), 399.
14. Augustus Buell, *The Cannoneer Recollections of Service in the Army of the Potomac* (Washington, D.C.: The National Tribune, 1890), 278–279.
15. 29th Reunion of the 77th New York State Volunteers Survivors Association, "The Survivors' Association of the Seventy-Seventh Regiment New York Volunteers,1901," United States Army Military History Institute Collection, Carlisle Barracks, Pa.; 44th Reunion of the 77th New York State Volunteers Survivors Association, "Report of the Forty-Fourth Annual Reunion,1916," National Archives, Washington, D.C.
16. Caroline Halstead Royce, *Bessboro: A History of Westport* (Essex County, N.Y.: Privately Published, 1885), 522–523.
17. Frederick David Bidwell, *History of the 49th New York Volunteers* (Albany, N.Y.: J. B. Lyon Company, 1916), 70–71.
18. Ibid., 73.
19. "From the 77th," *Saratogian*, Saratoga Springs, N.Y., October 1864.
20. Ibid.
21. Martin Lennon, Letters and Diary, *Fifth Annual Report of the New York State Bureau of Military Statistics,* New York State Library, Albany, N.Y.
22. Aldace Walker, *The Vermont Brigade in the Shenandoah* (Burlington, Vt.: Free Press, 1869), 70–88.
23. "From the 77th," *Saratogian*, Saratoga Springs, N.Y., September 24, 1864.

CHAPTER 19

1. Martin Lennon, Letters and Diary, *Fifth Annual Report of the New York State Bureau of Military Statistics,* New York State Library, Albany, N.Y.
2. Donald Chipman, "An Essex County Soldier in the Civil War: The Diary of Cyrille Fountain," New York History: Quarterly Journal of the New York Historical Society (Cooperstown, N.Y., 1985), 313.
3. Bell Irvin Wiley, and Hirst D. Milhollen, *Embattled Confederates* (New York: Harper & Row Bonanza Books, 1964), 48.
4. John William DeForest, *A Volunteer's Adventures: A Union Captain's Record of the Civil War* (New Haven, Conn.: Yale University Press, 1904), 209.
5. Henry Steele Commager, *The Blue and the Gray,* vol. 2 (Indianapolis, Ind.: Bobbs-Merrill Co., 1950), 1052–1055.
6. Aldace Walker, *The Vermont Brigade in the Shenandoah* (Burlington, Vt.: Free Press, 1869).
7. Ibid.
8. 28th Reunion of the 77th New York State Volunteers Survivors Association, "The 77th New York Veteran Association in Gansevoort, 1900." City Historian, Saratoga Springs, N.Y.
9. Aldace Walker, *The Vermont Brigade in the Shenandoah* (Burlington, Vt.: Free Press, 1869).
10. John William DeForest, *A Volunteer's Adventures: A Union Captain's Record of the Civil War* (New Haven, Conn.: Yale University Press, 1904), 217.

11. Henry Steele Commager, *The Blue and the Gray, vol. 2* (Indianapolis, Ind.: Bobbs-Merrill Company, 1950), 1052–1055.
12. Douglas Southall Freeman, *Lee's Lieutenants, A Study in Command* (New York: Charles Scribner's Sons, 1944), 3–604.
13. Official Records, Series 1, Vol. 43/1 (S#90) Aug. 7-Nov. 28, 1864, The Shenandoah Campaign, No. 46, Reports of Lt. Col. Winsor B. French, Seventy-Seventh New York
14. Larry Tagg. *The Generals of Gettysburg* (Campbell, Calif.: Savas Printing Company, 1998), 221.
15. George T. Stevens, *Three Years in the Sixth Corps* (Albany, N.Y.: S. R. Gray Publisher, 1866), 419.
16. Charles E. Stevens, Letter to the Editor of the *National Tribune*, "Sketch of the 77th New York, 1908."
17. 46th Reunion of the 77th New York State Volunteers Survivors Association, "The Forty-Sixth Annual Reunion of the Saratoga Regiment, the 77th Infantry Volunteers at 1861–65, 1918," City Historian, Saratoga Springs, N.Y.
18. 29th Reunion of the 77th New York State Volunteers Survivors Association, "The Survivors' Association of the Seventy-Seventh Regiment New York Volunteers,1901," United States Army Military History Institute Collection, Carlisle Barracks, Pa.
19. Aldace Walker, *The Vermont Brigade in the Shenandoah* (Burlington, Vt.: Free Press, 1869).
20. Ibid.
21. Frederick David Bidwell, *History of the 49th New York Volunteers* (Albany, N.Y.: J. B. Lyon Company, 1916), 120.
22. Bruce Catton, *A Stillness at Appomattox* (New York.: Anchor Books, Doubleday, 1951), 314.
23. Edward H. Fuller, "Battles of the Seventy-Seventh New York State Foot Volunteers," United States Army Military History Institute Collection, Carlisle Barracks, Pa.
24. "When Caw and Cramer Were Defending the Union," *Schenectady Union Star*, April 30, 1912.
25. Richard O'Connor, *Sheridan the Inevitable* (Indianapolis, Ind.: Bobbs-Merrill Company, 1953), 229.
26. Larry Tagg, *The Generals of Gettysburg* (Campbell, Calif.: Savas Printing Company, 1998), 289.
27. Nathaniel Bartlett Sylvester, *History of Saratoga County, New York* (Interlaken, N.Y.: Heart of the Lakes Publishing, 1979), 114.
28. George T. Stevens, *Three Years in the Sixth Corps* (Albany, N.Y.: S. R. Gray Publisher, 1866), 425.
29. "When Caw and Cramer Were Defending the Union," *Schenectady Union Star*, April 30, 1912.

CHAPTER 20

1. "The 77th," *Saratogian*, Saratoga Springs, N.Y., January 7, 1864.
2. Ibid.
3. John Michael Priest, *Turn Them Out to Die Like a Mule: The Civil War Letters of Hospital Steward John N. Henry, 49th New York, 1861–1865* (Leesburg, Va.: Gauley Mount Press, 1995), 407–413.
4. Thomas W. Hyde, *Following the Greek Cross or Memories of the Sixth Corps* (Boston, Mass.: Houghton Mifflin and Co., 1894), 238.

5. George Parsons, *Put the Vermonters Ahead: The First Vermont Brigade in the Civil War* (White Mane Publishing, Shippensburg, Pa., 1996), 138–139.
6. John Michael Priest, *Turn Them Out to Die Like a Mule: The Civil War Letters of Hospital Steward John N. Henry, 49th New York, 1861–1865* (Leesburg, Va.: Gauley Mount Press, 1995), 407–413.
7. Ibid.
8. Ibid.
9. "The 77th Battalion," *Saratogian,* Saratoga Springs, N.Y., January 19, 1865.
10. Thomas W. Hyde, *Following the Greek Cross or Memories of the Sixth Corps* (Boston, Mass.: Houghton Mifflin and Co., 1894), 238.
11. Timothy B. Mudgett, *Make the Fur Fly: A History of a Union Volunteer Division* (Shippensburg, Pa.: Burd Street Press, 1997), 115.
12. Lewis A. Grant, "The Old Vermont Brigade at Petersburg," 1887, A paper read before the Minnesota Commandery of the Military Order of the Loyal Legions (M.O.L.L.U. S.), 10.
13. Thomas W. Hyde, *Civil War Letters of General Thomas Hyde* (Privately Printed, 1933).
14. Donald Chipman, "An Essex County Soldier in the Civil War: The Diary of Cyrille Fountain," New York History: Quarterly Journal of the New York Historical Society (Cooperstown, N.Y., 1985), Dec. 25, 1864.
15. Thomas W. Hyde, *Following the Greek Cross or Memories of the Sixth Corps* (Boston, Mass.: Houghton Mifflin and Co., 1894), 238.
16. "The 77th Battalion," *Saratogian,* Saratoga Springs, N.Y., January 19, 1865.
17. Ibid.
18. Thomas W. Hyde, *Following the Greek Cross or Memories of the Sixth Corps* (Boston, Mass.: Houghton Mifflin and Co., 1894), 241.
19. Hazard Stevens, "The Battle of Sailor's Creek," Papers of the Military Historical Society of Mass, vol. 6, 1907, 409–436.
20. Thomas W. Hyde, *Following the Greek Cross or Memories of the Sixth Corps* (Boston, Mass.: Houghton Mifflin and Co., 1894), 244.
21. Ibid., 245–246.
22. Hazard Stevens, "The Storming of the Lines at Petersburg by the Sixth Corps, April 2, 1865," Papers of the Military Historical Society of Massachusetts, vol. 6, 1907.
23. George T. Stevens, *Three Years in the Sixth Corps* (Albany, N.Y.: S. R. Gray Publisher, 1866).
24. Edwin Bearss, "The VI Corps Scores A Breakthrough," n.d. (pamphlet) Petersburg National Battlefield.
25. Ibid.
26. Ibid.
27. Elisha Hunt Rhodes, *All for the Union: The Civil War Diary and Letters of Elisha Hunt Rhodes* (New York: Orion Books, 1985), 224–227.
28. Hazard Stevens, "The Storming of the Lines at Petersburg by the Sixth Corps, April 2, 1865," Papers of the Military Historical Society of Massachusetts, vol. 6, 1907, 409–436.
29. Frank J. Welcher, *The Union Army, 1861–1865, Organization and Operations, vol. 1: The Eastern Theater* (Indianapolis, Ind.: Indiana University Press, 1989), 416; Edwin Bearss, "The VI Corps Scores A Breakthrough," n.d. (pamphlet) Petersburg National Battlefield.

30. 24th Reunion of the 77th New York State Volunteers Survivors Association, "Veterans Reunion, The Gathering of the Survivors of the Seventy-Seventh, 1896," City Historian, Saratoga Springs, N.Y.
31. Hazard Stevens, "The Storming of the Lines at Petersburg by the Sixth Corps, April 2, 1865," Papers of the Military Historical Society of Massachusetts, vol. 6, 1907, 409–436.
32. 39th Reunion of the 77th New York State Volunteers Survivors Association, "Report of the Thirty-Ninth Annual Reunion of the Survivors Association of the Seventy-Seventh Regiment, 1911," Saratoga Springs Public Library, Saratoga Room, Saratoga Springs, N.Y.; War Rebellion, A Compilation of the Official Records of the Union and Confederate Armies (Washington, D.C.: Government Printing Office, 1891, Official Reports, Series 1, vol. 95/1.
33. Ibid.
34. Ibid.
35. Hazard Stevens, "The Battle of Sailor's Creek," Papers of the Military Historical Society of Massachusetts, vol. 6, 1907, 447.
36. Bruce Catton, *A Stillness at Appomattox* (New York: Anchor Books, Doubleday, 1953), 372–373.
37. Frank J. Welcher, *The Union Army, 1861–1865, Organization and Operations vol. 1: The Eastern Theater* (Indianapolis, Ind.: Indiana University Press, 1989), 416.

CHAPTER 21

1. William Caw, Letter to E. Z. Carpenter, May 5, 1865, Schenectady County Historical Society, E. Z. Carpenter Papers, Schenectady, N.Y.
2. 20th Reunion of the 77th New York State Volunteers Survivors Association,"The Seventy-Seventh, Official Report of the Twentieth Reunion,1892," City Historian, Saratoga Springs, N.Y.; Thomas W. Hyde, *Following the Greek Cross or Memories of the Sixth Corps* (Boston, Mass.: Houghton, 1894), 267.
3. Frank J. Welcher, *The Union Army, 1861–1865, Organization and Operations, vol.1: The Eastern Theater* (Indianapolis, Ind.: Indiana University Press, 1989), 547.
4. 39th Reunion of the 77th New York State Volunteers Survivors Association, "Report of the Thirty-Ninth Annual Reunion of the Survivors Association of the Seventy-Seventh Regiment, 1911," Saratoga Springs Public Library, Saratoga Room, Saratoga Springs, N.Y.
5. James Moore, M.D., *History of the Cooper Shop Volunteer Refreshment Saloon* (Philadelphia, Pa.: Jas. B. Rodgers Publishers, 1866), 199.
6. 39th Reunion of the 77th New York State Volunteers Survivors Association, "Report of the Thirty-Ninth Annual Reunion of the Survivors Association of the Seventy-Seventh Regiment, 1911," Saratoga Springs Public Library, Saratoga Room, Saratoga Springs, N.Y.
7. "The 77th," *Saratogian,* Saratoga Springs, N.Y., June 24, 1865.
8. Edward H. Fuller, "Battles of the Seventy-Seventh New York State Foot Volunteers," United States Army Military History Institute Collection, Carlisle Barracks, Pa.
9. New York Monuments Commission, *New York at Gettysburg, vol. 2* (Albany, N.Y.: J. B. Lyon Co., State Printers, 1902), 237.
10. 39th Reunion of the 77th New York State Volunteers Survivors Association, "Report of the Thirty-Ninth Annual Reunion of the Survivors Association of the Seventy-Seventh Regiment, 1911," Saratoga Springs Public Library, Saratoga Room, Saratoga Springs, N.Y.

11. George T. Stevens, *Three Years in the Sixth Corps* (Albany, N.Y.: S. R. Gray Publisher, 1866).

CHAPTER 22

1. 39th Reunion of the 77th New York State Volunteers Survivors Association, "Report of the Thirty-Ninth Annual Reunion of the Survivors Association of the Seventy-Seventh Regiment, 1911," Saratoga Springs Public Library, Saratoga Room, Saratoga Springs, N.Y.
2. "First Reunion," *Saratogian*, Saratoga Springs, N.Y., October 21–22, 1873.
3. 28th Reunion of the 77th New York State Volunteers Survivors Association, "The 77th New York Veteran Association in Gansevoort,1900," City Historian, Saratoga Springs, N.Y.
4. 33rd Reunion of the 77th New York State Volunteers Survivors Association. "Veterans of Civil Conflict in Annual Reunion at Gansevoort, 1905," New York City Public Library, New York.
5. *Saratogian,* Saratoga Springs, N.Y., October 25, 1892; 20th Reunion of the 77th New York State Volunteers Survivors Association, "The Seventy-Seventh, Official Report of the Twentieth Reunion, 1892," City Historian, Saratoga Springs, N.Y.
6. 44th Reunion of the 77th New York State Volunteers Survivors Association, "Report of the Forty-Fourth Annual Reunion, 1916," National Archives, Washington, D.C.
7. Ibid.
8. 33rd Reunion of the 77th New York State Volunteers Survivors Association, "Veterans of Civil Conflict in Annual Reunion at Gansevoort, 1905," New York City Public Library, New York.
9. Cornelius E. Durkee, "Reminiscences of Saratoga," Reprinted from *Saratogian*, Saratoga Springs, N.Y., "77th Regt. N.Y. Vols.," *Saratogian*, September 20–22, 1875.
10. Ibid.
11. New York Monuments Commission, *New York at Gettysburg, vol. 3* (Albany, N.Y.: J. B. Lyon Co. State Printers, 1902), 1392.
12. Ibid., 620.
13. 44th Reunion of the 77th New York State Volunteers Survivors Association, "Report of the Forty-Fourth Annual Reunion, 1916," National Archives, Washington, D.C.

CHAPTER 23

1. William F. Fox, *Regimental Losses in the American Civil War 1861–1865* (Albany, N.Y.: Albany Publishing Co., 1889).
2. 20th Reunion of the 77th New York State Volunteers Survivors Association, "The Seventy-Seventh, Official Report of the Twentieth Reunion,1892," City Historian, Saratoga Springs, N.Y.; Augustus Buell, *The Cannoneer: Recollections of Service in the Army of the Potomac* (Washington, D.C.: The National Tribune, 1890), 302, 303.
3. Ibid.
4. Bruce Catton, *A Stillness at Appomattox* (New York: Doubleday, 1953), 348.
5. Richard E. Winslow, *John Sedgwick: The Story of a Union Corps Commander* (Novato, Calif.: Presidio Press, 1982), 86.
6. William M. Owen, *In Camp and Battle with the Washington Artillery of New Orleans* (Baton Rouge, La.: LSU Press, 1999), 221.
7. Ibid.

8. John Michael Priest, *Victory Without Triumph: The Wilderness, May 6th & 7th, 1864* (Shippensburg, Pa.: White Mane Publishing, 1996), 184–190.
9. Douglas Southall Freeman, *Lee's Lieutenants: A Study in Command,* vol. 3 (New York: Charles Scribner's Sons, 1944), 604.
10. Augustus Buell, *"The Cannoneer: Recollections of Service in the Army of the Potomac* (Washington, D.C.: *The National Tribune,* 1890), 302–303.
11. Military Historical Society of Massachusetts, *The Wilderness Campaign May-June 1864, vol. 4,* 192.
12. Ibid.
13. Aldace Walker, *The Vermont Brigade in the Shenandoah* (Burlington, Vt.: Free Press, 1869).
14. Nathaniel Bartlett Sylvester, *History of Saratoga County, New York* (Interlaken, N.Y.: Heart of the Lakes Publishing, 1979), 118.
15. 43rd Reunion of the 77th New York State Volunteers Survivors Association, "Report of the Forty-Third Annual Reunion of the Survivors Association of the Seventy-Seventh Regiment, 1915," Saratoga Springs Public Library, Saratoga Room, Saratoga Springs, N.Y.
16. "From the 77th," *Saratogian,* Saratoga Springs, N.Y., March 8, 1864.
17. 39th Reunion of the 77th New York State Volunteers Survivors Association, "Report of the Thirty-Ninth Annual Reunion of the Survivors Association of the Seventy-Seventh Regiment, 1911," Saratoga Springs Public Library, Saratoga Room, Saratoga Springs, N.Y.
18. 43rd Reunion of the 77th New York State Volunteers Survivors Association, "Report of the Forty-Third Annual Reunion of the Survivors Association of the Seventy-Seventh Regiment, 1915," Saratoga Springs Public Library, Saratoga Room, Saratoga Springs, N.Y.
19. Ibid.

Bibliography

20th Reunion of the 77th New York State Volunteers Survivors Association. "The Seventy-Seventh, Official Report of the Twentieth Reunion, 1892." City Historian, Saratoga Springs, N.Y.

21st Reunion of the 77th New York State Volunteers Survivors Association. "The Brave Seventy-Seventh, A Jolly Reunion held by the Boys at Schenectady, 1893." City Historian, Saratoga Springs, N.Y.

23rd Reunion of the 77th New York State Volunteers Survivors Association. "The Bemis Heights Battalion, Annual Reunion of the Seventy-Seventh Survivors, 1895." City Historian, Saratoga Springs, N.Y.

24th Reunion of the 77th New York State Volunteers Survivors Association. "Veterans Reunion, The Gathering of the Survivors of the Seventy-Seventh, 1896." City Historian, Saratoga Springs, N.Y.

25th Reunion of the 77th New York State Volunteers Survivors Association. "The Boys of the Seventy-Seventh, Full Account of their Annual Reunion, 1897." City Historian, Saratoga Springs, N.Y.

26th Reunion of the 77th New York State Volunteers Survivors Association. "The Fighters of 61, The Seventy-Seventh Boys Recall Their Battles, 1898." Saratoga Springs Historical Society, Saratoga Springs, N.Y.

28th Reunion of the 77th New York State Volunteers Survivors Association. "The 77th New York Veteran Association in Gansevoort, 1900." City Historian, Saratoga Springs, N.Y.

29th Reunion of the 77th New York State Volunteers Survivors Association. "The Survivors' Association of the Seventy-Seventh Regiment New York Volunteers, 1901." United States Army Military History Institute Collection, Carlisle Barracks, Pa.

30th Reunion of the 77th New York State Volunteers Survivors Association. "Reunion of Bemis Heights Battalion 77th foot regiment N. Y. S. vols. at Schuylerville, September 17, 1902." United States Army Military History Institute Collection, Carlisle Barracks, Pa.

31st Reunion of the 77th New York State Volunteers Survivors Association. "Reunion of Survivors Association, 77th Foot Regiment, N. Y. S. Vols. at Schenectady, Sept. 22, 1903." New York City Public Library, New York.

33rd Reunion of the 77th New York State Volunteers Survivors Association. "Veterans of Civil Conflict in Annual Reunion at Gansevoort, 1905." New York City Public Library, New York.

34th Reunion of the 77th New York State Volunteers Survivors Association. "Stories, Sketches, History of Saratoga Soldier Boys, interesting account of Annual Reunion Seventy-Seventh Regiment Survivors Association, 1906." Saratoga Springs Historical Society, Saratoga Springs, N.Y.

37th Reunion of the 77th New York State Volunteers Survivors Association. "Report Thirty-Seventh Annual Reunion, 1909." United States Army Military History Institute Collection, Carlisle Barracks, Pa.

38th Reunion of the 77th New York State Volunteers Survivors Association. "Report Thirty-Eighth Annual Reunion, 1910." United States Army Military History Institute Collection, Carlisle Barracks, Pa.

39th Reunion of the 77th New York State Volunteers Survivors Association. "Report Thirty-Ninth Annual Reunion

Bibliography 261

Survivors Association Seventy-Seventh Regiment, 1911." Saratoga Springs Public Library, Saratoga Room, Saratoga Springs, N.Y.

40th Reunion of the 77th New York State Volunteers Survivors Association. "Report Fortieth Annual Reunion, 1912." United States Army Military History Institute Collection, Carlisle Barracks, Pa.

42nd Reunion of the 77th New York State Volunteers Survivors Association. "Report Forty-Second Annual Reunion, 1914." United States Army Military History Institute Collection, Carlisle Barracks, Pa.

43rd Reunion of the 77th New York State Volunteers Survivors Association. "Report Forty-Third Annual Reunion Survivors Association Seventy-Seventh Regiment, 1915." Saratoga Springs Public Library, Saratoga Room, Saratoga Springs, N.Y.

44th Reunion of the 77th New York State Volunteers Survivors Association. "Report Forty-Fourth Annual Reunion, 1916." National Archives, Washington, D.C.

46th Reunion of the 77th New York State Volunteers Survivors Association. "The Forty-Sixth Annual Report Saratoga Regiment, the 77th Infantry Volunteers at 1861–65, 1918." City Historian, Saratoga Springs, N.Y.

Adjutant General's Report. Seventy Seventh Infantry, Official Roster, Micro Film Reels, New York State Archives, Albany, N.Y.

Ambrose, Stephen E. *Upton and the Army*. Baton Rouge, La.: Louisiana State University, 1964.

Babcock, Nathan S. Letter to Mort Brockway. June 21, 1864. Jerry Babcock's Private Collection, Omaha, Nebr.

Bauer, Daniel. "They Also Serve Who Only March, And March—The Veteran VI Corps Fights With Its Feet First." Civil War Magazine, Volume 17, Carlisle Barracks, Pa.: United States Army Military History Institute Collection, 1989.

Bearss, Edwin C. *The VI Corps Scores a Breakthrough*. N.d. (pamphlet) Petersburg National Battlefield, Va.

Best, Isaac O. *History of the 121st New York State Infantry*. Chicago, Ill.: Published by Lieutenant Jas. H. Smith, 1921.

Bidwell, Frederick David. *History of the 49th New York Volunteers*. Albany, N.Y.: J. B. Lyon and Company, 1916.

Billings, John D. *Hardtack and Coffee: The Unwritten Story of Army Life*. Williamstown, Mass.: Corner House Publishers, 1973.

Boatner, Mark Mayo. *Civil War Dictionary*. New York: David McKay Company, 1921.

Bolton, George. Letters to his Wife, Dec. 1863. Rita O'Brien's Private Collection, Woodstock, Ill.

Boritt, Gabor S. *Lincoln's Generals*. New York: Oxford University Press, 1994.

Branch, Erskine B. *A Brief Sketch of the Experience of a Union Soldier in the Late War*. United States Army Military History Institute Collection, Carlisle Barracks, Pa.

Britten, Evelyn Barrett. *Chronicles of Saratoga*. Saratoga Springs, N.Y.: Privately Published, 1959.

Buell, Augustus. *The Cannoneer Recollections of Service in the Army of the Potomac*. Washington, D.C.: *The National Tribune*, 1890.

Bushong, Millard K. *Old Jube, A Biography of Jubal A. Early*. Boyce, Va.: Carr Publishing Company, 1955.

Catton, Bruce. *A Stillness at Appomattox*. New York: Anchor Books, Doubleday, 1953.

———. *Mr. Lincoln's Army*. New York: Doubleday, 1951.

Caw, William. Letter to E. Z. Carpenter. May 5, 1863. Carpenter Papers, Schenectady Historical Society, Schenectady, N.Y.

Chipman, Donald. *An Essex County Soldier in the Civil War—The Diary of Cyrille Fountain*. Cooperstown, N.Y.: New York

History, *Quarterly Journal of the New York Historical Society*, 1985.

Clemens, Cyril. *Josh Billings—Yankee Humorist*. Webster Groves, Miss.: Mark Twain Society, 1932.

Coggins, Jack. *Arms and Equipment of the Civil War*. Garden City, N.Y.: Doubleday & Company, 1962.

Cooling, Benjamin F. *Symbol, Sword, and Shield: Defending Washington during the Civil War*. North Haven, Conn.: Archon Books, 1975.

Contant, George. *Path of Blood*. Savannah, N.Y.: Seeco Printing Services, 1997.

Davidson, Homer K. *Black Jack Davidson, A Cavalry Commander on the Western Frontier: The Life of John W. Davidson*. Glendale, Calif.: Arthur H. Clarke Company, 1974.

Day, Donald. *Uncle Sam's Uncle Josh*. Boston, Mass.: Little Brown and Company, 1953.

DeForest, John William. *A Volunteer's Adventures: A Union Captain's Record of the Civil War*. New Haven, Conn.: Yale University Press, 1904.

Durkee, Cornelius E. *Reminiscences of Saratoga*. Saratoga Springs, N.Y.: Reprinted from the *Saratogian*, 1927–1928.

Executive Committee. *Maine at Gettysburg—Report of the Maine Commissioners*. Portland, Maine: Lakeside Press, 1898.

Foote, Shelby. *The Civil War: A Narrative—Vol. 2 Fredericksburg to Meridian*. New York: Random House, 1958–74.

Ford, Christopher. *Over the Wall—The VI Corps Fredericksburg*. Fredericksburg, Va.: Fredericksburg Press, 1996.

Fox, Norman Jr. Letter to his brother, May 1863. Louise Barker's Fox Family Collection, Winchester, Mass.

Fox, William F. *Regimental Losses in the American Civil War*. Albany, N.Y.: Albany Publishing Company, 1889.

Frassanito, William A. *Grant and Lee, The Virginia Campaigns 1864–1865.* New York: Charles Scribner's Sons, 1983.

Freeman, Douglas S. *Lee's Lieutenants: A Study in Command.* New York: Charles Scribner's Sons, 1944.

Frothingham, Washington. *History of Fulton County.* Syracuse, N.Y.: D. Mason and Company Printers and Publishers, 1892.

Fuller, Edward H. *Battles of the Seventy-Seventh New York State Foot Volunteers.* Carlisle Barracks, Pa.: United States Army Military History Institute's Collection, 1901.

Fuller, T. Scott. Letters to his mother, March and Dec. 21, 1863. Saratoga Springs Historical Society, Saratoga Springs, N.Y.

Furgurson, Ernst B. *Chancellorsville 1863: The Souls of the Brave.* New York: Alfred A. Knopf, 1992.

———. *Not War, But Murder: Cold Harbor 1864.* New York: Alfred A. Knopf, 2000.

Grant, Lewis A. *The Old Vermont Brigade at Petersburg.* A paper read before the Minnesota Commandery of the Military Order of the Loyal Legions (M.O.L.L.U.S.), Minneapolis, Minn.: Minnesota State Library, 1887.

Greiner, James M., Janet L. Coryell, and James R. Smither. *A Surgeon's Civil War: The Letters and Diary of Daniel M. Holt.* Kent, Ohio: Kent State University Press, 1994.

Gross, Edward F. *Centennial History of the Village of Ballston Spa.* Ballston Spa, N.Y.: Ballston Journal, 1847.

Hebert, Walter H. *Fighting Joe Hooker.* New York: Bobbs Merrill Company, 1944.

Hyde, Thomas W. *Civil War Letters of General Thomas Hyde.* Privately Printed, 1933.

———. *Following the Greek Cross or Memories of the Sixth Corps.* Boston, Mass.: Houghton Mifflin and Co., 1894.

Jewel, Altus. Letter to his sister. June 18, 1863. Warren K. Tice Collection at the United States Army Military History Institute, Carlisle Barracks, Pa.

Judge, Joseph. *Season of Fire: The Confederate Strike on Washington*. Berryville, Va.: Rockbridge Publishing Company, 1994.

Lennon, Captain Martin. Letters and Diary. *Fifth Annual Report of the New York State Bureau of Military Statistics*. New York State Library, Albany, N.Y.

Lewis, Thomas A. *The Guns of Cedar Creek*. New York: Harper & Row Publishers, 1988.

Lodell, Isaac. Letter to his wife. May 12, 1864. Jerry Babcock's Private Collection, Omaha, Nebr.

Lowry, Thomas P. *The Story the Soldiers Wouldn't Tell: Sex in the Civil War*. Harrisburg, Pa.: Stackpole Books, 1994.

Luvaas, Jay, and Harold W. Nelson. *The U.S. Army War College Guide to the Battles of Chancellorsville and Fredericksburg*. New York: Harper & Row Publishers, 1988.

Marvel, William. *Burnside*. Chapel Hill, N.C.: University of North Carolina Press, 1991.

Mather, William D. *If It Takes All Summer*. Chapel Hill, N.C.: University of North Carolina Press, 1988.

Moore, James, M.D. *History of the Cooper Shop Volunteer Refreshment Saloon*. Philadelphia, Pa.: Jas. B. Rodgers Publishers, 1866.

Mudgett, Timothy. *Make the Fur Fly: A History of a Union Volunteer Division*. Shippensburg, Pa.: Burd Street Press, 1997.

New York (State) Monuments Commission. *New York at Gettysburg*, vol. 2. Albany, N.Y.: J. B. Lyon Company, Printers, 1902.

O'Connor, Richard. *Sheridan the Inevitable*. Indianapolis, Ind.: Bobbs Merrill Company, 1953.

Owen, William M. *In Camp and Battle with the Washington Artillery of New Orleans*. Baton Rouge, La.: Louisiana State University, 1999.

Papers of the Military Historical Society of Massachusetts. *Campaigns in Virginia 1861–1862.* New York: Houghton Mifflin Company, 1895.

Parsons, George. *Put the Vermonters Ahead.* Shippensburg, Pa.: White Mane Publishing, 1996.

Phisterer, Frederick. *War of the Rebellion, 1861 to 1865, vol. 1.* Albany, N.Y.: L. B. Lyon Company, State Printers, 1913.

Priest, John Michael. *Antietam: The Soldiers' Battle.* Shippensburg, Pa.: White Mane Publishing, 1989.

———.*Victory Without Triumph: The Wilderness, May 6th & 7th, 1864.* Shippensburg, Pa.: White Mane Publishing, 1996.

———. *Turn Them Out to Die Like a Mule: The Civil War Letters of Hospital Steward John N. Henry, 49th New York 1861–1865.* Leesburg, Va.: Gauley Mount Press, 1995.

———. *Nowhere to Run, The Wilderness, May 4th and 5th, 1864.* Shippensburg, Pa.: White Mane Publishing, 1995.

Reid, James E. *Curtis Scrap Book of Clippings from Ballston Journal.* Saratoga Springs Public Library, Saratoga Room, Saratoga Springs, N.Y.

Rhea, Gordon C. *The Battle of the Wilderness, May 5th and 6th, 1864.* Baton Rouge, La.: University of Louisiana Press, 1994.

———. *The Battles for Spotsylvania Court House and the Road to the Yellow Tavern.* Baton Rouge, La.: University of Louisiana Press, 1997.

Rhodes, Elisha Hunt. *All for the Union: The Civil War Diary and Letters of Elisha Hunt Rhodes.* New York: Orion Books, 1985.

Royce, Caroline Halstead. *Bessboro, A History of Westport.* Essex County, N.Y.: Privately Published, 1885.

Rugg, Orrin. Letter to his parents. April 9, 1862. David Handy Collection, Cobleskill, N.Y.

Saratogian, Saratoga Springs, N.Y.

———. *Our County and its People, A Descriptive and Biographic Record of Saratoga County*. The Boston History Company Publishers.

Schenectady Gazette, Schenectady, N.Y.

Schenectady Union Star, Schenectady, N.Y.

Schiller, Herbert M. *Autobiography of Major General William F. Smith 1861–1864*. Dayton, Ohio: Morningside, 1990.

Scott, Robert Garth. *Into the Wilderness with the Army of the Potomac*. Bloomington, Ind.: Indiana University Press, 1985.

Sears, Stephen W. *To the Gates of Richmond, The Peninsular Campaign*. New York: Ticknor & Fields, 1992.

———. *George B. McClellan—The Young Napoleon*. New York: Ticknor & Fields, 1988.

———. *Landscape Turned Red, The Battle of Antietam*. New York: Ticknor & Fields, 1992.

Sedgwick, John. *Correspondence of John Sedgwick, Major General vol. 2*. Privately Printed, 1903.

Shaw, Henry W. *The Complete Works of Josh Billings*. New York: G. W. Dillingham Publishers.

Siegel, Alan A. *For the Glory of the Union: Myth, Reality, and the Media in Civil War New Jersey*. Rutherford, N.J.: Fairleigh Dickinson University, 1984.

Skinner, Robert H. Letters to Adam Clark Works. Dec. 23, 1861; Jan. 16, 1862; Mar. 28, 1862; Jul. 11, 1862; Oct. 1, 1862. Rochester, N.Y.: Adam Clark Works Papers, University of Rochester, Rush Rhees Library, Department of Rare Books, Manuscripts, Archives.

Steere, Edward. *The Wilderness Campaign*. Harrisburg, Pa.: Stackpole Company, 1960.

Stevens, Charles E. Letter to friend Cone. Dec. 17, 1863. Ed Italo's Private Collection, Ojai, Calif.

Stevens, Hazard. "General Getty Saves The Day," *The Blue and the Gray. vol. 2.* Ed. Henry Steele Commager, New York: Bobbs-Merrill Company, 1950.

———. "The Battle at Cedar Creek," *Papers of the Military Historical Society of Massachusetts. vol. 6. The Shenandoah Campaigns of 1862 and 1864, and the Appomattox Campaign of 1865*. Cadet Armory, Ferdinand Street, Boston, Mass.: Military Historical Society of Massachusetts, 1907.

———. "The Storming of the Lines at Petersburg by the VI Corps, April 2, 1865," In *Papers of the Military Historical Society of Massachusetts. vol. 6. The Shenandoah Campaigns of 1862 and 1864, and the Appomattox Campaign of 1865*. Cadet Armory, Ferdinand Street, Boston, Mass.: Military Historical Society of Massachusetts, 1907.

———. "The Battle of Sailor's Creek," In *Papers of the Military Historical Society of Massachusetts. vol. 6. The Shenandoah Campaigns of 1862 and 1864, and the Appomattox Campaign of 1865*. Cadet Armory, Ferdinand Street, Boston, Mass.: Military Historical Society of Massachusetts, 1907.

———. "VII—The Sixth Corps in the Wilderness," In *Papers of the Military Historical Society of Massachusetts. vol 4. The Wilderness Campaign May–June 1864*. Cadet Armory, Ferdinand Street, Boston, Mass.: Military Historical Society of Massachusetts, 1905.

Stevens, George T. Letter to his wife. Jul. 12, 1864. George T. Stevens Papers, University of Michigan, Ann Arbor, Mich.: William L. Clements Library, Schoff Civil War Collection.

———. *Three Years in the Sixth Corps*. Albany, N.Y.: S. R. Gray Publisher, 1866.

Sylvester, Nathaniel B. *History of Saratoga County, New York*. Interlaken, N.Y.: Heart of the Lakes Publishing, 1979.

Tagg, Larry. *The Generals of Gettysburg*. Campbell, Calif.: Savas Printing Company, 1998.

Bibliography

Tyler, Mason W. *Recollections of the Civil War.* New York.: G. Putnam's Sons, 1912.

Walker, Aldace. *The Vermont Brigade in the Shenandoah.* Burlington, Vt.: Free Press, 1869.

War of the Rebellion: A Compilation of the Official Records of the Union and Confederate Armies, Washington, D.C.: Government Printing Office, 1880.

Warner, Ezra J. *Generals in Blue.* Baton Rouge, La.: Louisiana University, 1964.

———. *Generals in Gray.* Baton Rouge, La.: Louisiana University, 1959.

Watson, William G. Diary for 1862 & 1863. Robert E. Lingow Family Papers, Archives and Special Collections, Eastern Washington University Libraries, Cheny, Wash.

Webb, Alexander S. *The Peninsula: McClellan's Campaign of 1862.* New York: Charles Scribner's Sons, 1862.

Welcher, Frank J. *The Union Army, 1861–1865, Organization and Operations. Vol 1. Eastern Theater.* Indianapolis, Ind.: Indiana University Press, 1989.

Wert, Jeffry D. *From Winchester to Cedar Creek: The Shenandoah Campaign of 1864.* Mechanicsburg, Pa.: Stackpole Books, 1997.

Wetherwax, David. Newspaper clipping. *Army Reminiscences.* Saratoga Springs Public Library, Saratoga Room, Saratoga Springs, N.Y.

Wheeler, Captain Luther. Letter to his mother. April 12, 1862. Cris Morley's Private Collection, Ballston Spa, N.Y.

Wiley, Bell Irvin, and Hirst D. Milhollen. *Embattled Confederates.* New York.: Harper & Row Bonanza Books, 1964.

Winslow, Richard E. *John Sedgwick: The Story of a Union Corps Commander.* Novato, Calif.: Presidio Press, 1982.

Index

A

Allen, Henry, 63, 66
Allen, James G., 131–32, 190
Andrews, Judson B., 7
Antietam, Maryland, battle of, 60–64
Armstrong, Edward S., 21
Arnold, Reed, 5

B

Babcock, Nathan S., 7, 66, 93, 103–4, 150
  at Antietam, battle of, 59, 63
  at Fredericksburg, second battle of, 77
  at Wilderness, battle of, 108–10
  at Spotsylvania, battle of, 113
Baker, William A., xiii, 54, 130, 134, 204
Ballston Spa, New York, 2, 7, 9, 16
Banks Ford, Virginia, battle of, 81–83
Barnes, James, 131–32, 190
baseball, 101
Battalion, 77th, 170
Beach, Albert, 5
Belding, John W., 54, 57, 165
Bemis Heights, New York, 3
Bemis, Isaac, 47
Bidwell, Daniel D., 21, 95, 112, 116, 137, 164, 200
Blanchard, Charles, 31
Boice, Isaac, 46
Bolton, George, 124, 129
Bowe, Halsey, 53
brigade commanders. See Casey, Silas; Davidson, John W.; Irwin, William H.; Vinton, Francis L.; Neill, Thomas H.; Bidwell, Daniel D.; Upton, Emory; French, Winsor B.; Hyde, Thomas W.
Bowers, Hermanus, 124
Branch, Erskine B., 80
Brandy Station, Virginia, 107
Briggs, Benjamin Alonzo, 139–40, 166–67
Bull Run, Virginia, first battle of, 1
Bull Run, Virginia, second battle of, 56
Burnside, Ambrose, 65–71

C

Cameron, John J., 7, 10
Campbell, Augustus, 18
Campbell, Sanford, 92
Camp Griffin, Virginia, 18, 21, 22, 23
Camp Hillhouse, Washington, D.C., 14, 18, 19, 21
Camp Misery, Virginia, 24
Camp Schuyler, New York, 3, 5–6, 9
Carr, John, 8
Casey, Silas, 15
Caw, David, 65, 170–71, 178, 191
  recruiting, 53
  at Fredericksburg, second battle of, 80
  at Petersburg 1865, battle of, 175–76
Caw, Willliam G., 176, 182
Cedar Creek, Virginia, battle of, 159–67
Charlestown, West Virginia, battle of, 148
Christmas, William C., 172
Clayton, Henry, 167
Clements, John, 203
Cold Harbor, Virginia, battle of, 127–31
Coleman, Oped, 102
Cooper Shop, Pennsylvania, 12–13, 65, 183
Corps, VI, 23, 53, 59, 197–98
corps commanders. See Keyes, Erasmus D.; Franklin, William B.; Smith, William F. "Baldy"; Sedgwick, John; Slocum, Henry W.; Wright, Horatio G.
Cowan, Andrew, 78, 117, 199
Cramer, Abram, 9, 167–68
Crampton's Gap, Maryland, 59–60
Cromack, Sidney O., 96
CSS *Teaser*, 27–28, 35

D

Danville, North Carolina, 182
Davidson, John W., 21–22, 25, 28, 47–48, 52–53
Davis, Charles H., 145
Davison, James, 105
Deep Run Crossing, Virginia, battle of, 86

Index

DeLong, William, 163–64
Deyoe, Seth W., 56
Deyoe, William, 84
disease and sickness, 6, 17–18, 22–23, 33, 44, 88
division commanders. See Smith, William F. "Baldy"; Howe, Albion P.; Getty, George W.; Neill, Thomas H.
drill, 5, 14, 22, 100

E

Early, Jubal A., 76, 135–36, 158
Essex County, New York, 2, 5
Evans, John E., 40, 121, 164, 189

F

Finch, William W., 78, 81
Fisher's Hill, Virginia, battle of, 151–53
flags
  77th's guidons, 187
  77th's national flag, 8, 133, 185, 187
  77th's regimental flag, 12
Fletcher, Leonard, 103
foraging, 55, 99, 148
Fort Fisher, Virginia, 175–78
Fort Stedman, Virginia, battle of, 173
Fort Stevens, Washington, D.C., battle of, 144
Fountain, Cyrille, 58, 101, 110, 120, 202
Fowler, Thomas H., 16
Fox, Norman Jr., xiii, 94, 99, 100, 105, 191, 199–200
  at Fredericksburg, second battle of, 77
  at Wilderness, battle of, 110
  at Spotsylvania, battle of, 122
Franklin, William B., 59, 136
Fredericksburg, Virginia first battle of, 69–71
Fredericksburg, Virginia, second battle of, 74, 85
French, Winsor B., 4, 8, 13, 21, 67–68
  recruiting, 2–3, 7, 53
  at Peninsular campaign, 44, 53–54
  at Fredericksburg, second battle of, 79
  at Fort Stevens, battle of, 139–41
  at Winchester, battle of, 149–51
  at Fisher's Hill, battle of, 151–53
  at Cedar Creek, battle of, 162–63
Fuller, Edward H., 64–65, 78, 91
Fulton County, 2
Fursman, Willliam H., 53–54, 65, 91

G

Getty, George W., 143, 150, 160–61, 168
Gettysburg, Pennsylvania, battle of, 97

Gloversville, New York, 7
Goldings Farm, Virginia, battle of, 47
Gordon, John B., 111–12, 162, 198
Grand Review in Washington, 182, 186
Grant, Lewis A., 77
Grant, Ulysses S., 130–31, 177, 191
  Wilderness, battle of, 106, 115
  Spotsylvania, battles of, 117
  Early's Raid, 135, 143
  Shenandoah campaign 1864, 146, 149, 157
  Petersburg Siege, 171
Greek Cross, 75, 141
Green, James O., 22

H

Ham, John W., 47–48
Harrison's Landing, Virginia, 52–53, 55
Hastings, Stephen S., 54
Henderson, Joseph C., 6, 7, 24, 44
Hetzel, Selden, 52–53
Hill, Clement, 5, 7
Hooker, Joseph, 36, 69, 72, 75–78
Horton, Stephen S., 2, 6, 7, 62, 78
Howe, Albion P., 68, 76–77, 79–80
Hulburt, John, 22
Hyde, Thomas W., 172–73

I

Irwin, William H., 59, 61

J

Jeffords, Francis, 30
Jennings, Edward, 120
Jewel, Altus, 84
Joyce, Thomas, 6
Judson, Benjamin F., 5, 11, 17

K

Keck, Jeremiah, 190
Keenholtz, Fred, 118
Keesville, New York, 7
Keyes, Erasmus D., 43
King, Sidney, 16
King, Thomas, 159

L

Lamey, Michael, 79
Lansing, Wendell, 7
Lawrence, James J., 131–32, 190
Lee, Robert E., 45
Lees Mills, Virginia, battle of, 32
Lennon, Martin, 57, 158, 163
Lincoln, President Abraham, 1, 70, 136, 139, 140

liquor, 3, 17, 131, 132
Love, Matthew, 141
Loveland, Joseph H., 54, 58

M

Maine Regiments
  1st, 184
  7th, 21, 69, 93, 102, 109
Malvern Hill, Virginia, battle of, 50
marches
  Mud, 71
  Gettysburg, 89–92
  Shenandoah Valley, 154
  Danville, 182
McClellan, George B., 26–27, 36
McKean, James B., 4, 15, 17, 30–31, 199
  organization and recruiting, 1–3, 7
  at Mechanicsville, battle of, 39–40
  at Peninsular campaign, 43
  sickness and fever of, 44, 56
McLain, Allen, 40
McMichael, Richard H., 6, 16, 181
McNaughton, Charles H., 81
Meade, George, 89
Mechanicsville, Virginia, battle of, 38–40, 41
Mechanicville, New York, 7, 181
Mine Run, Virginia, battle of, 95
monuments
  dedication at Gettysburg, Pennsylvania, 191–92, 195
  dedication at Saratoga Springs, New York, 191, 194
  monument at Saratoga Springs, New York, 196
Mustered
  in—77th Regiment, 8
  out—77th Battalion, 184
  out—77th Regiment, 181–82
  pay—77th Regiment, 18

N

Neill, Thomas H., 69–70, 79, 82, 91, 94, 134
New Jersey Regiment
  21st, 69, 81
New York Battery
  1st. See Cowan, Andrew
New York Regiments
  20th, 45, 52, 61, 69, 80
  33rd, 21, 39, 47, 62
  43rd, 69, 109, 112, 113, 119, 184
  49th, 21, 69, 94, 109, 123, 152, 184
  122nd, 184
Nickerson, Albert, 110
Norton, Franklin, 40

O

Oakley, Sumner, 174, 180
Orr, George S., 94, 164

P

Patterson, John, 30
Pennsylvania Regiments
  61st, 95, 101, 109, 114, 184
Perkins, Frederick N., 16, 37–38
Perry, John L., 6, 17
Petersburg 1864, Virginia, siege of, 131–32
Petersburg 1865, Virginia, battle of, 179
picket duty, 28–29
Pierce, Stephen, 173
punishments, 14–15

Q

Quivey, Aaron B., 22, 124

R

reconnaissance, 22–23
recruiting, 1–3, 5–8, 53–54
Reed, Henry, 167
Reid, Albert J., 132
reunions, 195, 201
Rice, Calvin, 7
Riley, John D., 10
Rockwell, John R., 53, 65
Rowe, Carlos, 63–64, 121–23
Rugg, Orrin F., 8, 57

S

Sailor's Creek, Virginia battle of, 177
Salem Church, Virginia battle of, 81–82
Saratoga County, New York, 2
Saratoga Springs, New York, 181
Savage Station, Virginia, battle of, 47–48
Scott, James G., 115
Sedgwick, John, 72, 73, 90, 111–12, 118
Seeley, John, 46
Seven Days, battles of, 51
Seven Pines, battle of, 43
Shenandoah Valley, 156
Sheridan, Philip, 146–47, 150–51, 165, 169
Shurtleff, Lucas F., 13
Skinner, Robert, 5–6, 8, 16, 22, 26, 37–38
Slocum, Henry W., 91
Smith, Dennis B., 99
Smith, William F. "Baldy," 23, 27, 36, 43, 51, 59, 92–93
snowball fighting, 101–2
Snyder, Albert, 121, 160

Index

sojering, 8, 200
Spotsylvania, Virginia, battle of,
   the angle, 122–23
   the Salient, 126
   Upton's Charge, 119–22
Stevens, Charles, 162, 185, 200
Stevens, George T., 27, 30, 35, 91, 106, 129, 147
Stillwell, Frank, 121
Stuart, James Ewell Brown, 90
sutlers, 18
Sweet, Milton F., 60

T

Taber, William J., 165
Temple Grove Seminary, 8
Thomas, Gilbert, 167
Thompson, Justin, 115, 116
Three One-Legged Jims, 131–32
Tully, David, 16–17, 20, 50, 181

U

Upton, Emory, 119–22

V

Van Anden, Barnard, 129–30

Vermont Troops, 27, 28, 32, 100–102, 118, 123, 141
Vinton, Francis L., 69

W

wagering, 98–99
war meetings, 54
Watson, William G., 109
Westport, New York, 5
Wetherwax, David, 31, 203
Wheeler, Luther, 57, 78, 81, 83
White Oak Church, Virginia, 71
White Oak Swamp, Virginia, battle of, 49, 51
White, Thomas M., 103
Wilderness, Virginia, battle of, 107–14
Williamsburg, Virginia, battle of, 36–37
Wilton, New York, 5, 7
Winchester, Virginia, battle of, 155
Wood, Lewis, 5, 7
Worden, William W., 111
Wright, Horatio G., 119–21, 174–75
Wright, Willliam H., 23–24, 25, 176

Y

Yorktown, Virginia, siege of, 29–30

973.7 Mor
Morrow, Robert F.,
77th New York Volunteers
:
$29.95 10/08/04 AGV-6631

SHENENDEHOWA PUBLIC LIBRARY, NY

0 00 06 0250497 9